CW00540137

'Finally, a book to dispel the myth
an exclusively childhood condition.
this valuable contribution to the fi
understanding of the nature and far-reaching effects of ᴏᴍ, ⸱⸱
help mobilise Health Services to provide appropriate support
for both children and adults.'

– *Maggie Johnson, FRCSLT, co-author of*
Can I tell you about Selective Mutism?

'This must-read book educates about the emotional challenges
of Selective Mutism experienced by all involved. From being
bullied to overcoming obstacles, Sutton and Forrester expertly
weave heartbreaking and uplifting moments through personal
stories that read like journal entries. This is a resource that
should be on all clinician's shelves.'

– *Joleen R. Fernald, PhD, CCC-SLP, BCS-CL,*
Selective Mutism Expert

of related interest

Tackling Selective Mutism
A Giude for Professionals and Parents
Edited by Benita Rae Smith and Alice Sluckin
ISBN 978 1 84905 393 8
eISBN 978 0 85700 761 2

Can I tell you about Selective Mutism?
A guide for friends, family and professionals
Maggie Johnson and Alison Wintgens
Illustrated by Robyn Gallow
ISBN 978 1 84905 289 4
eISBN 978 0 85700 611 0

SELECTIVE MUTISM IN OUR OWN WORDS

EXPERIENCES IN CHILDHOOD AND ADULTHOOD

Carl Sutton and
Cheryl Forrester

Foreword by Donna Williams

Jessica Kingsley *Publishers*
London and Philadelphia

First published in 2016
by Jessica Kingsley Publishers
73 Collier Street
London N1 9BE, UK
and
400 Market Street, Suite 400
Philadelphia, PA 19106, USA

www.jkp.com

Copyright © Carl Sutton and Cheryl Forrester 2016
Foreword copyright © Donna Williams 2016

Front cover image courtesy of Kimberly Gerry-Tucker.

Library of Congress Cataloging in Publication Data
Names: Sutton, Carl. | Forrester, Cheryl.
Title: Selective mutism in our own words : experiences in childhood and
    adulthood / Carl Sutton and Cheryl Forrester ; foreword by Donna Williams.
Description: London ; Philadelphia : Jessica Kingsley Publishers, 2016. |
    Includes bibliographical references and index.
Identifiers: LCCN 2015029307 | ISBN 9781849056366
Subjects: LCSH: Selective mutism.
Classification: LCC RJ506.M87 S88 2016 | DDC 618.92/855--dc23 LC record
available at http://lccn.loc.gov/2015029307

British Library Cataloguing in Publication Data
A CIP catalogue record for this book is available from the British Library

ISBN 978 1 84905 636 6
eISBN 978 1 78450 114 3

Printed and bound in Great Britain

In memory of Carl's mother, Maureen, and Cheryl's mother, Evelyn, who both passed away within a short space of time in 2014, while this book was being written.

Contents

Some days my rusted tongue is freed, set free
upon a breath of light and chink of air –
in whispers first, as whispers are the key
to later, raging, roaring like a bear.
Some days the rusted door is left ajar,
and out the shadows of my whispers waft –
my face is near but voice is from afar
at first, but then I sing and hoot aloft.
Some days I hoot of silence to the sun;
I hoot, uncaged, of freedom of the tongue
but yet, by dusk, unfree, I am undone:
my mouth rusts shut each evening and I'm wrong.
Some days my rusted tongue is freed, I rage
until the iron nighttime of my cage.

Carl Sutton

Foreword

Condition and personhood enter a dance in which one shapes the other. None of us is solely our condition. We have our own characters, identifications, motivations, experiences, cultures, genders, capacities and opportunities which all change the unique ways we each live with a seemingly comparable condition. Selective Mutism is one such condition. It can affect those from any background, those with or without other disabilities, those from privilege and care and those from challenge and trauma. This book presents that diversity, exploring the commonalities and the differences, how it affected lives at different stages, their opportunities, what has worked for them, what has compounded their Selective Mutism. The accounts within the book present Selective Mutism from so many angles – as an involuntary self-protection response, as habit and compulsion, as addiction, as investment and security, as anxiety disorder, as identification, as a product of interplay with the environment, as predisposition, as weakness, and as perceived strength. Selective Mutism presents challenges to a speaking world which is frustrated by those with it. And it presents challenges to those living with it in a speaking world. Most promising are the stories of those determined to challenge their own limitations in either overcoming their Selective Mutism or learning to live more constructively with it; and those determined that Selective Mutism alone will not define them.

Donna Williams, BA Hons, Dip Ed.
Author, artist and presenter
www.donnawilliams.net

Acknowledgements

Our sincerest and most special thanks to every person who contributed his or her own life experience to this book. This book would never have been written without you. Special thanks also to those who collectively proofread the book, including many of the same contributors; and also Rae Smith and Alice Sluckin (of the Selective Mutism Information and Research Association – SMIRA); Paz Lopez Herrero (University of Granada, Spain); and Anita McKiernan (City University, London). Special thanks also to Michelle Tytherleigh, who supervised Carl's exploratory study on Selective Mutism in Adults (University of Chester, UK) and to Astrid Schepman (University of Chester, UK). Sincere thanks to Maggie Johnson (Kent Community Health NHS Foundation Trust) for numerous e-mail discussions on Selective Mutism. Special thanks also to Donna Williams for writing such an inspiring and beautiful foreword for us; and to Kimberly Gerry-Tucker for creating the cover art. Last but not least, sincere thanks to Lisa Clark, Sarah Hamlin, Lucy Buckroyd, Sarah Minty and Emma Holak, our editors at Jessica Kingsley Publishers, who did a fantastic job at each and every stage of making this book become a reality.

Preface

This book came about because, as someone with a very long history of Selective Mutism (SM) myself, I did not feel there was sufficient personal experience of this anxiety disorder in published literature. This point is noted by academic writers on the subject too:

> The voices of people who have been selectively mute are still largely missing from follow-up reports – and, in fact, from the literature on the subject as a whole. (Cline and Baldwin, 2004, p. 213)

In particular there is a dearth of outcome studies[1] on children with SM, which serves to give the impression that SM universally remits in early childhood with or without support. It is imperative to highlight the severe difficulties that teenagers and young adults with SM can experience in particular. SM does not necessarily remit in early childhood and the result can be education difficulties; further anxiety disorders and depression; difficulty finding or maintaining employment; and severe social isolation.

Without being too graphic about it, for me, as I entered young adulthood, Selective Mutism was a grossly unpleasant experience which I can only liken to being a mute prisoner in my own head. As such, another motivation for the book is that I had a deep need to convey my own experience openly in order to finally free myself of it. Thus, for me, this book is, also, the end of a personal journey after which I can fully understand

---

1 Only two outcome studies appear to exist: Remschmidt *et al.* (2001) and Steinhausen *et al.* (2006).

and position my own experience within the context of many others.

The intention of the book is to explore SM via the life experiences of many people who have experienced it and their parents and caregivers; to explore the difficulties people with SM experience from their early lives, all the way to adulthood; and to highlight the fact that successful interventions are possible.

This book is written for and by people who have experienced SM; their parents, carers, friends, and relatives; and professionals with personal experience of working with this condition. For readers who have experienced SM themselves and parents, the message that I hope this book conveys is that, while SM may appear to be rare, in fact you are far from alone with this kind of experience. For readers in a position to help (e.g. teachers, SENCOs, psychologists, psychiatrists, speech therapists, and so on) this book intends to highlight the need to provide intervention early on in a child's life to avert the worst of the experience later on. For those reading the book due to a personal interest, I believe that you will find many of the stories deeply moving, as I do myself.

My main hope is that the voices of those who personally experienced SM and their caregivers and helpers resound from the pages and that the book provides a wide array of insights into how it feels to live with SM for years at a time.

Carl Sutton (co-ordinator of iSpeak.org.uk)

CHAPTER 1

An Experiential Introduction to Selective Mutism

Carl Sutton

Selective Mutism (SM) is a situational anxiety disorder of communication which affects around 1 in 150 younger children, the incidence rate reducing with age to around 1 in 1000 adolescents (NHS, 2015). Furthermore, my own research on SM in adults (Sutton, 2013) estimates that SM affects greater than 1 in 2400 young adults. My belief, however, is that the incidence rate in adults is likely to be an underestimate, particularly as SM is a common comorbidity of autism spectrum disorders (e.g. Williams, 2015). As with most anxiety disorders, females are more likely to experience SM than males.

A person with SM is phobic of initiating speech/being overheard in the proximity of a given trigger person or collection of people. A person with SM may be able to speak in one situation (e.g. at home with close relatives) but be unable to speak, frozen, and timid in another (e.g. at a social event, at school or college, with doctors or dentists, or even in a work meeting.)

While SM principally affects speech, all avenues of communication can be involved:

- People with SM may also not be able to put pen to paper, particularly when writing about themselves. Thus SM can affect written language.

▶ People with SM may also feel that their own body movements expose their anxieties, so they tend to move rather woodenly or freeze. Thus SM can affect body language.

▶ People with SM tend to hide their true emotions, facially, in trigger situations, hence they may tend to either smile or maintain fixed facial expressions, regardless of how they are truly feeling. Thus SM can affect expressive body language.

While SM may seem like something people choose or elect to *do* (the old names for this condition used to be Aphasia Voluntaria then Elective Mutism) this is absolutely not the case. Muteness/freezing/hiding is triggered by the proximity of specific individuals or groups of people. Triggers may be generalized: strangers, other students, teachers, shopkeepers, or even work colleagues. Or triggers may be more specific: aunts, uncles, siblings, stepparents, or even parents. Most people with Selective Mutism have a mixture of generalized and specific triggers.

It is most frequently noticed in the school environment (a situation where some children do not speak for the entirety of their school lives). However, most children who are mute at school are also mute with others outside the school environment such as strangers or relatives who are encountered infrequently. Many children with SM simply do not speak outside the home at all. Less frequently, muteness can also occur inside the home. The formal diagnostic criteria for SM in the DSM-5 (APA, 2013, p. 195) dictate that mutism should occur consistently in situations where there is an expectation for speech (such as educational, occupational or social settings); a child or adult is able to speak in other situations; the disorder lasts for more than a month (excluding the first month of a child's school life); mutism is not better explained by a communication disorder, autism, schizophrenia or a psychotic disorder; and that there is no more appropriate explanation for mutism such as a lack of knowledge or comfort with the spoken language in a given setting (e.g. if the child or adult has recently moved into a new culture).

Note, however, that there are a number of issues with the formal criteria: They preclude a diagnosis of SM when a child or adult cannot speak in all situations. In fact, there are cases where SM can *progress* such that a child or adult cannot speak to anybody at all (as we see later in the book). I spent months, myself, mute in all situations.

Additionally, SM is a common comorbity of autism spectrum disorders (notably Asperger Syndrome); and Williams (2015) suggests that people with more severe autism sometimes describe an inability to speak due to anxiety too.

While children who find themselves in a foreign culture do experience an adjustment period which frequently includes 'mutism', such an adjustment can be a trigger for the onset of SM also.

Research on SM in children by Steinhausen and Juzi (1996), Cunningham *et al.* (2004), Black and Uhde (1995), and Elizur and Perednik (2003) describes a range of mean onset ages from 2.7 to 4.1 years. In agreement, my own research on SM in adults also reported a mean age of onset of 3.8 years (Sutton, 2013). Thus SM is an anxiety disorder/communication phobia with an extremely early age of onset.

A diagnosis of SM is generally made when a child is between 5 and 8 years old (Wong, 2010), hence children with SM may often have experienced the condition for a number of years, their condition markedly worsening in that time, before receiving help.

Adults with SM are significantly less likely to have received diagnoses or help as children; however, diagnosis and intervention rates are improving (Sutton, 2013).

While SM may seem to be a relatively innocuous behaviour in young childhood, by late adolescence and adulthood, should

SM persist for that long, there can be serious mental health repercussions – such as depression, social anxiety disorder (SAD), generalized anxiety disorder (GAD), agoraphobia, and so on. Additionally, there can be serious social ramifications to the persistence of SM, such as young adults with SM being unable to leave the house unless accompanied, being unable to work, being entirely reliant on aging parents, and so on.

In my own case I have been affected by significant mental health difficulties directly due to SM, among them clinical depression, GAD and an element of post traumatic stress disorder (PTSD). Note that I identify PTSD primarily as the result of, rather than the cause of my SM. However, I believe that most experiences of SM like my own, which persist to adulthood, are avoidable if children with SM receive sufficient help or interventions in childhood.

I thus include my own story to highlight the main points of this book: take SM in both children and adults seriously, and treat SM as early in a child's life as possible, even if it may seem to be a relatively innocuous behaviour, to avoid potentially serious outcomes in later life.

To summarise the story which follows: while SM was part of my life as far back as I remember, my SM became much worse in my teens after my parents' divorce, continued to adulthood and eventually culminated in my experiencing a nervous breakdown when I was a PhD student. At that stage I had been mute in my home environment for a decade. While the story is about the distress that I experienced, which some readers may find upsetting, I must add that I have, subsequently, lived a fulfilled and productive life, although I could not achieve many of my life goals – one of which was to be an academic.

MY (CARL'S) STORY

I was born in 1969. As a young child, it was my instinct to be non-vocal in certain situations, as it is for many children, including those who don't develop SM. I would not say my muteness began, rather it was a natural behaviour, shaped by my environment, that became more and more problematic as I got older.

As a young child, I was mute with all adult relatives besides my mother. I could speak to other adults provided they were no relation or potential relation to me, if nobody I was mute with was present, and if my mother was not present either. As a result, none of my grandparents heard my voice before they died. Until I was an adult, no aunt or uncle heard my voice either. I generally could speak to other children at school individually; and often I could also speak to teachers. Contrary to the majority of children with SM, communication was often easier for me in less rather than more familiar environments.

My mother experienced mental health issues throughout my childhood. While she did her best and I was never in any doubt that I was important to her, this did, however, strongly impact upon me. She was often verbally and potentially physically aggressive. One particular aspect of her behaviour is that she couldn't tolerate 'noisy' children. When I was a child she would berate the parents of children who were boisterous and loud – to their faces. And she would often make it clear to me when she couldn't stand the sound of a child either crying or enjoying itself. She would also view me positively for being quiet and restrained in comparison with other children. As such I feel that my muteness was significantly shaped by my mother's behaviour.

Towards the end of her life my mother revealed to me that she could hear a horde of voices, and had done so for years – her critical mother's being the most prominent among them. I wonder, reflecting back, whether she could always hear voices, and this was one of the reasons why she would control my volume switch, not needing yet another voice jangling in her head.

My mother and birth father were also strict disciplinarians. For instance, as children, my brother and I would be threatened with the strap if we 'answered back'. As such, as a young child I lived in an environment where being quiet and compliant was the most sensible, safest way to be. I very quickly learnt that speaking up for myself would never be tolerated and was, in fact, unsafe. I would (I was told) 'have my block knocked off' if I spoke up for myself.

While I was compliant inside the home environment, I would steal from school and local shops. On an almost daily basis – as a primary school child – I would steal an exercise book or a pen from the school storeroom at the end of the day. In my early school life I was a mixture of unconfident and bolshie, bursting into tears because I stuttered and failed when giving oral presentations to classmates, yet verbally demanding of the teacher to be in the school play. Furthermore, I recall shouting at a bemused primary school teacher for being spendthrift and throwing a worn-out paintbrush in the bin (mirroring my mother's kind of behaviour).

Out of the blue, at primary school I was singled out and sent to the headmistress's office without my parents' awareness, and intrusively examined by someone I assumed to be a doctor, with other present, for signs of sexual abuse. At the time I did not understand what this was done for (in my naïveté I believed they were checking my cleanliness); however subsequently I did not take this experience in my stride. In fact, this experience gave me profound issues with 'body' for quite a few years. I would say that it was probably just about the worst thing a school could do to a child such as myself who had problems with speaking. It also made me much more ashamed of 'being a physical entity' and vastly more secretive with my wants, needs and wishes. Subsequently, not only did I have an issue with speaking, I would also hate to run taps or flush toilets in earshot of other people and I would attempt to do these things silently.

In stages, my SM worsened over the years, changing from something I just 'did' to something that ruled my life and made it unbearable. When I was 14 my mother and father divorced. As a teenager, having supported my mother through the process, I felt like I had been through a divorce myself. Subsequently my to-be stepfather (a stranger) moved into the household and we moved to an old cottage that needed much renovation. There was no heating and there was only one bedroom – theirs. I was without a bedroom and my non-existent personal 'space' was shuffled round the house for several years. For months my bed was in the living room. Next it was at the top of the stairs, on the landing. I had no privacy, and, with a new figure in the house, I was unable to talk at all.

The beginning of my mother and stepfather's marriage, particularly, was a very unpleasant time for me. My mother and stepfather argued almost constantly, often violently. My heart felt continually in my throat in their proximity. I would, for instance, return from school on the bus to see them raging at each other in the street. One evening my stepfather began to strangle my mother, while I stood silently by – effete, mute, and unable to do anything about it. Later, my mother punched his tooth out. Our two border collies used to sit mutely in their basket, never stepping out unless invited to, and never barking. It was not just me who was so affected by my mother and stepfather's behaviour. Even the dogs were mute.

I was regularly threatened with being 'sorted out' by my stepfather as his means to retaliate to my mother who was paranoid and psychotic at times. My stepfather threw crockery at me, simply for being in the living room, sitting on my bed, with nowhere else to go. As a manual worker, he would also often call me an 'educated idiot' – deeming the education that I was trying to gain worthless.

Despite their relationship improving after a couple of years, I continued to find myself mute in my home environment for almost a decade. I felt as though my voice had been swallowed, irretrievably, by a black hole located at the centre of my head. It was as though my voice was inaccessible. Sometimes I used to feel there was a dead thing in the centre of my head (which I conceived as a bloodless, dead egg-shaped object) that blocked my ability to connect my inner voice, which was ever alive, to my vocal chords. The process of speaking felt inconceivable and impossible. It was as though a fuse had blown in the mental circuitry between my inner voice and whatever mental process powered my speech. There was no voice to use.

While many teenagers and young adults retreat to their bedroom and are reticent, particularly with their parents, I was unable to speak even if I wanted to. I was trapped in a profound state of muteness. I could merely nod, shake my head, shrug, smile and use basic mime. Without let-up I was mute every second of every evening, weekend, school holiday, birthday, Christmas, and so on. During the summer holiday – whether from school, sixth form or eventually university – I would be entirely mute for weeks or months at a time. I was ashamed of myself, but nodding and mime were the best I could do.

Throughout the decade I lived a double life. I could speak at school, to an extent. However, I was ashamed of my inability to speak at home therefore I kept it entirely secret from my friends at school, sixth form, then university. In the late 1980s, still mute at home, I headed off to London on the bus to do a degree in Computer Science. I would return home and be mute still at weekends and during holidays. I lived a double life – speaking in London but mute a two-hour train journey away, in my home city.

I became utterly desperate to speak in the end, not least because I wanted a normal life. I wanted a relationship and a family, and I believed that nobody could possibly want someone who couldn't speak to his own parents or other relatives.

I came to believe that if I made myself suffer so much that my silence became intolerable then I would be forced to overcome my inability to speak. I decided the way to break my silence was to become mute everywhere, all the time; and to make my life so unbearable that I would be forced to speak to my parents, through emotional pain inflicted on myself. The way to achieve both things was to cut myself off from everyone I could speak to – all of the friends I had. This was the only way forward that I could think of. I couldn't recommend this decision less, but I felt I had no alternative.

I coincided this decision with starting my PhD in another city, where I knew no one. I could have gone to another university with my friends. Instead, I deliberately isolated myself with a view of somehow, though I had no plan and had no idea how horrible it would become, breaking my own self in order to speak. Over the next two years of mute isolation, my mental health deteriorated and, without over-egging the experience, by 1992 I was utterly tormented. Living alone and mute, I envisioned myself as behind an insurmountably high wall – me on one side and everything worth having on the other. All I had to do was speak and ask for help to get through to the other side but there seemed no way to do it. I desperately wanted to be normal (if there is such a thing) and to speak – particularly to my parents.

To my mind, being mathematically inclined, speaking was an equation, speech = suffering – fear of speaking. In other words, if I suffered enough I could speak; if I suffered more than the insurmountable wall was high I could speak. If I didn't suffer enough I would be trapped and isolated forever, be permanently mute, never have a family of my own, and there would be zero point to my existing.

I felt as trapped and as isolated as it is possible to be. There seemed to be no possibility of escape from my own solitude and my own silence. I was entirely trapped by my speech rules – unable to speak to my parents and unable to reveal my inability to anyone else. Something had to give eventually – either the veins in my head, which were constantly protruding and sore, or my system of speech rules.

I started to believe I was having 'astonishing', 'revelatory' thoughts. On one occasion, stepping onto a train, for instance, I received an intense idea (which was extraordinarily physically painful) that I could see beyond things – and that life and the existence, as I had previously perceived it (and everyone else continued to), was a delusion designed to keep my and everyone else's mentalities safe. Frankly, it felt as if my mind was splitting excruciatingly into pieces. It's rather poetic, I suppose. I had not magically become a genius with remarkable insights into anything at all. Rather, I had become ill due to isolation, acute depression and SM. It became a very existential breakdown.

A day or so later, while I was a passenger on a train passing through Clapham Junction station, there was a 'violent' click in my head. I jolted, then blacked out briefly. No one seemed to notice. Coming to, however, I felt afraid for my life. I absolutely didn't want to die but I believed that a stroke was imminent. Only then did my basic survival instinct override every other fear I had. After holding my head all night (it was the only thing that seemed to help with the fear and stress and the 'rats crawling in my head'), the next morning I left my flat to walk to a nearby psychiatric resource centre. Luckily this happened to be only a few minutes from my flat. Walking there, I couldn't focus my eyes properly. The walls at the side of the road seemed to be moving to and fro; buildings were throbbing; and everything seemed to be imbued with strange colours – especially the sky, which was, very literally, yellow.

After ringing the bell and being led into a small waiting room, a psychiatric nurse, who was very respectful, initially assessed me. I don't recall any of the interim but I saw a psychiatrist a day or so later. He was fantastic. He helped me over the next few months – as an outpatient (telling me that I should avoid coming into hospital because of the stigma I would encounter in later life) – just by being emotionally present, primarily.

Such is the nature of my own SM that I didn't actually have any problem speaking either to him or the nurse. I was never helped for SM directly because I didn't exhibit silence in the helping situation. Rather I was treated for chronic, acute depression – via a mixture of paroxetine, an SSRI antidepressant, which was new at that time, and, far more importantly, basic human kindness.

I went home to see my mother a couple days after seeing the psychiatrist for the first time. To demonstrate the absurdness of SM,

I telephoned her to say I was coming and, to an extent, what had happened, then, once home, I couldn't speak again. I sat in a state of fugue on the settee for days – dawn until dusk – unable to move. However, then my mother instinctually devised a method to enable me to speak. At this moment in time she knew precisely what to do.

My mother suggested I take a specific book down from her bookshelf. It was *Our John Willie* by Catherine Cookson, which, ironically, is about the relationship between Davy and his 'deaf-mute' (not my term) younger brother, John Willie. To begin with, and encouraged by my mother, who became my natural 'speech therapist', I whispered a few sentences each day. While it may seem bizarre to anyone who has not experienced SM, I can't express how difficult it was even to whisper. However, I gradually began to increase my volume. When speaking again, my voice didn't feel connected to me. It was like an out-of-body experience. A few days after being able to read at a reasonable volume to my mother, I answered my stepfather for the first time since he'd moved into the house a decade before that. While my speech remained functional rather than expressive with both of them for the remainder of their lives, at least I could speak if and when I wanted to.

Only a matter of weeks later I joined an amateur dramatic society then appeared in *The Sound of Music*, with a speaking part, to prove to myself that I could speak everywhere and that my speech trap was over.

Very soon after that I met my future wife and stepdaughter through a family friend. I have been married ever since – and I got the loving family of my own I had so wanted. Cheryl, my wife, is the co-editor of this book.

Less importantly, after this experience, I continued on and completed my PhD, which was a huge personal achievement – not academically, emotionally. I have subsequently had a successful working life in industry and I count my blessings.

Challenging myths and stereotypes about Selective Mutism

It is very important to remark that, despite the stereotype of SM being a childhood-only disorder, SM sometimes extends into adulthood. To demonstrate this fact, this book includes the testimonies of teenagers with SM, plus adults with SM from their early 20s up to their late 50s. My own research demonstrates that for those whose SM continues into adulthood, peak severity generally occurs during their early 20s, although some report significant or even undiminished speech and social difficulties all the way into their 50s (after which I have little data).

The second stereotype to challenge is that SM is a school-only issue. My own research (Sutton, 2013) demonstrated that SM occurs in a wide spectrum of situations – with strangers, teachers, peers, doctors and dentists, aunts and uncles, grandparents, stepparents and, in rarer circumstances, parents also.

While it should not need stating, the third stereotype that *most or all* children with SM have been abused is false. Unfortunately the idea that SM is always the direct result of neglect or abuse still pervades the general public's view of this condition due to the way muteness was portrayed in the past – as a universal result of psychological trauma. As such, while simply doing the best for their children, some parents encounter inappropriate and prejudiced questioning from teachers and others.

Julia writes about her experience as a parent – teachers intimating that her daughter's SM was her fault:

> We had a private meeting with a teacher who said, 'Something must have happened to Nicky when she was little.' That, to me, was accusing us, as parents, of child abuse in an indirect way.
>
> The teacher also said I never kissed my daughter when she went into school. I felt horrified that they thought it was my fault. Other parents never wanted to speak to me.

Also, Julie writes about her experience as a parent as follows:

Relative strangers have often said to me loudly, and in Justine's earshot, 'What happened to her then?' As if I am going to tell them some terrible story about something that suddenly made our beautiful daughter stop speaking. Nothing did.

Fantastic, loving parents have children with SM. To such parents, questioning of their behaviour toward their children is, understandably, repugnant. Very often the onset of SM is inexplicable and/or the trigger is small (at least from an adult point of view).

There is no evidence to suggest that children with SM are either more likely or less likely to have experienced abuse or emotional ill-treatment compared with other children.

Quoting Alice Sluckin and Rae Smith[1] of the Selective Mutism Information and Research Agency (SMIRA):

> More complex problems exist in some families and must be addressed if suspected. It is a common mistake to assume that all cases, or no cases, indicate abuse or emotional ill-treatment. (Sluckin and Smith, personal communication, 2015)

Given SM is an anxiety disorder, it is clear that it can be worsened by anxiety-provoking life experiences. In fact, disruptive life experiences of various kinds – relocation, parental conflict or divorce, parental mental illness, bereavement, bullying, shame, feeling different, and so on – compound mutism in children and adolescents with SM. Examples of various kinds of compounding factor are found throughout this book.

Other environmental factors which can bring about SM include geographic isolation – such as a child having few opportunities for socialization prior to going to school for the first time.

---

1 Editors of *Tackling Selective Mutism*, Jessica Kingsley Publishers (2014).

Children who find themselves in a different culture, faced with a foreign language (for instance Japanese children in London) may develop SM also.

Selective Mutism – a compulsion to be silent

A compulsion to be silent is ordinary behaviour for many young children, not just those who develop SM, when they experience stranger anxiety (Lesser-Katz, 1988), when they feel vulnerable, or when they are separated from their primary caregiver. SM becomes a diagnosis, as such, when it continues well into a child's early school life or causes significant social difficulties. Hence the first month of a child's early school life is formally precluded from a diagnosis, as is a duration of situational muteness which lasts for less than a month. SM often lasts for years rather than months and is, in practice, a very easy diagnosis to make for someone with the experience or understanding to recognize it. Quite simply, a person with SM *cannot* speak in certain situations.

From an evolutionary point of view, mutism under threat may simply be a throwback to avoiding the attention of predators. We are, after all, animals regardless of apparent sophistication. Lesser-Katz (1986) contrasted SM with the freeze defence in animals and, from an experiential point of view, I would concur that, for a young child, SM feels just like that. As a young child, there was no thought involved in my reaction of silence to certain people. It was all trigger (proximity of an overwhelming person) and response (silence).

Much like an animal in the jungle that becomes silent and on tenterhooks when a hungry predator approaches, children with SM avoid 'threat' – albeit the threat of feeling vulnerable and overly perceived rather than being eaten! – automatically and subconsciously, via instinctive muteness. Children with SM don't choose to behave in this way. Their fight or flight response compels them to be silent when they feel physically, emotionally or psychologically vulnerable. There is thus a direct link between 'being perceived' (i.e. social exposure) and silence. Likewise there is also a direct link between separation from a primary caregiver and silence because, particularly for younger children, separation can engender a sense of danger and discomfort.

Based on this description of the roots of SM, there does not need to be a stressor or any kind of trauma for SM to come about. Some children are, simply, more predisposed to the anxiety of feeling exposed and vulnerable. This is particularly the case for children with autism and significant anxiety.

The speech trap (explained through my own experience)

Writing from experience, I always found certain people to be impossible to speak in earshot of. I would feel 'overwhelmed' and trapped by a trigger-person's proximity and it would feel as if they had encroached on my private space even if they were the other side of the room. I could not cope with the thought of their hearing my voice.

For a child (or adult) with SM, speaking can feel like a very intimate, unnerving, embarrassing, threatening act. Children with SM are generally risk-averse, and it often feels much safer to keep shtum. So much so that speaking at all, in a trigger situation, can be unfeasible. In my own experience, saying one word would have felt as if I was giving others the key to the whole of my private inner world – my thoughts, feelings, wants, desires and needs. These were things I felt very uncomfortable sharing at all.

Even if I did eventually begin to feel comfortable with someone, I would still remain unable to speak to them. While I would usually have dearly loved to speak, challenging my inability felt impossible. As a child the maintaining factor (what kept me silent) felt unfathomable. I did not understand why I could not speak. In retrospect, however, it seems to have principally been the fear of re-inviting the attention of someone who I originally found overwhelming. I was safe if I did not speak. If I spoke I would be overwhelmed, more so than ever. I was certainly very change-averse, particularly when such change would encourage personal attention or scrutiny.

After being silent for a while, there becomes little expectation on a child or adult with SM to speak. As such the fear of initiating speech (i.e. the speech trap) is deepened due to other people ceasing to expect anything but silence. This makes the thought of speaking even more difficult. Speaking, when all expectation has gone, would feel like being a jack-in-the-box and hollering 'surprise' to everyone whose presence triggered muteness in the first place.

One, perhaps, would have to personally experience SM to understand how distressing it can be to be trapped in such a way. Compounding that distress, however, is that SM can engender very little sympathy or support because it is wrongly perceived to be a choice – namely a 'refusal to talk' – when in fact nothing could be further from the truth.

Speech behaviour = separation and attachment behaviour (sometimes)

I have already described an association between silence, 'threat' and separation, silence being an entirely natural response to threat and separation from caregivers in young children. It seems to be the case that many young children with SM also have comorbid separation anxiety and/or attachment disorders. In fact, SM has been likened to an insecure attachment style (Kolvin et al., 1997).

To demonstrate the association (at least in my own case) between speech behaviour and attachment behaviour, I would consistently find myself muted by associates and relatives of people I knew well. As such I was rendered mute by the proximity of my stepfather in relation to my mother; the proximity of partners and friends in relation to my friends; the proximity of my daughter's fiancé or friends in relation to my daughter; and even my mother-in-law and wife's friends in relation to my wife. I could only speak when a third-party associated with someone I cared for was not around. Particularly when I was an adult, if the third-party had no association with an 'attachment figure' at all I would probably be able to speak to them – for instance a person visiting the house to fix the boiler.

There was thus a triangular/triadic pattern to this part of my behaviour: myself at one corner, an attachment figure at another, and an associate of the attachment figure at the third. Introspectively, it appears that I expect to be 'socially exposed' (thus in need of the support of an attachment figure) and also to 'lose someone I care for' when a semi-stranger is on the scene.

This kind of triangular pattern can also explain so-called 'progressive mutism' (a variant of SM when a child gradually ceases to be able to speak to anyone at all). When I was younger my muteness tended to spread/progress because rather than be able to overcome my inability to speak to a third-party, I would, instead, cease being able to speak to the attachment figure long term. As an example, when my brother married I ceased to be able to speak to him, having been unable to speak to his fiancée. I also ceased to be able to speak to my mother, as a child, when my stepfather-to-be moved in. Given I also could not speak to any associate of anyone I could not speak to already, SM rapidly spread to just about every person in my life.

I still very much feel the compulsion to cease speaking when any similar triadic relationship pattern occurs.

I am not suggesting that this kind of pattern is the case for every adult or child who experiences SM, however I believe such 'triangulation' to be quite common. In Chapter 13, a parent (Louise) writes about 'triangulation' in regard to her daughter also. One could suggest that the therapeutic technique called Sliding-in™ (Johnson and Wintgens, 2016) works directly on this kind of triangle – gradually moving a third-party trigger into the emotional space, and hence relationship, between child and trusted person.

The Sliding-in Technique™ is a therapeutic procedure by Maggie Johnson and Alison Wintgens in which a person to whom a child cannot speak, for instance a teacher, moves gradually into hearing range of a child (through a door which is initially ajar, for example). The child is accompanied by a trusted person they can speak to already, and all the while is quietly counting. For further information on Sliding–in™ and other therapeutic techniques, see Chapter 10 of Johnson and Wintgens' *The Selective Mutism Resource Manual* (2016).

In my own experience (see my life story) – I began to speak again to my mother by increasing volume while reading a book to her – whispering at first, eventually using my full voice. This could be likened to a second procedure deemed shaping. Both the Sliding-in Technique™ and shaping are means of graded exposure and phobia elimination.

For those children who are mute with their own parents/stepparents, as I was, parental divorce is commonly involved (c.f. A. Sluckin, personal communication, 2015). The results of divorce are, of course, a huge amount of anxiety in the home environment followed by (if one or other parent remarries or sees other people) the introduction of a stranger directly into an already anxious child's personal space. For children who have SM already this can be very difficult to deal with, even more so if the stepparent turns out to be controlling or hostile. Note, however, that even the kindest, gentlest stepparent can encounter difficulties creating a relationship with a child with SM in which speech is reciprocated. While my SM existed long before my parents' divorce, their divorce made it much deeper.

Introduction of a stepparent into the home environment is a potentially difficult process when there is a child with SM. Specific advice on this topic is given by Vivienne (who contributes in numerous places in this book) and Maggie Johnson[2] in Appendix A.

Complex speech rules (explained through my own experience)

Children and adults with SM can be riven with speech rules – basic rules (instincts) about who can be spoken to and who can't, and when and where, all derived from specific anxieties about the person who can't be spoken to. Analyzing my own rules, I had five types as follows:

▶ *Rule 1* – With certain people I was compelled to be mute every single time I encountered them (the instinct to be mute).

▶ *Rule 2* – Those who had never heard me speak would never hear me speak, even if I had known them for years (the speech trap).

▶ *Rule 3* – With a few exceptions, anyone related or associated with anyone who I couldn't speak to couldn't be spoken to either. (I could only rationalize being mute with one person if I was mute with all their associates too.)

▶ *Rule 4* – Those who didn't know I was mute in other situations could never be allowed to find out about my muteness. (My inability to speak had to be my secret from those I could speak to.)

▶ *Rule 5* – Those who *only* knew me as mute couldn't discover I could speak in other situations. (My ability to speak had to be my secret from those I couldn't speak to.)

---

2 Principal Speech and Language Therapist, Kent Community Health NHS Foundation Trust, UK.

I must add that none of my rules was consciously derived or maintained, though there is, on reflection, logic to them once one has developed the compulsion not to speak. I will now explain each of the types of rule.

RULE 1: WITH CERTAIN PEOPLE I WAS COMPELLED (IT WAS MY INSTINCT) TO BE MUTE EVERY SINGLE TIME I ENCOUNTERED THEM

When mute, this was my instinct or compulsion not choice. I would liken SM to being a fish circling around its bowl which automatically 'plays dead' every time a gigantic human eye peers in at it. Muteness is both a physiological and psychological reaction to vulnerability and feeling over-perceived by others, silence being an intrinsic part of the fight or flight response. In my own case I have explained that this was, in a large part, based on childhood attachment fears – even as an adult when the fears ought not apply.

Walker (2014) suggests that the fight or flight response has four main behavioural components: Fight, Flight, Freeze and Fawn (the so-called 4Fs). Of the four, I experienced three prominently: Flight, Freeze and Fawn.

Being silent is a means of 'fleeing' which rouses less unwelcome attention than physically fleeing. I would also 'freeze' physically sometimes, find myself feeling stiff and uncomfortable moving. I would remain in an unpleasant situation rather than remove myself from it. Regarding 'fawning', when I was mute I was entirely unable to be disagreeable. I would agree to almost any question, regardless of how contradictory my chain of 'yeses' (i.e. nods) happened to be.

RULE 2: THOSE WHO HAD NEVER HEARD ME SPEAK WOULD NEVER HEAR ME SPEAK, EVEN IF I HAD KNOWN THEM FOR YEARS

Selective Mutism has a memory of its own. In my own experience it had its own way of making very consistent associations and rules regarding those I could and could not speak to. If I encountered someone I had been mute with before, I would find myself unable to change my behaviour because doing so would also make me feel very uncomfortable.

Frankly, it was too frightening to try to speak having developed a pattern of muteness. If I spoke I would also be stepping out into the unknown. I would potentially rouse the overwhelming attention of a person who I had originally found overwhelming. I would also be afraid of how I might feel to hear my own voice again in a circumstance where I'd become unaccustomed to hearing it. I believed I hated my voice, and that it was strange.

This trap can last for months, years, decades, or a lifetime in situations, and with people, where a pattern of muteness has already developed. The trap can, sometimes, be successfully broken by switching environments and making a fresh start – as Danielle's story of recovery shows in the final chapter of this book.

RULES 3, 4 AND 5: MAINTAINING SAFETY AND AVOIDING CHALLENGES TO MUTENESS

The final three rules (Rules 3, 4 and 5) are each derived to avoid every possible future eventuality that could result in an expectation of speaking to someone I couldn't speak to. These rules are as much to do with avoidance of humiliation as avoidance of speech. Together they tautologically cover every possibility of being placed in a position where speech is expected. SM can become very 'watertight' and very difficult indeed to escape from – or break into, if you are a parent, therapist or teacher.

While these communication rules relate to my own experience, many other people with SM report similar rule-making. As such, given all these kinds of communication rules, children and adults with SM live in a precarious space where almost everything they try to do or achieve can feel impossible.

Living a double life

Speech rules can clash, placing multiple conflicting speech demands at the same time on a child or adult with SM and resulting in horrid emotional stress. For this reason children and adults with SM tend to live a double life – switching from one life and personality[3] to another on a daily basis. Most children with SM are silent at school and noisy at home. I was silent at home and speaking at school. Either way, it is still a double life.

Regarding my speech rules, should I have been in the same place as a person who had only ever known me as mute and, also, someone who had only ever known me as speaking, I would have needed to be both mute and demonstrably not mute at the same time. This was a logical and emotional impossibility. In essence, if I were mute I would be ashamed of being mute in front of those who only knew me as speaking; and, yet, if I were to speak (which I could in some situations) I would be ashamed of speaking in front of those I couldn't. I am unclear whether speaking or muteness would win. I would feel 'found out' because SM is something I would always try to hide wherever I could speak.

To avoid clashes of speech demands, I used to have to keep my two lives entirely separate. This is a common theme for people with SM. In my case I had to keep my mute home life secret from my friends (they were never invited back, of course). For many children who are mute primarily at school they often feel the necessity to keep their mute school life secret from their families. As such, parents are often very surprised to receive the first call from school to hear their child isn't speaking and that, at school, he or she isn't the ebullient, loud, vocal child they know. This is particularly the case if a child is being bullied

---

3 Of course, a child's intrinsic personality does not change between situations – merely their ability to 'be themselves'. That said, it was impossible for me to be disagreeable while mute, thus, at some levels, even my basic personality traits were tested.

and the child feels that speaking, plus getting their bullies into trouble, would make their situation worse.

For some, maintaining a double life can be impossible and they succumb to total muteness – besides, for instance, whispering to the family cat sometimes. This is an extreme solution to avoiding all clashes of speech rules and avoiding all possible stresses, all possible humiliations, and so on. They are mute in all circumstances and thus feel, to a degree, 'safe' – although it can't be underestimated how isolating, stressful and 'unsafe' in other ways this is.

Note that it is entirely possible to be mute in all circumstances and to still be suffering from 'selective' mutism. In fact, this is a state that a minority of young adult males (in particular) find themselves in. Selective Mutism is a poor name for this condition. I would prefer the condition to be called Situational Mutism as it is situational rather than selective. That said, for some, all situations can become triggers thus is can even cease to be situational per se. For an example, read Janice writing about her son, Owain, in Chapter 9.

As an example of conflicting speech demands: consider a little girl with SM who enjoys dance classes after school. She is relatively comfortable in that environment and, though reticent, speaks a little. She has even made a couple of friends. One day a classmate from school, who has only ever seen her mute, shows up at the dance class. Immediately, she has the conflicting demands of hiding her muteness from all the other children in the dance class, particularly her friends and, at the same time, hiding her ability to speak from the girl from school. This is extremely stressful for her, and in all likelihood she will never be able to go the dance class again. Her parents will never be able to understand why this happened or why their daughter is distraught.

How the remainder of this book is organized

This chapter provided an experiential rather than academic or professional introduction to Selective Mutism. The remainder of the book explores specific aspects of SM through a multitude of first-hand experiences.

In Chapter 2 ('Selective Mutism – What it is in Our Own Words') 13 people who have personally experienced SM explore what SM is and how it feels.

In Chapter 3 ('Early Life and Selective Mutism') parents of children with SM and people who have experienced SM themselves explore early life experiences.

In Chapter 4 ('Early School Experience and Selective Mutism') early school experiences are explored from both a personal and a parent's perspectives.

In Chapter 5 ('High School Experience and Selective Mutism') high school experiences are explored by 10 people with personal experience of SM in their high school years.

In Chapter 6 ('Parents' Experiences of High School and Home-Schooling') three parents write about SM during the high school years, including a decision to home-school.

In Chapter 7 ('Becoming an Adult with Selective Mutism') seven people whose SM continued into adulthood explore their adult lives.

In Chapter 8 ('Bullying and Selective Mutism') bullying in relation to SM is explored, including issues for some children with SM being targeted because of their inability to speak.

In Chapter 9 ('Mutism, Family Relationships and the Home Environment') the impact SM has on the home environment and family relationships and vice versa is considered.

In Chapter 10 ('Those Who Spoke for Me') a parent writes about speaking for her daughter and an adult with SM writes about having been spoken for, particularly as a child.

In Chapter 11 ('Selective Mutism and Asperger Syndrome') four people with personal experiences of both SM and AS and three parents write about the two conditions.

In Chapter 12 ('Selective Mutism and Learning Difficulties') a parent (Ann) explores her personal experience of parenting a child with SM and learning difficulties, and the pride she has in her daughter.

In Chapter 13 ('Parents' Experiences of Selective Mutism') six parents write about their personal experiences of having a child with SM.

In Chapter 14 ('Therapists' Experiences of Selective Mutism') two therapists (Marian Moldan and Judith Rosenfield) explore their personal experiences of helping children and adolescents with SM.

In Chapter 15 ('A Teacher's Experience of Helping a Child Find Her Voice') a teacher (Hélène Cohen) explores her personal experience in helping a child with SM.

In Chapter 16 ('How Different Life Would Have Been Without Selective Mutism') adults who experienced SM into adulthood write about how different they perceive their lives might have been without SM; and a parent writes about her hopes and fears for the future.

In Chapter 17 ('Life Stories') people with personal experience of SM and parents of SM children include their life stories, to share with the reader a variety of lived experiences.

CHAPTER 2

Selective Mutism – What it is in Our Own Words

Carl Sutton; Kimberly, Danielle, Helen, Ashley, Chris, Alison, Wendy, Kerrie, Sara, Vivienne, Sonja, Justine and Betty

At the present time, the majority of existing literature on SM is written from professional perspectives. This goal of this book, on the other hand, is to convey what it is like to live with SM, in childhood and adulthood, in the words of people who have personally experienced it.

In the introduction I presented my own thoughts about SM and highlighted my own experience. In this chapter, however, I explore the thoughts and perspectives of a number of people who have experienced SM, in order to present an overall view of the condition.

As such, following are the personal descriptions of SM by 13 people who have experienced it. All but two (Danielle and Kerrie) would say they still have SM. Contributors were asked to avoid the formal definitions of SM in their descriptions of SM, repetition of which would be uninformative. Rather they were asked to describe their own feelings and conception of SM in their own way.

It is worth remarking how expressive people with SM can sometimes be – on paper – even if they often or sometimes can't speak.

Selective Mutism is not a choice

The first thing to say is that children and adults with SM are not wilfully mute, when they can't speak. In fact the opposite is true. Without exception (I have yet to encounter an exception, at least) children and adults with SM desperately want to speak in the situations they can't.

Kimberly, who is an artist and writer,[1] has had SM all her life. She describes her own SM as follows:

Speaking from experience, I tell you this condition is not wilful. That is to say: children and adults are not silent on purpose.

I compare the throat and the voice to an elevator. The voice works well enough a lot of the time (especially in one-on-one interactions and with a select handful of people), but there are times that the elevator car snaps its cables. It is then that the voice seems to free-fall down the throat and there's no accessing it.

SM is not a 'controlling' behaviour. Why would anyone who is filled to the brim with words choose not to utter them? Nor is SM a 'stubborn' refusal to talk. It's an inability to speak.

Although SM can be caused by trauma, most people with SM don't have a history of trauma. In fact, SM can have a genetic component – it often runs in families.

I can tell you how SM feels: overwhelming sensory-integration issues, autism, severe anxiety… In my case, I've got all of the above in addition to SM.

Can a person outgrow it? Many people will tell you they have done just that. There are ways to cope. But I think, for the majority, including myself, it will always be there.

---

1   Kimberly Gerry-Tucker is author of *Under the Banana Moon: A True Story of Living, Loving, Loss and Asperger's* (2012).

Why indeed would someone as expressive and lyrical as Kimberly choose not to speak? Muteness is not a conscious choice. As Kimberly points out, SM affects many adults of all ages, as well as children, although adults with SM are seldom heard of in academic or any other kind of literature.

Danielle, who is a mathematics student, reinforces this:

SM is commonly defined as the 'failure to speak in certain social situations'. However, to me, it is so much more than that. On the surface, it appears as though the sufferer is choosing when and where to speak; however, the truth is that rather than being deliberately silent in certain situations, it feels as though you physically can't talk, like the words will not come out.

Danielle featured in the BBC TV documentary *My Child Won't Speak* (Goddard and Peel, 2010) and also the BBC Radio 4 programme *Finding Your Voice* (Tzabar, 2015). She recovered from/overcame SM when she was 15. Danielle's story of recovery is included in Chapter 17.

Likewise, Helen writes:

SM is a part of who I am. It is not a choice. It is an anxiety condition that I have learned to live with. But it does not have to define me. There is more to me than SM.

Helen makes the very valid point that SM defines nobody. SM is a behaviour, or mental health issue, depending on your interpretation of it. However, behind each situationally silent face is an extraordinary human being – as creative, intelligent or expressive as any other.

Physiological responses and initial triggers

Regarding what happens, physiologically, when an adult or child is first mute, there appear to be two related physiological experiences. The first is an anxiety/panic reaction based upon the physical presence of key individuals or groups of people. The panic response can be intense and profound and much like the Amygdala Hijack referred to by Goleman (1996). Each of us have two amygdalae – one in each side of the brain. The amygdalae contribute to threat detection. In conjunction with other brain structures, such as the hippocampus, they are also involved in forging and responding to emotional memories, mood and social cognition. In much the same way that someone can make a rash or thoughtless decision due to an Amygdala Hijack (regretting their actions immediately after, when their conscious thoughts catch up sufficiently to reflect on what they have done), I feel that muteness in Selective Mutism is an instinctual reaction, which is faster than or bypasses rational decision making. Having had an uncontrollable, immediate urge to be mute in a given situation, a person with SM subsequently worries 'why is this?', 'what am I afraid of?', 'why can't I stop doing this?' and 'what do people think about me, mute like this?'

To reiterate, one of the key points of the introduction, mutism in SM is not a choice. Rather, people with SM have fixed instinctual 'rules' forged into their emotional memories about who or what triggers muteness. In much the same way that an Amygdala Hijack hijacks one's actions, SM can hijack one's voice.

Ashley writes:

There have been circumstances where I have forgotten my age, or even my name. And there have been many situations where I indeed am expected to speak and fail to. I try with all my will to speak, but when it comes to it I am overcome by anxiety and it is as if I have no voice. I try to smile and often begin blushing in my humiliation, while I feel everyone's eyes drilling into me, and I seek any exit from the situation as soon as possible.

The second, seemingly related, experience is that of a 'slowness to react'. This has nothing to do with intelligence it has to be said – on the contrary it may be to do with so-called sensory overload or stress. After all, few perform well under stress. For instance, Chris writes:

> *I have had to figure out for myself what is wrong with me, as my SM was not diagnosed in childhood. My SM arose out of mild autism (Asperger Syndrome) with an inability to understand situations, a slowness to react and not having things explained lovingly by my parents. I found it impossible to talk with teachers due to the inability to process and answer questions quickly enough. I feel that my brain has reduced the empathy I feel so that I can cope.*

When we are mute it feels as though something switches off in our heads. Our voices feel disconnected from our thoughts. In my own past experience I have likened being mute, as a teenager, to my voice disappearing into a void in the centre of my head. My voice felt irretrievable.

The panic/physiological response to be mute is automatic. And, as such, the cause of it can be very difficult to fathom or explain – even by the person experiencing it. For instance, as Alison writes:

> *SM is like having your voice trapped inside your own mind. It's feeling as if your throat is physically locked when you're put in a position in which you are expected to speak and want to speak, but can't. It's feeling alone, because you're 'that kid who doesn't talk' and most people have never encountered anyone like you before, and they don't understand why you can't speak. It's not being able to explain why you don't talk, because even if you were able to speak to answer them, you don't fully understand it yourself.*

However, there will sometimes be an identifiable trigger – usually a specific individual or group of people. Ashley cites the presence of a new unfamiliar person as a trigger:

> As soon as any new person is introduced into a situation it is as if a switch goes off in my head. I become inhibited and my voice shuts off.

Whereas Wendy, having this in common with me also, cites potential hostility or disapproval as a trigger:

> If I am challenged, or if I sense hostility or disapproval from someone I usually become mute in those situations where I most need to stand up for myself. I don't feel as though I have ever grown up, and I am embarrassed to have reached the age I now am and to still be this way.

Sometimes the trigger can be very specific. For instance, Alison cites her grandfather as her initial trigger:

> I developed SM at about age four. At first I couldn't talk to or in the presence of my grandfather, and, after I started school, I couldn't speak in school either. I was never diagnosed nor received any treatment for SM. It caused me to feel so anxious in school that I felt physically ill, and stayed home from school frequently. I dropped out of school at the age of 16. I had trouble developing basic social skills and still struggle with social interaction. As an adult it has made finding and maintaining employment difficult.

Note, however, that Alison had a very good relationship with her grandfather. He was not a 'threat' in any conscious sense:

> Every weekend, my mother would take me and my siblings to visit our grandparents. When my grandfather was present, I wasn't able to speak in front of him, or to him. I remember my grandmother chastising me for being 'rude'

to him, but my grandfather himself was understanding and never made me feel guilty about it.

On the other hand, Kerrie cites fear of negative evaluation, a marker of Social Anxiety Disorder, as a trigger:

SM made me feel like I was someone different. I felt very isolated and cut off from other people. I also felt very sad and lonely. I was afraid to talk. SM is a fear of talking and also a fear of what other people think of you. I always believed that other people thought I was weird or different in some way. I was constantly anxious around other people and couldn't look them in the eye. I also had problems doing anything in front of people that would draw attention to me. I felt anxious in rooms full of people and while out shopping with my mum. I couldn't eat in front of people in the school canteen or anywhere in public. I experienced a constant fear of interacting with people.

SM seems to be based on situational fears and anticipatory anxiety

One should not underestimate how difficult starting to speak again after developing SM is, however. It sounds very easy. A child or adult just has to speak – a very human thing. SM is seemingly solvable in an instant to the observer; and this thought doesn't pass by someone experiencing SM either. However, to speak again the child or adult has to overcome both (a) the initial, usually inexplicable, fear that rendered them mute in the first place – a fear that lost its shape and understandability many years ago but still returns as a shapeless terror when they try to speak; and additionally (b) the anticipatory fear of beginning to talk again when nobody is expecting it – changing profoundly and becoming a vocal, social person. SM can be a hellish trap to break out of.

Danielle believes she was born with anxiety and explains that SM was her way to control her anxiety:

I believe that I have suffered with severe anxiety from birth and this was the reason why, when I started school and social interaction became an important part of everyday life, I developed SM as a way of keeping my anxiety at bay. By not talking, I was allowing myself to be in control of my anxiety, leading people to make the incorrect judgement that I was selecting when and when not to speak. Due to the extent of my anxiety, this 'coping strategy' very quickly developed into SM, meaning that however hard I tried, I couldn't speak at all.

Likewise, Ashley writes about anticipatory anxiety in relation to SM:

Going into public and social situations, I will often begin to experience anxiety in anticipation of any situation where I will be expected to speak. I will attempt to make myself as low profile as possible and avoid eye contact so as not to invite conversation. Though sometimes I will be forced into these situations anyway. In this event I will feel my heart rate and breathing increase, I will picture myself answering and play it over and over in my head, but fear no words will come out when I open my mouth. I will try my best to stay relaxed and clear my throat in preparation, and in some cases from time to time I am successful and can give a one-word answer.

Anticipatory anxiety is a maintaining factor in SM in a number of ways. First of all the anxiety experienced in anticipation of speaking, when mute, makes speech very difficult. It becomes very difficult to differentiate between a genuine trigger for muteness and becoming mute due to the anticipation of being mute.

Speech rules and anxieties are very frustrating

As a complex system of 'rules', anxieties and triggers, SM can be very difficult, constricting and frustrating to navigate around and live inside. Sara likens SM to a maze that she will, one day, escape from:

> *I see SM as a complex maze-like obstacle, preventing me from ever reaching the outside. Every step I take, trying to overcome my speech difficulties by attempting to accomplish what seem like simple tasks such as speaking to a classmate or professor, or talking about my week with my cousins, I hit a wall: Selective Mutism. When I hit this wall, I divert onto another path, down which I just hit another wall. SM is an anger instigator and knows how to get under my skin and bring the worst out of me. In time, I will learn the maze's blueprint, and I will be able to escape.*

Sometimes our voices feel trapped in our throats or sound strange

Males with SM seem less likely to experience unpleasant physical sensations when trying to speak than females. In my own experience I have never experienced any physical sensation in relation to trying to speak (besides a feeling of anxiety in my stomach and at the back of my mind, if I were to contemplate trying). This may be due to it being more socially acceptable for males to be reticent. I would expect that there were fewer situations that I would have been expected to speak than a comparative female.

Alison describes the unpleasant feelings thus:

> *It's feeling as if your throat is physically locked when you're put in a position in which you are expected to speak and want to speak, but can't.*

Likewise, and I have experienced this, when we do speak we can perceive our voices as sounding strange. As Vivienne writes:

> *To me, my voice sounded loud and incongruous, even though I was really only whispering, speaking always caused me to blush and made my palms feel sweaty.*

And, as Wendy writes, children and adults with SM can lose touch with what their voice sounds like and it can feel very strange to hear it, including through a voice recording.

> *When I am in a situation where I feel uncomfortable about speaking but it is necessary for me to speak, or if I feel 'put on the spot' my voice sounds strained, really weird, and it feels as if I have no control over how I sound in these situations. Sometimes then my voice is barely audible and I am frequently asked to repeat myself. Attempts at speaking are often embarrassing, shaming experiences for me. I sound quite different when speaking with someone I am more relaxed with, but I don't like the way my voice sounds at the best of times; I was horrified when I heard a recording of myself. Because of this inhibition about speaking, I have never learned to project my voice or to use it effectively. I often feel that I could no more use my vocal cords to break a silence, to get somebody's attention or to initiate an interaction than I could run through fire or do something dangerous in my life.*

I am assured that disliking one's voice is a common phenomenon, even for people who don't have SM. I have found that sometimes I can't judge volume correctly and I feel as if I have a different voice for every occasion where I can speak. This may be because my speech still feels relatively unpractised. I constantly feel I have rather a lot of catching up to do, regarding the count of words I have spoken in my life.

SM is situational: we tend to live double lives

Most commonly, children with SM tend to be mute at school and speak at home, keeping their two lives entirely separate. Sonja writes:

> *I spoke normally at home. There I was sometimes loud, even bossy, but I was barely able to speak to people outside my immediate family from the age of 12 for a period of eight years. I didn't tell anyone about this at the time, I didn't ask for help, I didn't know that I needed help. Most times I desperately wanted to speak, but I couldn't. My family didn't know because I talked at home.*

Because I have been so ashamed of being mute, I have tended to keep my muteness a secret from anyone who would not guess that I experience this behaviour.

For instance, my friends at sixth form never witnessed my muteness because I was mute primarily at home. I was mute in one life, and couldn't do anything about it, and because I was ashamed of my muteness I kept it a secret in my more 'public' life. Mine was the opposite pattern to most, of course. For most people with SM, home is their haven – the place they can relax and talk. Even so, children and adults with the ordinary pattern still live a double life though they, perhaps, don't always have the desperate need for secrecy that I had.

SM is tough to live with and dominates one's whole life

Justine is 16, an excellent musician, and has been home-schooled by her mum, Julie, for the last few years. Justine's writes about her experience of SM:

> *The only people I can talk to freely are my closest family, which comprises of three people: my mum, dad and sister.*

I have no friends my age. I yearn to meet like-minded people who I can develop strong bonds with, and feel safe with.

Everyday life is an arduous challenge. I am anxious when I think of what the day contains, what situations I will be put in and where I will have to go. I find it so difficult to cope in any social environment. Every fibre of me wants to run and hide in a dark cave where no one can judge me or speak to me.

When I go out anywhere I am tense. I avoid eye contact and hide in the shadow of my mother to evade attention. Since I am unable to speak, if a person were to address me, it would be profoundly distressing. I struggle to avoid any such incident and try to be insignificant.

If a stranger were to approach me, they would be greeted by my total silence. They think I am being insulting or rude, but that is not true. They don't understand that I don't want to offend them – that something within me prevents me from speaking. A dominant force in my brain stops me from speaking. Panic freezes me to the spot. I can't control what I do. I can't think about the situation and resolve it. I feel like a paralyzed deer in the headlights.

A person I know well will get a smile, perhaps a quiet 'hello'. However, I find it tough to make eye contact. When I do that I feel the need to move back several paces. I feel asphyxiated by the other person's presence. Then I will awkwardly look away or look at mum, moving away from the person's possible passage of exit, smiling mutely if I am addressed.

SM can be a very lonely experience

Clearly, SM can cause a good deal of loneliness. Betty eloquently describes the lifelong loneliness that SM can bring with it:

Aloneness – that is what SM feels like to me. Isolated, alone, separated, left out as I silently stand by watching others experience life while the words freeze inside me, afraid to speak up or join in a conversation. Actually feeling the anxiety shaking inside my chest as I try to get up the courage to speak to someone or call or text a friend. SM feels like the child standing alone behind the door watching the other kids in the playground – afraid to ask, 'may I play?' It feels like the teenager standing silently against the wall, listening to classmates laugh and chat, invisible to everyone and wondering what it would be like to have a friend. It feels like the 50-year-old office worker, alone in her cube while others chat and laugh in the aisle, still left out. I live inside a shell, a mask that looks like me, but isn't me. I am in here, but it is really hard to let others see.

I'm so grateful for the few dear friends I have now. Most people, though, only see the shell and assume I'm aloof and uncaring because I am quiet. I feel very deeply. I feel others' joy and pain intensely, yet they rarely know. I'm not quiet because I am uncaring. I'm silent because I'm afraid.

SM can feel very trapping and isolating

For those whose SM continues into adolescence or adulthood there very often comes a point in life where it becomes unbearable – notably when a person with SM feels overwhelmingly isolated, trapped, scrutinized, humiliated by their inability to speak, and absolutely barred from the ordinary things in life such as forming their own family.

As a teenager and young adult, I found being mute intensely isolating and dehumanizing. I felt truly like I was just a pair of eyes and ears – an entity without a body, without a face, and without a mouth. I felt as though I was barely a physical being. At this stage, SM can become an execrable experience. Describing this part of the experience, Sonja writes:

I was a prisoner inside my own body. I felt desperate, angry, stupid, confused, ashamed, hopeless and absolutely alone… and that this was of my own making. I could speak at home, how come I couldn't outside it? I have never been able to find the right words to describe what it was like. Imagine that for one day you are unable speak to anyone you meet outside your own family, particularly at school/college, or out shopping, etc., have no sign language, no gestures, no facial expression. Then imagine that for eight years, but no one really understands. It was like torture, and I was the only person who knew it was happening. My body and face were frozen most of the time. I became hyperconscious of myself when outside the home and it was a relief to get back as I was always exhausted. I attempted to hide it (an impossible task) because I felt so ashamed that I couldn't do what other people seemed to find so natural and easy – to speak. At times I felt suicidal.

SM can leave us feeling traumatized years later

While SM may be uncommonly caused by trauma, I would certainly say that my own experience of SM was traumatic to live through. I felt extremely trapped and isolated by SM and the speech rules that I had which meant that I could speak in one situation but not another or I couldn't speak if a certain person (usually the partner of a friend or a parent) was there. My life felt at risk due to the stress that I was under, feeling so isolated due to my inability to speak. Without exaggeration I would say that, in my late teens and early 20s, I found being mute thoroughly torturous. Echoing how I feel about my own past experience, Sonja writes:

I still feel traumatized by my experience, and certain stressful situations at work trigger my being mute again. It is extremely distressing. I re-experience the torture and become 13 years old again at school and the girl who does not speak. I feel incredibly ashamed because I can't control it and still don't know how to deal with it. I look at other people and wonder at how natural speech is for them. For me it is always a conscious process, unless I am with people I know very well or am in a 'flow' about something that really interests me.

CHAPTER 3

Early Life and Selective Mutism

Carl Sutton; Vivienne, Andrea and Bronwen
(parents); Wendy, Danielle, Liz and Kat

While most anxiety disorders, including Social Anxiety Disorder, begin in adolescence or early adulthood, SM has a very early mean age of onset, as discussed in the introduction. In fact, many adults with SM would say that they were 'born' with the condition – often because their parents informed them this was the case.

Given the very early age of onset of SM, many children develop/have SM before they begin preschool, nursery, kindergarten or school. Many children with SM are unable to speak to aunts, uncles, grandparents, other extended relatives visitors and/or family friends before they start school. Prior to going to preschool or kindergarten, however, their inhibitions are often put down to shyness. As such the behaviour is usually (but not always) well tolerated by their parents, other relatives, and strangers. I recall myself, as a very young child, often hiding behind my mother's trouser legs in the proximity of adult strangers who would remark that I was 'taking everything in'. At such times, I felt acutely alert and I did indeed listen to everything everyone said and watched everything everyone did. When I became a teenager and still couldn't speak, however, I soon realized that I was no longer 'cute' and I felt very alienated by my own behaviour.

SM usually becomes remarked on when a child first enters a communal environment outside the family home for the first time – such as preschool or kindergarten. A behaviour that seems unremarkable and natural to parents and relatives in the family home seems stark and highly remarkable to teachers and child minders who find themselves faced with a child behaving very differently from their peers – a young child who is mute, expressionless, perhaps even physically frozen in the presence of all adults, peers or both.

SM in early childhood may be marked by a fear of adults, separation anxiety, anxiety or freezing during routine medical checks, sensitivity to touch, loud sounds, and so on. As such children with SM often seem to be of an innately sensitive nature – both psychologically and physiologically. In my own case, I recall disliking many physiological sensations when I was a child. For instance, I couldn't stand 'feeling full' after eating, walking barefoot on grass or sand, certain textures such as wet or rough paper, being touched or hugged, and so on. These are common dislikes for children with SM, ADHD, Sensory Processing Disorder, autism and so on. Such dislikes are markers of a number of developmental disorders as well as SM, which is not deemed a developmental disorder.

To begin this chapter, Vivienne writes about her daughter, Hazel. Vivienne has her own history of SM too, which means that she has an understanding of SM both first-hand and as a parent, which is a very valuable combination.

Hazel was born at home. She was a contented baby who fed well and made lots of eye contact with us. Hazel soon began imitating our facial expressions and mouthing words, although of course she was far too young to speak. She consistently smiled at us from one month onwards, although the health visitor claimed she was too young to do this. Hazel was a communicative and affectionate baby with her immediate family. She loved to sit and watch her older sister play and Hazel's eyes would follow her attentively around the room. She was equally at home with some of our extended family who she saw regularly.

Developmentally, Hazel gave no grounds for concern. In fact she was ahead in many ways. She was an early walker and had perfect balance and coordination, right from day one; and she never seemed to totter or fall on her bottom like other toddlers did. She was an early talker too and had no trouble learning colours, numbers, the alphabet and nursery rhymes etc. Rather strangely, she also had an extraordinary sense of smell.

Anecdotally, having a heightened sense of smell, along with being sensitive to touch, sound and taste, seems to be common among infants who go on to develop SM, which may, again, indicate that children with SM are innately more physiologically sensitive than average. From an evolutionary point of view, there are advantages to this of course, in terms of avoiding predators and keeping safe. Some research suggests that children with SM (along with children with autism and anorexia nervosa) have enlarged amygdalae – structures in their brains that automatically activate under threat, with connections to memory, the senses, and, interestingly, given Vivienne's contribution, the olfactory system (one's sense of smell).

Andrea writes about her daughter:

Jennifer's interaction with people seemed normal up until about six months of age. She was a happy baby, smiling and hardly crying.

Over time she seemed to get more and more withdrawn, hiding behind me if approached by anyone, and getting very distressed if I moved too far away from her. I was told it was probably extreme shyness and she would grow out of it, which was untrue.

Toddlers who develop SM can often initially be happy and contented. However, they seem to develop separation anxiety and/or stranger fears quite early in their lives – generally between six months and three years. From an evolutionary point of view there are advantages in maintaining proximity with a parent for safety, of course, and also in maintaining silence when under 'threat'. As was indicated in the introduction there is a relationship between 'safety', silence and attachment – they are each related via the survival instinct and the fight or flight response.

Continuing the theme of attachment and a need for proximity, Vivienne writes:

> *Hazel didn't like to be placed in her cot to sleep. She really loved attachment and liked to sleep in my arms. This presented a problem at bedtime as I had to let Hazel fall asleep in my arms and then, ever so gently, lower her into her cot. Hazel woke up on many occasions, as I tried to place her in her cot, so I would have to start over again. This sometimes made bedtime quite exhausting. Her afternoon nap was equally difficult as, unlike her older sister, who would settle down and sleep on her own for a couple of hours, Hazel needed to be held all the time.*

Stranger fears/fear of adults

Parents of children with SM often notice their children exhibiting stranger fears from a young age. Andrea writes:

> *In her early years, Jennifer's main difficulty was communicating with adults. She was a lively, happy girl at home with her family but in situations away from her family she was withdrawn and found it difficult to express her feelings to any adult. She was withdrawn when being talked to and showed extreme stress when attention was put on her. She had no problems communicating with children. She was fun loving and all her peers wanted to play with her, but when an adult approached she became silent and frozen, not able to move or speak. When visiting friends or family Jennifer would be clingy, unable to leave our side.*

Selective Mutism being apparent during routine health tests

Very often signs of SM become apparent in young children during routine health tests – at least in hindsight. Often this is when hearing tests and sounds are part of the process. Again, health tests are occurrences where young children are placed outside the ordinary safety of their home environment. Vivienne writes:

> When Hazel was about nine months old we attended our local health centre for a routine hearing test. This was performed by a health visitor, together with a nurse. Hazel sat on my lap while the health visitor sat in front of us and distracted Hazel with a toy, meanwhile the nurse quietly positioned herself behind us holding a small bell. When the nurse rang the bell I felt Hazel tense up. She then began fidgeting uncomfortably. The test was repeated three times as Hazel didn't turn to look in the direction of the sound. The health visitor concluded that Hazel had heard the bell, as she was definitely reacting to the sound. However, she seemed to be showing discomfort rather than curiosity. I had held Hazel's older sister when she was Hazel's age and the same test was performed. Hazel's sister immediately turned to see who was ringing the bell; she seemed curious and, unlike Hazel, didn't seem bothered by the possibility of eye contact or the fact that there was a stranger behind her.

Fear of loud noises (the startle response)

In common with Hazel's fear of hearing a 'bell' during a routine health check, a fear of loud noises (such as vacuum cleaners, kettles, and fireworks) is a common issue for young children who have or go on to develop SM. Wendy writes:

I remember that I was a very nervous, anxious child and I felt scared a lot of the time. I was scared of any machine or appliance that made a noise. That included the vacuum cleaner and the whistling kettle we had. There was one shop that had a machine, which ground coffee beans. The noise that it made sounded very loud to me at the time and I wouldn't go in that shop. I used to insist on waiting outside if my mother went in there!

Issues at nursery and playgroup

SM is often first noticed and picked up at nursery or playgroup – the first social/group situation outside the home where a parent tends to leave a child, giving rise to separation anxiety. In fact, Danielle recalls experiencing her first panic attack at a very early age, at playgroup:

I distinctly remember having my first mini panic attack. My great grandparents had taken me to a playgroup one day and, as I realized that they were leaving, I started crying uncontrollably. I didn't stop until, and after what seemed like hours but was realistically no more than five minutes, they came back and took me home. I didn't attend the playgroup after that and had no social interaction with anyone my age until I started school when I was three.

Potential triggers for SM in young children

There are, sometimes, anxiety-raising triggers in the lives of young children. This chapter does not contain a definitive list of such experiences – this is not intended to be an academic study. Nonetheless there are themes among the variety of stories of young children and their parents.

Separation from a primary caregiver as young children

Writing from my own experience, my maternal grandfather died when I was around three years old. I was sent to live with extended relatives for a few months because my mother could not cope, entering a period of 'abnormal' grieving. Although I do not recall this period at all, I am certain that I would have been mute and profoundly anxious throughout. When I was around the same age, my father accidentally severed an artery in his wrist. I recall hiding behind the settee when he eventually returned from hospital. In my own experience, there were therefore traumas (from a young child's point of view) which may have contributed to the inception of my SM as well as other factors in my home environment which I described in the introduction.

Hospitalization as young children

A relatively common trigger for SM in young children can be hospitalization. While parents are permitted to stay in hospital with their children nowadays, even in the relatively recent past this was not the case. Childhood hospitalization can be a strong trigger for attachment or separation anxiety, and relatedly mutism too – particularly for children between two and four years of age.

Liz writes about her experience of hospitalization in the 1960s:

> As a very young child I was confident, and frequently wanting to be the centre of attention. I was a 'Daddy's girl', I would be cheeky and do things which I wouldn't dare have attempted in later years. But one of my first memories was being in a hospital bed. I still have the letter from the hospital agreeing that, in spite of my tender years, my tonsils and adenoids should be removed – I was two and a half years old at the time and had suffered from very

*bad problems with ear, and throat infections. My memory
was of being in a hospital bed, which looked more like
a cot, the nurses were asking me questions and I would
not answer. Later I found myself in a different bed on the
hospital ward. My parents had come to visit me – but then
they left, and I couldn't understand why they hadn't taken
me home with them.*

Vicarious experiencing

Anxiety-raising home environments can, potentially, be a
trigger for SM. Most children can and do experience a parent's
stress vicariously. For instance, death of grandparents can affect
young children via the emotional effects on their parents. This
is part of my own experience too. Bronwen writes about her
son, Haydn:

*Haydn had observed me caring for his dying grandmother
and we spent a lot of time with her. Within three months
he also saw my husband's uncle die on the ward where I
worked as a nurse and a close friend of his unexpectedly
died. Haydn had spent a lot of time with this child as the
mum and I had shared child care. Haydn was aged six
at this point and, while I am not convinced these events
caused him to become selectively mute, his levels of anxiety
certainly increased around this time and he became
increasingly self-reliant as a form of self-protection.*

As Bronwen indicates, mutism can rapidly become a
psychological tool of choice in order to avoid experiencing
anxiety and to maintain a sense of safety.

Geographic location and social isolation

In addition to environment stressors, geographic location can
be a factor in the development of SM. For instance, children
who have fewer opportunities to interact with their peers prior

to starting school seem to have more difficulty when entering school. For instance, Liz writes:

> *We lived in the country: an idyllic place for a child to grow up in, but I didn't have much contact with other children. My brother would tease me, I was an easy target. I was sensitive and would often take things literally but I still looked up to him. When my brother started to attend school, I couldn't wait to go with him. But the reality was very different from what I imagined. Being three years younger I was in a different class from him and I wasn't prepared for the company of children I didn't know: I felt lost and frightened. There were very few people I felt comfortable talking to and I was constantly anxious and self-conscious. I became a very serious, fearful and introverted child. I started to build a protective barrier around myself, but far from protecting me it contained and fuelled my fears and anxieties and was sapping my energy and self-confidence.*

Relocation

Likewise upheaval and relocation, particularly between countries and cultures, can be factor in the development of SM. When I was a child my own family relocated a number of times, because my mother was aspirational in terms of where she wished to live. I would say that repeatedly moving areas impacted on my ability to interact at school, particularly the more times it happened. Regarding relocation between continents, Kat writes:

> *Exactly one month before my second birthday my brother was born. I was a 'happy little thing' and I loved my brother. I played well by myself, chattered away and generally was a normal, happy two-year-old. It was 1981.*
>
> *My parents were working out how to tackle the economic crisis and stress levels were high. I'm not sure if it had an impact on me at this stage, but my baby brother definitely noticed. He cried and cried – and cried.*

Four months later we moved from North East England to the 35th floor of the Ponte City Apartments in Johannesburg.

During those first six months we moved house five times. Each time, I made new friends and started again. I was two – and that seemed to be okay. However, it became apparent that I was not talking to my own friends and that I no longer spoke to anyone outside my own family. Alongside my difficulties with speaking, I also found it hard to make eye contact with people and I simply couldn't smile for the camera if it was anyone other than my parents on the other side of it. It is really difficult for me to truly connect back to this time of my life and then attempt to decipher what was going on for me. However, it does make a lot of sense today to think that I was picking up on the high-stress feelings around me, and my reaction was one of silence.

Home environment

While it may be uncommon for issues in the home environment to compound SM, many such stories do exist. Given SM is an anxiety disorder it can be further compounded, obviously, by anxiety arising from any part of a child with SM's life. I have written that my own difficult home environment (see my life story in the introduction) strongly impacted on my ability to speak.

Vivienne's story is similar to mine in that her SM was compounded by her new stepfather entering the family home, though she experienced it much earlier in her childhood than I did. Vivienne writes:

When I was a little girl, my world felt safe. At home I could be a veritable chatterbox with my immediate family. Then I started kindergarten class at school and, at the same time, a new and unfamiliar person entered the family: my stepfather. I was suddenly struck dumb, as the world had suddenly overwhelmed me. What had once felt safe now felt threatening and unpredictable. School just induced a fog of anxiety within me, and for a long time, I never uttered a word.

Vivienne also provides a very valuable contribution about successfully incorporating a stepparent into the home environment in Appendix A.

The reasons for tackling SM early on in life

One might suggest that during early childhood, when being selectively mute is acceptable behaviour for a child, the people who suffer most with it are parents and other relatives. Parents are often worried about their children's future at this age, when the children aren't themselves, and grandparents and other extended relatives often feel upset because they can't be spoken to. For the most part, SM is ordinary behaviour for the children themselves and, generally, it does not cause unhappiness to them at this age, unless, that is, the behaviour is challenged and then they can feel discomforted. Kat writes about her own experience and her own parents:

> *I was not talking to my friends. I no longer spoke to anyone outside my own family. Yet I'm not sure it was really an issue for my young friends or me at this stage. So much communication between young children is non-verbal, and I had no problem with communicating in this way. I'm told that I played happily and that other children completely accepted me. We found our way to make our little friendships work without the need for words. It was more difficult for the teachers at my nursery school, but I am told that we found ways to make it work too. I imagine that the people who struggle the most with SM in young children are the parents. When your child does not speak to people other than you it can pose any number of questions, worries and fears.*

That said, SM is best tackled when a child is young, otherwise it can develop into a potentially lifelong disorder – as it did for me. By way of example Andrea writes about the progression of her now adult daughter's SM:

Jennifer has a loving family (mother, father and older sister) and although we have always given her full support, we have not been able to reduce her fears, anxiety and ever-increasing progression of SM. We feel this is mainly because she was misunderstood by the various professionals she came into contact with, being branded as stubborn and oppositional when she was the complete opposite. Jennifer always wanted to please, getting distraught when people thought she was rude or when they got angry with her – all because she couldn't reply or show any emotion in front of them.

For more information about SM in adults, see Chapter 7.

CHAPTER 4

Early School Experience and Selective Mutism

Carl Sutton; Dawn (parent); Marian, Vivienne, Kat, Danielle,
Kerrie, Sara, Nicky, Alison, Betty, Adriane and Wendy

Following on from the previous chapter, which was about early life experience, this chapter describes the experiences of young children with SM in their early school environment. To begin this chapter, Marian Moldan,[1] who now uses her own life experience to work with anxious children and children with SM in New York, writes briefly about an episode in her own early school life.

> *Thomas proudly said, 'Jane'. Martha sat up straight when it was her turn and said, 'run'. Lynn said a loud and clear, 'see' as the next card was held in front of the teacher. The class of first grade children sat in a circle as Mrs Beasley showed the uniformly cut white flashcards with the words each child would read as she went around the circle. They were new to school and eager to please. Nothing but the sound of the cards flipping followed by the sound of a young child's voice could be heard over and over again.*
>
> *Then it was my turn. I loved school. I loved my teacher. I knew those words – each and every one of them. I felt smart. I wanted Mrs Beasley to smile at me. I wanted her to nod. I desperately wanted to hear her say, 'Good,*

---

1   Marian also contributes to the therapists' chapter – see Chapter 14.

Marian,' just as she had done with my classmates before me. In my head I said the sight words over and over while practicing for when it was my turn. It finally was my turn and there was nothing. Nothing. There were no words coming from my mouth. There was nothing!

I stared straight ahead at that card for what seemed like hours. No one around me said anything. Mrs Beasley said nothing at all. She stared at me, waiting and waiting. There was no help forthcoming, just a feeling as if the life had been sucked out of me. I couldn't breathe. I was trying not to cry. I couldn't say anything. What was worse was that my card had nothing on it!

Mrs Beasley had mistakenly drawn one of those white vocabulary cards that didn't have a word written on it. I couldn't tell her. 'Don't cry. I can't tell her that the card has no word. Don't cry. Just help me. Why can't you help me, Mrs Beasley? Look at the card Mrs Beasley. Can't you see it's blank? Please move onto to someone else…please. Just don't cry. They will look at you more.' The room couldn't have been more still. Finally, and thankfully, Lynn said, 'Mrs Beasley there's nothing on the card.'

Mrs Beasley broke her stare, nodded, smiled, and said, 'Oh, good Lynn.' I got nothing except burning eyes, a face reddened by embarrassment and a feeling that Mrs Beasley hated me. In that moment, I hated her. I hated her stupid cards and I really hated the children who could talk.

When I returned home at the end of the day, I promptly had a tantrum. I wasn't sure why I was angry and my poor mother had no idea what caused such an outburst filled with screaming, throwing, and stomping my right foot. I wanted my mom to know how smart I was. Instead, I felt like I had failed. I couldn't tell her what happened in school, partly because I was ashamed and partly because I just didn't know why I couldn't talk.

What was wrong with me? My mother looked at me with that same look as when one of her friends asked 'what's wrong with her?' It was a look of confusion, anguish, and desperation.

I wanted her to be so proud of me like my brothers and sisters. Instead I felt that I had caused her agony. She knew I was smart. She told me that every day. She told me a story of how the doctor who delivered me told her that I was special…and I was smart beyond my years. He told her my reflexes were not only on target but better than other babies. I loved this story. For an instant I felt special. I felt smart. I felt understood and loved.

However, those wonderful feelings melted each day when I walked silently to the bus stop. This walk was the beginning of my prison of silence each day. Every day I had a similar experience in reading and circle time – filled with humiliation. At least once a day, I wet my pants and looked down at the floor to a puddle of urine because I couldn't ask to go to the bathroom.

On those days, my mother's confusion turned to irritation, 'I'm writing a letter to that teacher and insisting that she let you go to the bathroom anytime you need to go.' That seemed like a great solution to the problem, but I couldn't just get up and go to the bathroom. I never could find the right time to just get up without interrupting my teacher or having everyone look at me.

Day after day I came home with my floral dresses sewn to perfection by my mother, only to be stained and damp. I got used to the teacher saying, 'Why can't you just get up and go to the bathroom?' This teacher, who I had loved, didn't understand. She didn't understand me. She didn't help me. In fact, I sensed her irritation with me. I was just too much work.

There are many themes in Marian's text which are repeated by many others who have experienced SM when they recall their early school lives, as shall be discussed in the remainder of the chapter.

The significance of SM is often not realized

Transient mutism among anxious and sensitive children who are just starting school is, in fact, relatively common. Among this population, most do begin to speak within the first months, after adapting to the hustle and bustle of the school environment. Thus a diagnosis of SM is precluded during the first month of a child's school life.

However, mutism at school can last for a very long time and turn school into a torrid experience. Writing about Tom, her son, Dawn explains:

> *Tom's time at school never got any easier; although academically he was very bright, through the primary years he never managed more than a nod or shake of his head or even when he was at his most relaxed, the faintest of one-word whispers. He would stop talking to me the minute we parked the car, and would give me a death stare if I talked to him walking up the path into school. Tom was never able to answer a question in class even when he was bursting with the answer. Quite often, at primary school, he was overlooked as he always just got on with his work. He was the 'ideal pupil' – bright, quiet and willing to just get on with it. He was forgotten about.*

When the behaviour persists, the significance of a child's mutism is often not realized – either by the child's school or, sometimes, by the parents. Unfortunately, years may elapse between a child starting school and a child receiving a formal diagnosis of SM, or relevant intervention, due to assumptions that children will simply grow out of the behaviour.

SM is often confused with ordinary shyness. Vivienne writes:

> *I don't believe the school or my mother realized the significance of these difficulties; they simply thought I was painfully shy, something that I would get over in my own time.*

Because children with SM are likely to be genuinely the least disruptive children in any classroom, their behaviour may go unnoticed because they don't and in fact can't cause any trouble! Sara writes:

> *People noticed my quietness. Every teacher I ever had mentioned it to my parents. However, because I excelled in class, it was never brought up as something needing to be taken seriously. I speak at home so my parents didn't take any action either.*

Relationships with other children

There is a mixture of responses to children with SM in the classroom. Many are perfectly accepted by their peers who find alternative ways to communicate them; but some are bullied – occasionally by teachers as well. Bullying is only briefly mentioned in this chapter, as Chapter 8 is dedicated to this issue.

Some children find those who can't speak objects of curiosity, at least to begin with. Kat, who relocated between continents as a child several times, writes:

> *I felt quite different to the other kids when I first started school. I think the other kids thought I was interesting...*
> *I remember never being short of people wanting to sit next to me, or play with me – even though I didn't talk back to them. We found ways to play and communicate where words were not necessary, and this seemed perfectly acceptable at the tender age of five. A friend's understanding was made apparent when she introduced me to her Mum at a birthday party, 'This is Kathryn. She doesn't talk because she's from Africa!' Perhaps it was true – in part. I was already selectively mute when I lived in South Africa, but the move back to Northern England was a big, scary change for me. Not only was I moving countries and*

cultures, I was starting school, age five, in a place where I was also 'the new girl'.

Regarding having had a good relationship with some of her peers, despite being silent, Danielle writes:

I had a good group of friends who somehow always managed to include me in everything and have full-blown conversations with me, even though they knew I would never answer them back, adapting any questions they had so that they could be answered with a simple 'yes' or 'no' which I could answer by either nodding or shaking my head.

Kerrie developed a simple code to communicate with one friend in particular:

I made a friend at school and she would talk to me by touching hands. It was touch once for yes and two for no.

In fact, many children with SM use others to speak for them. In my own case I sometimes used my brother for this purpose.

Sometimes mutism is not total and a child with SM may be able to speak to one or two children in particular. Sara writes about the inexplicability of why she should be able to talk to one child but not another:

I remember a classmate who I befriended, the only person I have ever befriended outside my family circle during my years in grade school and high school. I met her in the fourth grade. I spoke little to her (outside of class only) through the two years we were friends for the fourth and fifth grade. Until this day, I still don't know why I was able to talk to her and not to the others. I can't recall if anxiety played a part.

Other children can be unpredictable for a child with SM, who tends not to cope well with unpredictability. In Nicky's case she had an ambivalent friendship with a girl who was friends in one situation, but not in another:

> *Another girl in my class was friends with me outside school, but picked on me in school. I remember being upset and confused by this. Maybe she was like this because she probably didn't want other children in the class to see that she was a friend of the weird, unpopular girl.*

Alison writes about a young friend who she attempted to maintain a friendship with, who snubbed her and caused her to lose all ability to speak again at school:

> *In third grade, a girl at school made attempts to befriend me. It was the first time any of my classmates took a real interest in me and over time I gradually began trying to communicate with her. It started with passing notes, progressing to whispering single word answers if she asked me questions. Then, one day the teacher sent us both to work on something in the teacher's office that was adjoined to the classroom, and in the privacy of that room I worked up the courage to try to start a conversation with my friend. She snapped at me and told me that I was being annoying, and from that day on I never spoke another word to any classmate at school.*

Feeling isolated, alienated and sidelined

When a child can't speak at school, they tend to feel not included. Rather they tend to feel isolated, alienated and sidelined. Describing the isolation that Betty experienced at school, she writes:

> *I wanted to have friends more than anything, but was afraid to talk or laugh out loud or go up to another person. People just thought I was extremely shy. Kids would ask me why I didn't talk and I would just shrug my shoulders.*

I had no clue. Most games at young ages didn't require talking, so if someone invited me to play, I would chase in game of tag or take turns on swings or slide or softball. I was fine as long as talking wasn't required. But if no one invited me to join them, I was alone. I was afraid to go up and ask to play. I would often stand behind the propped back door on the north side of the building just watching the other kids playing. Once I remember sitting in a swing alone on edge of playground and imagining what it would be like to stand up on the stage and sing and everyone would be amazed that I had a voice. I did a lot of daydreaming!

Adriane writes about feeling sidelined because she couldn't communicate in the same way as the other children:

During group assignments, 'she's not helping' would be a constant refrain from classmates who had to work with me, even when I had ideas I wanted to contribute.

There were days when the Pledge of Allegiance was the only thing I was able to say at school. At recess I would play with the toys provided, but as we grew older, children played less with toys and moved onto bigger group-oriented games. I eventually stopped playing and just watched from the sidelines. I feel I missed out on a normal childhood because of insufficient screening for and treatment of SM.

As children who can't speak move through their early school life, they can feel very different and alienated from their peers. Wendy writes about having SM and entering puberty very early on – something that drew even more attention to her:

When I was around seven years old, I entered puberty. In this respect I was years ahead of my peers. From the beginning of school I had stood out as different because I didn't speak and interact normally. But my very early puberty was just one more thing that made me stand out even more. It gave me a reason to be very self-conscious from a very young age, making me feel even more that I was not normal in any way. It also drew a lot of attention to me – turning me into even more of a curiosity and making me even more of a target for mickey taking. I can remember at the age of about nine, painstakingly trying to arrange my clothes so that my developing bust didn't show.

Teachers

As a profession, teachers can react in all manner of ways to a selectively mute child in their classroom. On the one hand, examples exist of wonderful teachers who make every effort to include a selectively mute child in class activities and treat children sympathetically; and, on the other, there are some teachers who seem to go out of their way to make school life even more difficult for children with SM.

Danielle writes about the supportive teachers she had in her early school life. Though she was mute at school, her teachers still included her as much as they could in classroom activities:

My years in infant school were probably my happiest as I was oblivious to any problems that I had. The teachers always did their best to include me in everything; I was always given good parts in school plays, just without any spoken lines and I used to record myself reading on tape so that the teachers could assess my progress. Even without knowledge of SM, my teachers were always very supportive and tried to help me as best they could. Despite my lack of oral activity, I was not treated any differently to any of my classmates, and so they also accepted me as I was. Although I was included in everything non-verbally, my infant-school teachers also did their best to try and get me to talk, but in a way that I would be comfortable with.

Vivienne also writes about a school secretary who took it upon herself to help her get included with other children:

After a difficult year at kindergarten, my mother remarried. I started a new school at age five and a half. This was the best school, by far, that I ever attended. By chance, an acquaintance of my stepfather (I will call her Mrs W) happened to be the school secretary. I met Mrs W before I started school. She told me that I would be attending a really great school with lots of friendly children and added that I was not to worry as she would look after me. As it turned out, Mrs W was always true to her word! I started school in June. Most of the children had been there for almost a year and were already in established friendship groups. During my first playtime, I briefly stood outside alone, feeling lost and watching the other children play. However, after a short time, Mrs W came out of her office. She took me around the playground introducing me to some of the children (there was no pressure to speak, as Mrs W did all the talking). She found a group of girls playing together whom she knew lived in my vicinity and asked me if I would like to join them. In this new environment, I suddenly found that I could speak to other children, as long as I didn't have to initiate. Mrs W intervened on several more occasions. She seemed to have made it her mission to make sure that I always had the company of friends. My form teacher was good too, as she seemed to keep a discreet eye on me, giving individual attention when I appeared stuck. This school radiated a warm and welcoming ethos and as sensitive child I really thrived there. My reading improved in leaps and bounds and I became confident with numbers. I also started to speak outside school during this period.

Some teachers will try everything to help a child to talk. Some of the better examples of this are through the use of rewards.

This is not an incorrect thing to do but, in fact, a child's anxiety may not be reduced through rewards alone and one should be wary of too much praise and making too much of a child's attempts to speak. Doing so can raise a child's anxiety levels and make the process more difficult. Adriane writes:

> *I was so quiet outside the home that by first grade my teacher would pull me out of class to put me in a small group and have a teacher's aide try to encourage me to speak up more. I would give one-word answers to questions and she'd reward me with a bead to add to a bracelet at the end of each session.*

Note, however, that rewards and bribes often don't work because children can see them coming! For example, Nicky writes:

> *They used bribes within this school as a way to try to get me to speak. Anyone who has an understanding of SM now would know that bribes don't work. One attempted bribe that amuses me now, when I think about it, was that if I talked I would be able to have an ice cream. I remember thinking 'I won't get an ice cream anyhow, as there is no ice cream van for a start!'*

Unfortunately, teachers can take a much less wise approach and try to trick children into speaking, which will always backfire. Danielle writes:

> *Although I wouldn't speak during the school day, there were occasions after school where I would stay in the yard playing with my grandfather after everyone had gone home and I would talk normally, despite still being in the school grounds. On one occasion, the teachers hid behind one of the walls so that they could hear me talking. As we were going to leave, they came out from their hiding place and told me how nice it was for them to hear me talk, causing me to once again retreat into my silent shell. By letting*

me know that they'd heard me, I immediately clammed up and became even more introverted than I was before. As there was no awareness of SM at the time and the teachers thought that they were doing the right thing by encouraging me; however, in hindsight, doing the opposite would probably have had a more positive effect on me.

While many teachers try their best, examples also exist of teachers who appear to take it on themselves to be deliberately cruel, and single out the selectively mute child in their class. This is not a historical issue either; it still seems to happen. Some teachers can find the silence of a selectively mute child threatening or challenging at some levels.

Alison writes about a teacher accusing her of being rude and yelling at her:

In fifth grade, I had a teacher who repeatedly accused me of being rude for not speaking. On several occasions she would start yelling at me in front of the class when I couldn't answer her after she called on me, reducing me to tears. After a few months in her class, I begged my parents to have me transferred out of her class, which I was, but I'll never forget that teacher and how cruel she was to me.

Wendy writes about being singled out and excluded by a teacher due to her SM:

I never joined in at song time, but I knew all the words to all the songs and I used to give my toys singing lessons at home. However, I remember having to sit outside the room for not answering the register, while the rest of the class were read a story. I also remember the teacher tried to make me ask for my workbook, and when I didn't ask for it I was made to stand out in front of the class while the other children did their work.

Finally, Vivienne writes about a teacher taking exception to her facial expression (a frozen, emotionless facial expression being one of the markers of many children with SM):

> *One teacher took a particular dislike to my frozen facial expression, which she interpreted as a smirk. She had been exasperated with my class for not lining up promptly after playtime. However, it was my frozen facial expression that became the focus of her intense anger.*

The toilet

Older literature on SM indicates an almost mysterious, ethereal link between enuresis (i.e. wetting oneself) and SM, particularly in younger children. Quite obviously, however, the issue of young children with SM wetting themselves is due to a school's or individual teacher's inadequacy to cater for their physical needs when children can't *ask* to go to the toilet – hardly a mystery! As such, many young children unfortunately do have accidents, which can only serve to make their SM worse because of the embarrassment that it causes. It's not their fault – it's the school's fault, plainly and simply. Providing a straightforward, discreet arrangement for a younger child with SM to get to the toilet is one of the very first accommodations that a school should do to make the school lives of younger children with SM more bearable.

I have only included one example here (of many I received while writing this book), but this is a very common issue for children with SM. Privation of straightforward access to the toilet could easily be deemed a form of institutional oppression, given SM can be thought of as a disability. Kat writes:

> *There was one girl who I would talk to at the time. She acted as translator between me, my teacher and our classmates. There were some things, however, that I couldn't say to her either. Going to the toilet was my biggest fear – and*

asking to go was impossible. I used to try to time it with playtime and lunchtime, but it wasn't always that easy. I remember one time, when I was about seven, I needed the toilet and I was trying to summon the courage to ask. By now I could talk a little more – most often in whispers. I heard another child ask to go, and I saw my opportunity to just say, 'me too!' Before I could move in that direction, the teacher's response left me frozen, 'the question is not can you go – we all know you can do that! You should be asking, 'may I go to the toilet?" After that there was no way I was asking, so I put all of my concentration into holding on. Unfortunately, shortly after this was assembly and we all filed into the hall. I remember sobbing uncontrollably, sitting there in a big pool of wee. I was mortified as I was ushered out of assembly in front of everyone.

Parents and teachers can constructively work together to find solutions which meet the needs of individual children. For instance, a child could use a discreet gesture or signal that the teacher understands; or be given an opportunity to go to the toilet when most or all other children are not around. Helpful information on this topic can be found in *Can I tell you about Selective Mutism?* (Johnson and Wintgens, 2012, p. 46).

Eating

After the toilet, a second, very common preoccupation of children with SM is eating in public. Betty writes:

I remember being in the cafeteria afraid to get up and scrape my plate because I was afraid someone would see I didn't eat all my food. I waited and waited until I was the only person left in cafeteria except the cooks before I finally got the courage to sneak out and back to the classroom.

There is a relationship between eating and SM because it's all about 'mouth'. In fact, one feature of some of the young people with SM whom I have met is that they often touch or mask their mouths. I also recall doing so myself, though I had no particular issue with eating. Danielle writes:

> My SM became so severe that I couldn't even open my mouth to eat; I would have to try and eat while keeping my lips firmly together.

Kerrie writes about eating too, and describes further preoccupations about making a noise – such as coughing, sneezing, or laughing. These fears are all to do with trying to avoid the perception or thoughts of others. When I was acutely aware of sound, as a young person with SM I could, almost, palpably *feel* other people's thoughts. Kerrie writes:

> I was also very uncomfortable about eating in the school canteen and couldn't walk in assembly without being very self-conscious. It wasn't just talking that I was unable to do. I couldn't cough, sneeze, or laugh out loud either. In school assembly I felt frozen to my seat and found it hard to stand up and couldn't look ahead. I always looked down and felt as though I was weird or different in some way. I couldn't make eye contact with anyone.
>
> I always stood alone in the playground and couldn't join in with playtime. I couldn't eat my sandwiches at dinner in the canteen or would eat them very slowly and it would take me forever. I felt as though all eyes were on me.

Emotional problems

As I described in the introduction, underlying my own SM appears to be an attachment disorder, which has always manifested itself in the pattern of people I can and can't speak to. I find certain figures 'threatening', based on their relationship or association to the attachment figures in my life. I have also had a tendency to want to attach, emotionally, to virtual strangers, which I do my best (and sometimes fail!) to resist.

In my childhood my attachment disorder manifested in a need to steal books and pens from school.

As we will see in Chapter 3, attachment disorders and separation anxiety are common in young children with SM. Kerrie writes:

> *I used to cry a lot while at school and would be sent home as the teachers thought I was ill but I was just very uncomfortable, anxious, and fearful. I felt very unhappy, lonely, and different and confused as to why I couldn't talk and everyone else could. At this time in my life I had no idea what was wrong with me. I was just labelled as an 'Elective Mute,' which is what it was called at the time before they changed the name to SM.*

Because their school lives are so stressful, many children with SM commonly have meltdowns at the end of a very stressful day at school. Regarding meltdowns, Dawn, writing about her son, Tom, writes:

> *Tom couldn't cope with anything different. Non-uniform day would upset him so much he would just not go. His behaviour at home was that of a time bomb waiting to explode! All day he contained and controlled his feelings and when he got home he generally exploded at the slightest thing. He would shout and swear almost as if every word he had kept in all day had to be released!*

Some children with SM save their worst behaviour for their parents, it has to be said. They can feel so repressed at school that a blowout with parents and siblings is more or less inevitable. I would suggest that a few children – by no means all – with SM are not only hiding and bottling up anxiety by being mute but also virtually every other emotion they have, not limited to being happy, unhappy, loving, affectionate, tender or angry. There was no way I would have been able to have a meltdown with my parents. They would have not have

SELECTIVE MUTISM IN OUR OWN WORDS

tolerated my expressing any such emotion or behaviour. Thus I felt even more repressed I expect than most children with SM. Even in the recent past I have found myself swamped with just about every emotion going when I have been unable to speak. On such occasions I feel like a child again, swamped by feelings I can't deal with and bottled up years ago. My speech rules and emotions, while mute, are those of my much younger self.

Psychiatrists and psychologists

Given young children may cry at school or be overtly anxious (I didn't cry and was not, to the best of my knowledge, overtly anxious), children with SM receive psychologist or psychiatrist intervention. Most of the reports of psychiatrist and psychologist interventions I have received have been negative – they have been unable to help or have not known how to help. That said, I may have simply never heard about success stories for the very reason that the intervention worked. Much more research is needed into what works and what does not, how many children with SM recover and how many don't. Please note that some therapists (notably speech therapists and therapists with personal experience of SM, thus specific expertise) do work wonders with young children – see Chapter 14.

Regarding the numerous psychiatrists Danielle encountered in her early life, she writes:

> *I saw a long line of psychiatrists who didn't know what was wrong with me and so didn't really know how to help me. I saw one for a period of about two years; she even came into school one day, much to my embarrassment, to assess the situation as she really didn't know what to do to help me. At this point, I still had not had a diagnosis and so there was no clear plan of what to do next in order to help me move forward.*
>
> *I used to go to weekly appointments after school in the local hospital as the psychiatrists tried everything they could*

to get me to speak. These appointments normally involved them asking me questions and me writing my answers on a piece of paper, then about half an hour of relaxation exercises which involved me lying on the floor with my eyes closed listening to a relaxation tape which gave instructions of images to think about. For an adult, this probably would have been a good method, unfortunately, as I was only eight at the time, I was more interested in thinking about who I was going to go and play football with when I got home!

Nicky also writes about being observed in the classroom by an unidentified adult (a child psychiatrist):

My mum asked me when I was about seven years old why I didn't talk at school. Apparently I said, pointing at my stomach area, that I felt something there that stopped me from being able to talk at school.

I remember a man in the classroom going around the class to see what we were doing. I tried to hide my work from him, as I was stuck on a question, and I didn't want him to find out as I was embarrassed as I couldn't ask for help. I realize now that this man was actually a child psychiatrist called into observe me in the classroom. After observing me he told my parents not to worry and that I was not behind in my work and there was nothing 'wrong' with me. I think he had dealt with other children similar to me, but he had no advice for my mum to help me overcome it.

What one should note from each of these contributions is that the assessments and interventions achieved very little/ nothing. While SM can be successfully treated early on in life with sensitive, appropriate interventions, for instance through speech therapists, or – with a little training – primary school teachers themselves, many, many children fall through the system unaided for this condition with repercussions for, not only their education, but potentially (writing about myself, rather than Danielle or Nicky) their mental health.

Incorporating relatives into the school environment

Some primary school teachers try to incorporate relatives into the school environment. This avenue can, indeed, be worth pursuing in order to provide a further small step in enabling an SM child to speak in the school environment.

For Nicky, incorporating her older brother into the school environment was successful and may have been the key to unlocking her SM early in her school life had it continued:

In my first year of school I managed to make friends somehow, even though I didn't talk. The teacher treated me with sensitivity and patience. She suggested bringing my older brother into class to see whether I would read to him while she sat behind and listened. Although I do remember the teacher setting nearby, I felt at ease and would read quite happily to my brother in the classroom. My brother was also happy to come in to help with my reading, as he said he got to miss maths! I believe, to this day, that if I had stayed in that school I would have overcome my SM early on.

In Nicky's next school, however, the same approach was disregarded, which brought her progress to a full stop.

After having to move schools, however, I dreaded the school register every morning. The teacher would call my name out several times and when I couldn't respond would have to look for me and I think I would nod. I also got behind in my reading. I am still slow with reading and suspect that this is because I couldn't read to the teachers. My mum suggested the idea of getting my brother into class so that I could read to him like in the previous school, but they ignored her. I probably fell behind in other subjects due to my inability to 'talk' and ask for help when I was struggling.

Hearing

While collecting stories for this book I found that a number of the contributors had had ear, nose and throat (ENT) problems as children (for instance see Beth's life story in Chapter 17 and Kimberly's throughout this book).

Dawn, writing about her son, Tom, writes:

Tom had ENT problems and was a little deaf. His speech delay was, for many years, always attributed to this. When I look back, with the knowledge I now have, it was the start of not being able to communicate. Tom received speech and language therapy until he was about six and they believed his lack of speech was because he was shy and was spending periods being slightly deaf when his ears where bad.

Dawn continues, describing how Tom's SM meant that he didn't even make a sound during painful procedures.

When Tom was nine he had an operation on his ear to remove a benign growth. Basically they cut his ear from behind, peeled it forward, drilled into his mastoid bone, cleaned his ear bones then put it all back together. Painful! All without uttering a sound. Three weeks later Tom had a really bad tummy ache. In Accident and Emergency he was prodded and poked without showing any emotion at all. He made no sound and didn't flinch, despite having an acute appendicitis. It is on occasions like this when, as a parent, you realize the implications of SM. It's possible to be in agony and still be unable to speak!

Of course some children with Asperger Syndrome also tend to live in their own worlds and appear not to hear. Talking about her own experience, Wendy, who was diagnosed with Asperger's as an adult, writes:

My mother has told me that she was asked whether I had a problem with my hearing because when the teacher told us to put our toys away and go out to play I used to ignore her and carry on with my activity. There wasn't a problem with my hearing, and my mother replied, 'No, I'm afraid she's ignoring you!'

Getting older

In my own experience I recall being called 'cute' when I was small and unable to speak, but this perception of me naturally dissipated as I got older. In fact I felt rather disappointed to no longer be called 'cute' or to be accepted for who I was becoming. Kat writes about getting a little older at school and the change in acceptance of her as a person, due to her SM:

As I grew older, the acceptance I had once felt from my peers changed, and along with the adults in my life, I found myself more and more exposed to questioning. The big question has always been, 'Why?' And, as I grew a little older, it started coming more frequently. There is nothing more difficult for someone with SM to do than to explain themselves to others. All the times I was ever asked this question felt like they had been bundled up together and thrown into a time-warp which would explode back at me with every new asking. 'Why are you so quiet?' The words look so innocent here on the page. I have no idea how to write them so they can communicate the intensity that I used to feel when they were spoken. It truly is the most impossible question to answer, and would always leave me completely stuck, choked up with a big ball of emotion lodged in my throat. There was no way I could have unravelled those feelings into words back then, I truly felt frozen in time, confusion distorting my vision as life carried on about me. The biggest thing that I didn't understand was that I didn't ever truly consider myself to be quiet. At school, I was considered 'the quiet one' but inside my head I was so busy, creative and loud that the description never made any sense to me.

I've always been hugely sensitive and aware of the subtle ways we all communicate – through our faces, our bodies, our thoughts and our feelings. Sometimes this can be overwhelming, and the idea that I am expected to reply to all of that through a few well-chosen words seems like an incredible feat. My reply to the question today would be, 'I'm not quiet. You just aren't listening properly!' because, truly, my verbal silence was the loudest form of communication I have ever used. Unfortunately, I believe my true words were lost in translation for the rest of my childhood, and some of my adulthood too. I felt a tremendous amount of pressure to talk – and with my nature comes an eagerness to please others. This was my experience of becoming verbal in every situation. Once I began talking, it was so often so that I could fit in and find acceptance from others. I spoke to meet people's expectations; my words were not mine, I simply pretended that they were.

CHAPTER 5

High School Experience and Selective Mutism

Carl Sutton; Kerrie, Rosie, Karen, Kimberly, Vivienne, Danielle, Leanne, Tessa, Lesley and Liz

For many children with SM entering the high school environment is a challenge – progressing from a small, parochial primary school, where their speech limitations may have been accommodated or tolerated, and where the child may have only had one or two teachers in any year, into an impersonal, bustling high school replete with teachers who may not have the inclination or time to take heed of the emotional and educational needs of any one child. In fact, it is a transition that not all children with SM are able to make successfully. Thus an unknown, but not insignificant, proportion of children with SM are home-schooled, either immediately or when they can't cope with the high school environment any longer. For some examples, and to read about parents' experiences of high school age children with SM, including experiences of home-schooling, see Chapter 6.

Starting high school

SM can be a very long-term disorder. Children entering high school with SM are likely to have lived with SM for years already. However, while they may have been able to get by with SM at primary school, the high school environment can feel overwhelming. Kerrie, who recovered from SM as an adult, describes the duration of her high school experience as a time of grossly unpleasant isolation.

By this time I started secondary school I had already suffered from SM for nine years. I had not improved at all. I had only got worse. I found things more difficult than at middle school because there was more expectation to talk and more need to talk. I went through all four years without speaking a word. I was very isolated and lonely during these four years at secondary school. I didn't find teachers to be very understanding. They thought I was doing it deliberately for attention. Not only did I find it difficult to talk, I also found it difficult to even nod or shake my head. I was afraid of doing anything that would draw attention to me in some way. I found it hard to walk in and out of assembly. I would sit there and feel frozen, like I couldn't move. I was afraid to cough or sneeze in front of people. I used to try and hold it in. I couldn't laugh out loud either. I could only smile.

I so desperately wanted to join in but I just couldn't do it. It was not just talking I couldn't do, it was anything where people would be watching me, or anything that would draw attention to me. I couldn't eat in the school canteen at lunchtime. I felt so self-conscious. I would sometimes eat my dinner in the toilets. I couldn't make any eye contact at all with anyone. I would always look down at the floor when I walked along. I would always sit in class with my hand up to my face or over my mouth. I think I did this to try and hide myself.

Some can describe high school as one of the most difficult times of their lives. Others are disappointed that high school doesn't bring with it the personal change they are looking for. Rosie writes:

On my first day of secondary school I felt so grown up. I had been dropped off at a friend's house (one of only a rare few people whom I was able to talk a little to) and we walked into school together with a couple of other people. I felt included, I felt perhaps this was it; I could change.

Unfortunately it wasn't to be. As soon as I stepped into that school it was overwhelming; there were so many people crowded everywhere. I just about managed to utter an answer to the registration when my name was called but many of the teachers didn't hear me and soon learnt to start looking up to check I was there.

The other children didn't understand why I didn't talk so they joked about it. They soon got bored of being nice to me when I never answered and some could be very cruel about it. I started dreading certain classes and often spent lunchtimes eating my lunch in the toilets because I was too scared to sit on my own on the benches outside.

People would actually groan if they were told to sit next to me or if they were paired with me for a class activity. I went through each lesson on my own often not talking, laughing or even smiling. I'd just keep my head down, get on with the work and hope that the time passed quickly. It was lonely, sometimes unbearably so. I would have given anything to be normal like the rest of them, to be able to say the first thing that came into my head without a second thought. I used to hate myself for being different, for not being able to join in and talk like everyone else did.

Isolation

Naturally children with SM can feel very isolated and cut-off from other students and teachers at high school. They can feel like they stick out like a sore thumb, and as though the spotlight is forever shining down on them. Kerrie writes:

I made a couple of friends when I started high school. I never spoke to them but we used to communicate by touching hands. It would be right hand for yes and left hand for no or both hands for don't know. I found other people in my class to be a lot more helpful and understanding than the teachers. Even though I had these two special friends I still felt so different, lonely and isolated. I felt cut off from them. I really wanted to join in with the fun and laugh and talk to them but this terrible fear got in the way. I couldn't ask for help in lessons when I needed it. I would just sit there and hope and pray that someone would notice I needed help.

Karen writes about the anxiety and stress that being selectively mute in the school environment causes. Being perpetually watchful can be an exhausting experience.

Given the opportunity I would sit as near to the back of the large classrooms as possible. I felt safer there. It was a good position to see anyone who entered the room. I could see all the other pupils and hopefully hide behind their heads from the teacher's eye-line. When I was unable to sit near the back, my concentration was absent from most of the lessons. I had far more important things to think about – were they looking at me? Why were they looking? What were they looking at? What were they thinking about me? What had I done wrong? And so on and so forth! Every day felt like taking part in a marathon race, I felt exhausted. Obviously there were days that went relatively okay but not enough to make much difference.

Kimberly writes poignantly about her own high school experience, including self-harming:

In 'sheet metal shop', I'd used a machine to cut metal. Now I was trying to bend it with tools into a box. We would be graded on it. Some of the boys finished early and were going around helping the girls. That's when Giovanni approached, and he knew darn well the effect that lopsided grin had on girls.

'Need help?' he asked. 'There! Like this.'

I smiled. He thought I was as normal as any girl there! That's when he ruined everything.

'You're so shy. Don't you ever talk?' he asked.

I swallowed hard and found my voice.

'Don't you ever stop talking?' I asked, hoping to wound him as he'd wounded me.

He set down my box. I watched him step backwards away from me, his palms up. He never spoke to me again.

That night I burned half-moons into my arms with heated-up lighters pilfered from my mother. How could I explain how my voice fell away? That I wasn't shy, it was something big. I hated the word shy. It was like being clinically depressed and someone says to you, 'Cheer up!' Well I couldn't 'just talk'. The words got stuck. So many of my ideas, thoughts and feelings went unexpressed that I'd cry about the unfairness of it all every single night. I couldn't be any other way. And I was trying so hard! I was like an intricate origami swan. I felt beautiful on the outside, but origami rips. And crumples...

Daily stress

Being mute for the entirety of every school day is both exhausting and stressful, which can give rise to a child feeling disorganized and forgetful. Vivienne writes:

I was so anxious I became forgetful and disorganized, which led me to being late on several occasions. I seemed to be in constant trouble with the head teacher who frequently used to shout at me. I was in the reading recovery stream, which involved many intensive reading sessions. I particularly hated these because it meant reading out loud in class.

I had difficulty raising my voice to an audible level and when I concentrated on doing this, I seemed to stammer and frequently lost my place on the page. My reading must have sounded abysmal. However, in my own head I could recognize every single word.

Furthermore, experiencing muteness and stress on a daily basis can also give rise feeling utterly trapped, and to panic attacks. It can also rapidly give rise to a feeling of being unable to cope with the school environment, resulting in lost days, weeks or even years at school. Danielle writes:

Towards the end of my first year in comprehensive school, aged 12, my anxiety was the highest it had ever been, and I began to have panic attacks. Initially, we didn't know what was happening but soon it became apparent that something was very wrong. At first, I would start to feel really nauseous and get really bad headaches on the way to school and so whoever was taking me to school that day would just take me home where I would be feeling fine within an hour of getting back. However, after missing a week of school, my parents started to realize that this was something more than a simple stomach bug. I went to see my GP and was prescribed beta blockers for daily use and Valium for occasions when my anxiety was more extreme. I continued to take the beta blockers for the next 18 months; however, I only took the Valium a handful of times. My panic attacks carried on in this intensity for the next two years, resulting in me having to be taken into school every day by my head of year and the educational welfare officer at the school. She used to tell me that I had 'Monday morning blues' when I returned to school after the weekends. I wish it were as simple as that.

At my worst, I had up to 60 panic attacks a night, lasting between five and ten minutes each. It went on in this intensity for nearly three years, meaning I had to sit my

GCSEs, 'AS' Levels and 'A' Levels on less than two hours' sleep a night. Eventually, the anxiety became too intense, and I ended up missing most of years 12 and 13 because I was too anxious to leave the house, resulting in me failing my 'A' Levels and having to repeat year 13 in order to re-sit them.

As a child who was mute in my home environment, I also had panic attacks, yet I had to keep them to myself because I couldn't talk to my parents. I would sit in my bedroom clutching my chest and feeling like I was going 'mad'. From my own experience, even when a child recovers from SM itself, the panic attacks and indeed the stress itself can remain. Even now, over 20 years after the worst of my SM, I still re-experience the same stress (and relive much of the entrapment I felt) regularly.

Further emotional problems

Enduring high levels of stress and anxiety every day, children with SM can develop other issues such as depression and eating disorders. Many have low self-esteem because they feel so different from their peers. Others can develop compulsive behaviours such as nervous excoriation (skin picking). And, without wishing to alarm parents of younger children with SM, a few tend to misuse alcohol or drugs, or more seriously self-harm.

Vivienne writes about developing depression and a related eating disorder in her high school years:

My form teacher told me that I would not be moving up a form in September. She assured me that it had nothing to do with my exam results, rather that I needed to develop my confidence. I felt devastated and tried to tell her that I wanted to stay with my friends but she just laughed and said that I would love the new girls. I begged my mother to intervene but she was sick and tired of things not going right at school. Over time depression started to set in.

> *I didn't know that I had SM then, so I attributed my lack of confidence and failure to keep up with girls of my own age to a defective personality. I began hating myself. These negative thoughts began to eat away at me. I was obese and had been put on repeated diets over the years by my GP, to no avail. However, at the age of 13, I went on a very successful diet and achieved my target weight. Instead of feeling good about this, I felt ugly. I began binge eating and starving to compensate. This turned into an eating disorder, which began to dominate my life. I felt repulsive and couldn't bear to be seen in public. I stopped using the bus and began taking long detours to avoid meeting people.*

Karen writes about having low self-esteem at school:

> *While I became quite good at pre-empting the majority of my school difficulties unfortunately, however, school life actually got worse the older I got. Things got more complicated. My teenage years were well and truly here with all the physical and emotional changes all teenagers go through. If I lacked self-esteem before, it now went to a new low. My image was even more important, I was small, skinny and undeveloped (especially in the areas where a bra should've replaced my childlike vest!). It was a confusing time. I was unable to trust my own judgements. Girls who I thought were my friends, turned out to not be so nice. Boys wanted to 'go out' with me, even though I would avoid them like the plague! I hated my thoughts. I hated my feelings. I hated my life.*

Kimberly writes about hoping that starting high school would be the change she needed – high school being a situation where she knew nobody and could thus take on an alternative persona without the expectations of other people. The way she hoped to achieve this was through drinking alcohol:

One month before high school started, I nearly died, thinking that alcohol would give me the 'gift of the gab'. I downed too much Vodka and blacked out. At 13 years old I didn't know my body could be poisoned, go into a coma, and die. Luckily, my mother found me and called the paramedics. When I woke up from the coma I realized my experiment had failed. I was the same...

Finally, Leanne writes about alcohol use and self-harm:

About the age of 14 someone from my class who lived nearby invited me out. I just wanted a friend so I hung out with her. I figured that alcohol could make me talk but as drunk as I got I still couldn't speak. Not even illegal drugs could help me talk, hanging around the streets all night and getting into trouble. It was the only way I felt I could fit in. There was nothing I could do to help myself. My parents stopped me from bothering with these people anymore so I was back to being pretty much friendless, and on realising this I even self-harmed. I couldn't communicate with anyone and had a hard time displaying emotions. My parents still don't know about SM; I still haven't told them. I left secondary school to go to college, with four GCSEs and no friends.

Alcohol misuse also features in SM in adults (see Chapter 7). As yet, data does not exist to show whether alcohol or drug misuse is more likely for teenagers or adults with SM than the general population, although I would suggest that this is the case because this is a theme among such stories. Approximately 20 per cent of people with Social Anxiety Disorder suffer with alcohol abuse or dependence (Anxiety and Depression Association of America, 2015); alcohol abuse and dependence is a factor in most other anxiety disorders also; and, as such, there is every reason to assume that it is a factor in SM in older children and adults with SM.

Interventions

Given 'high profile' mutism can be very apparent in the school environment, in some cases professional help is sought. There is no data regarding the proportion of interventions for high school children that are successful (and which kinds of interventions are most successful) – this research has yet to be done. It should be added, however, that even for teenagers with SM, whose SM has become very ingrained, successful interventions are still possible and can be effective – see Chapter 14.

Regarding an unsuccessful act at helping, however, Kimberly provides her own experience:

The school noticed my high absenteeism and oddball behaviour. They 'evaluated' me by sending me to look at inkblots. I was made to see a shrink. Day one, he flipped on a tape recorder. I never spoke a single word in all our sessions.

Vivienne describes an experience similar to the unpleasant physical examination I experienced myself as a child, described in my life story in the introduction. Rather than 'help' at high school she was subject to a compulsory medical, which served no purpose.

My parents received a letter requesting that one of them should attend the school while the school nurse gave me a medical. There was another girl at this compulsory medical. We were put in an empty classroom and told to undress down to our pants. I knew the other girl and realized that they had singled out the 'two school misfits' (to put it politely). The other girl became distressed and began crying and would not remove her bra, so the supervising teacher sent for the deputy head and together they struggled to restrain the girl and remove her bra. I felt terribly anxious about the whole situation but I reluctantly got undressed and was led into the adjoining class, where a nurse was seated at a desk with my mother on the other side. I stood in front of the nurse and she looked me up and down but didn't examine me. Instead she began questioning my mother about my previous visit to the child guidance clinic (four years earlier) and demanded to know why we had not attended any follow-up visits. She ordered us to attend the local child guidance clinic the following week.

Subsequently Vivienne and her mother went to a child guidance clinic:

At the clinic my mother and I were split up and taken to separate rooms; this was the same every week. My first session was with an educational psychologist. He questioned why I was doing so badly at school, as the tests (taken four years previously) had indicated that I had a high IQ and reading age. I couldn't answer him. The following week I was passed to another professional. He asked me questions about my family and school life, which I tried hard to answer. I managed to say yes and no and sometimes use short sentences to answer his questions, but the intense eye contact and questioning left me taciturn. He took this very personally, as he kept asserting that I didn't trust him and that I was putting up a barrier. He repeatedly inferred that other girls at school were bullying me but I kept saying no. I wanted to talk about my teacher's behaviour; however, he kept saying, 'but you are being bullied by other girls'.

Tessa decided to seek out help for herself, with the help of her parents, via Child and Adolescent Mental Health Services (CAMHS). Unfortunately, as a service, CAMHS didn't even attempt to try for Tessa. In fact, the story of CAMHS being unable or unwilling to help teenagers with SM is one that I hear regularly thought my own support network, iSpeak.

It was in secondary school when I once again decided to 'try' to get help, as my SM was affecting me at school.

I went along with my dad to the local doctor's, to get a referral to go to CAMHS. We went to the doctor and she said she could sort the referral out. After months of waiting CAMHS came back saying we can't help you, which is never what you want to hear when you are desperate for help.

As an adult, while suffering from acute depression, I was referred to Improved Access to Psychological Therapies (IAPT) Services by my GP. I was allocated high-intensity Cognitive Behaviour Therapy (CBT), which came to an abrupt end after two face-to-face sessions when I specifically asked for help with SM. The therapist sought advice from the service as a whole, the response being, 'we have no experience of working with Selective Mutism, so we can't help'. Thus, for adults, there simply appears to be no help available. Tessa's story seems to demonstrate that teenagers with SM fare little better either via CAMHS.

Tessa subsequently sought help via the school counsellor. Because SM is poorly understood, however, this was not helpful to her either.

We decided to go another route and go through the in-school counsellor. It didn't really help. I had one half hour appointment every fortnight, and had to miss half a lesson in the first year of my GCSE year to go and see her, another person who didn't really understand, but if you have never suffered with SM you never really know what it is like.

Given the scarcity of sources of help for teenagers with SM, even in the present day (rather than my own when awareness of SM was non-existent) it should come as no surprise that many teenagers with SM become adults with SM.

Teachers

In some instances teachers at high school can have a substantial positive influence on the lot of teenagers with SM, even if they don't directly enable children to speak. For instance, Danielle writes about a superb head of year:

My head of year was extremely supportive and really seemed to understand the issues that I was having. At the time, I hated her as she was making me go to lessons – effectively sending the lamb to slaughter – but as the time has gone on, I've realized how much she did actually care and want the best for me, even when everyone else had written me off, and for that I will be forever grateful.

However, other teachers, particularly those who don't wish to understand SM, and supply teachers, who don't have the time to get to know children as individuals, can become objects of dread. Danielle continues:

Supply teachers were a great fear of mine. Due to the size of the school, it was inevitable that, if we had a supply teacher, they had not been told about my SM. This almost always ended up with me getting into trouble for not answering the register and then one of my friends having to stick up for me. Not only did this make me feel useless, depending on the level of the telling off, more often than not it made me extremely angry. I used to get asked if I thought I was being clever or if I was playing a game. As I couldn't verbally retaliate, we ended up in a vicious circle until one of my friends spoke up on my behalf. As I progressed up the school, going into year 9, I used to go and see my head of year, who was really supportive, with my best friend every time I had a run in with a supply teacher. At one stage, we were having supply teachers on a regular basis, and I used to dread going to school if I knew that we were going to have one that day, often feigning an illness so that I could stay home to avoid it.

Particular subjects

Because SM is a situational phobia of speech those subjects which have more emphasis on speaking or singing are, naturally, more problematic.

MUSIC

Danielle writes about music and singing lessons being a particular problem for her:

> *It was at Christmas time that I felt the most isolated. While everyone else was having a great time singing Jingle Bells, during our singing lessons, I would be sat looking out of the window, willing time to go faster. It was during these moments that the true extent of my SM hit me the hardest.*
>
> *Similarly, the run up to our annual school Eisteddfod also caused me a lot of extra anxiety. Each year, every house in the school had to learn a song to perform at the competition. There were daily choir practices that were compulsory. If I tried to avoid them, the sixth formers who ran the rehearsals would come looking for me. As they were so much bigger than I was, I used to be quite fearful of them and so, in my first year, I attended every choir practice – even though there was no way that I was going to be able to sing. Obviously, as I couldn't verbally retaliate, I just had to comply. The sixth formers would tell me off during every choir practice. It got to the point where I was too anxious to go to school because of these rehearsals.*

Even if reasonable accommodations are made for a child with SM, this can still leave them feeling isolated. It is difficult to say what better a teacher can do in this situation, however. Danielle writes:

> *Every couple of weeks, we would have a singing lesson, which, even though I couldn't take part, initially I still*

enjoyed. At first, my music teacher would just leave me out, which I didn't mind, but as she got to know me better, she started giving me various percussion instruments to play while everyone else was singing. Although the music side of this wasn't an issue for me, I hated the idea of being the only one playing an instrument. I felt as though the spotlight was on me, like I was the centre of attention because I was doing something different to everyone else. If I ever made a mistake in what I was doing, I used to get told off for it, bringing even more attention to myself. Once I moved into year nine, my teacher stopped giving me other things to do, and so I felt a lot more comfortable within the lesson. However, the feeling of isolation and being different to everyone else didn't go away.

CURRENT EVENTS/GENERAL STUDIES

Subjects involving group discussions are also very difficult for teenagers with SM. Kimberly writes about her dread of current event days, and having to speak to the class:

Current event days were bad. I would toss all night. In the morning I'd choose uninteresting articles to prevent the class from asking me follow-up questions. I chose the shortest articles so I wouldn't have to read for too long. In terror, I'd wait for my turn. Inevitably it came. In front of the class, I started the first sentence, 'On Tuesday…' The teacher interrupted me, 'Project your voice. Start again!' 'On Tuesday, fire broke out…' A boy called out, 'We can't hear her!' I was shaking. Jaimie whispered loudly to the girl next to her, 'She looks scared to death!' At last I finished, glancing at Jaimie before I sat down. She was trying not to laugh. 'I have to give a C for that,' said the teacher. 'A shame…you're so bright.' Jaimie went next. She was fluent, poised, engaging, and answered a million questions about her lengthy article in a loud, concise manner.

ORAL LANGUAGE EXAMINATIONS

In my own experience, I failed my English Language 'O' Level at school for the sole reason that I couldn't successfully participate in a group-based English oral examination. In hindsight it seems very oppressive to me that I was not enabled to bypass this. Someone with a hearing difficulty would not have been expected to do an English aural examination, so why was someone with a speech difficulty/an anxiety disorder forced to speak or marked on their inability? Given my English oral examination was the first exam of the summer of my 'O' Levels, it had a devastating effect on all my grades – except for technical drawing and maths. In fact, until I received my results late summer, I believed I'd failed everything.

Likewise, Leanne failed oral examinations because of SM. Leanne writes:

> *I failed all my oral and language exams because the only thing I could do was shake my head when they asked me if I had learnt anything. The thought of having a conversation was enough to give me a panic attack. I had a few panic attacks, but I didn't know that's what they were back then and of course I never told anyone. If teachers asked me questions I'd just shrug my shoulders and play stupid. The only subjects I enjoyed were art and gym – two things I was naturally good at. Out of school hours were spent in my room doing homework, playing computer games or exercising.*

DRAMA

Tessa found drama to be the most difficult subject. Again, it was because there was no escaping it and the expectation was to speak and perform in front of her peers.

> *One thing I hated was drama, a compulsory subject up until the end of year 9. Through my three years of drama I had to perform and speak in front of my peers. It was a*

> *terrifying experience. What made drama worse was that I had quite a small friendship group, so if we were put in groups, there was a very slim chance that I had someone I was friends with. This made drama worse, not feeling comfortable with people and being expected to speak and act with confidence.*

While Drama was Tessa's least favourite subject, I have also heard of and met young people who find that they can speak during drama lessons but in no other situations. This is due to the emphasis of speech being on the words of the play itself and on the character they are portraying rather than themselves. I know of one young person, a fabulous young actress, applying to the Royal Academy of Dramatic Art (RADA) though selectively mute.

Without suggesting he had SM, while Rowan Atkinson (the British comic actor) found social speech difficult at university, he was nonetheless a great performer once in role. One could even suggest that Mr Bean (Rowan Atkinson's best known character) is selectively mute – being sociable, inventive, yet grossly uncomfortable when speaking.

FRENCH

From my own experience, as a young teen, it usually didn't occur to me that I had an issue with speech. Nor did it occur to me that I could not or should not take part in school activities in exactly the same way as everyone else. I couldn't understand why my French teacher was so surprised that I signed up to go on the school exchange trip. Once I arrived in France, at the exchange student's home, however, I spent two weeks virtually mute. I could speak to the student, in private, but not his parents or other relatives. His parents vociferously complained to his teacher about me not speaking to them or eating their food. However, when his teacher approached me and began to criticize me directly, my own French teacher keenly defended me. I recall a few of the girls on the bus home, one of whom's pigtails I had the habit of pulling, saying '…are you going to start speaking to us now?' Even then I didn't understand the relevance of what they were saying. Being selectively mute was an inveterate part of my personality – something that I just did. It wasn't, at that age, something that I thought much about.

Making changes

There are a number of ways which young people with SM tend to overcome their difficulties at school: (a) by taking drastic action and changing schools; (b) by becoming more open about their SM to diffuse the anxiety around speech; and (c) by making many small steps to begin speaking.

Lesley writes about how difficult it is to make a change and be speaking at school, faltering over attempts to make a connection with a teacher.

Every day I passed a teacher, she always smiled at me, I smiled – at least I think it was a smile, could just have been a grimace. She said 'hello' and continued past. This happened for a few days and I began to feel more confident. I looked forward to our conversation (that is how I viewed the exchange of smiles).

After a few days/weeks/months I wanted to do more, expand the conversation. I went home and thought about it. This teacher was an ally, she never criticized, and she never expected a response. She seemed to know me, understand that I wanted to be polite but couldn't. I knew that I needed to say hello back. I thought about it for days. Eventually, one night I decided that's it. I'm going to do it. First of all I was going to say, 'hello miss, how are you?' Then realized that was too much. 'Hello miss,' that would be fine. Then it was down to, 'hello'. It would be a start and that is what I wanted.

The day came. I was walking to school rehearsing my speech. Then a thought popped into my head.

What happens if she is not there today? What happens if she doesn't say hello. What happens if…

No, I've got to do it. If she's not there, I can do it another day. If she doesn't say hello first I can start the conversation, I can still say hello. And it would be a start. It would be a good day even if I didn't speak again that day. I felt so good.

Then the teacher came into sight.

My throat tightened, my jaw ached, my stomach churned. The fear and panic must have shown on my face. She opened her mouth to say hello. I ran past her, I didn't even smile at her. The rest of the day was uneventful.

That night I lay in bed and cried.

The following day I saw the teacher approaching, I steeled myself. I wanted to run again but was able to hold it together. She walked past me. No hello, no smile, nothing…

She had given up on me and I had lost an opportunity.

I understand now that she probably didn't say hello because she thought she was frightening me. I realize that my body language betrayed me and created a barrier.

Danielle saw an end to her SM (but not her anxiety) by making the bold decision to change schools. The reason this can work is that in the new environment there is no expectation on a child with SM to be mute (the perceived expectation of others being one of the primary maintaining factors). It requires, however, that the child immediately speaks in the new environment to avoid the pattern starting all over again. Recounting her own experience, Danielle writes:

After another hellish day, I spoke to my parents and said that I thought I could beat my SM if I moved schools. As we looked into it, I quickly ruled out all the state schools in the area as some of my classmates from primary school who I didn't speak to attended them. We found a much smaller independent school slightly further away which, on the surface, seemed to be perfect. The only way my plan was going to work though was if I could speak the minute I walked through the door. I had my visit to the school within a couple of weeks and, somehow, I managed to talk to everyone, even taking an active part in a science lesson while I was there. For the rest of my time in comprehensive school, I had my ups and downs, but the not talking aspect of the SM was well and truly behind me. Within a year of leaving my old school, I'd taken part in two school plays, was reading out loud regularly in lessons, and had sat my first GCSE exams – something my teachers in my old school doubted that I'd ever be able to do. I even managed to get an A grade in my GCSE English oral exam when, two years before, I'd still been writing my answers on a whiteboard.

Rosie took a different route and had her speech anxiety difficulties explained for her by the teacher. This route works on diffusing the anxiety that a person with SM has regarding how others may perceive their muteness. It can lead to group acceptance, in the right setting, thus reduce a child or adult's fear of not being accepted due to their muteness, which can lead to a child feeling gradually more able to speak. Rosie writes about her own very positive experience:

In the second year of secondary school my parents found out about Selective Mutism. With a little bit of persuasion I wrote my classmates a short letter about Selective Mutism and why I didn't talk and the teacher read it out when I wasn't there on the last day of term. When we went back after the school break a few people came up to me and talked to me as if I was another human being. Previously some people didn't think I could understand them and would come up right to my face to check I heard them. But after I wrote that letter they didn't look at me with an odd expression wondering if I knew what they were saying. Instead they told me they understood; it was more than I could have wished for.

Things got a little easier after that. I began talking to some people from school on MSN messenger and they started to see my real personality for the first time. Talking to them over the Internet made it a little easier at school; I felt a bit more relaxed around them and they tended to include me more, even if I still wasn't talking to them face to face.

Another potential way to overcome SM in the school environment is to take small steps. In fact, this is something I did myself as a teenager, in my school environment. In the evenings I used to try to bolster my confidence by wearing headphones and listening to music while in bed. I used to try to infuse myself with the confidence and energy of the singer – Bruce Springsteen. The next day I would try to carry some of that energy around with me. Speaking more was slow going, but gradually I did, however, feel better about myself.

Children with SM can fail to reach their full potential

It has to be said that many children with SM don't reach their full potential at school. I didn't do particularly well in my own 'O' Levels as I said (because I found taking an English oral exam so stressful and I was suffering from childhood depression) but I caught up later. In sixth form, a smaller environment where I was focusing on subjects I enjoyed – maths and physics – and where there was less emphasis on either me or speech, academically I did much better than in the previous five years, despite concurrently being entirely mute at home. Liz writes:

I feel sorry for others who, like me, have not reached their full potential because of SM. It is a very debilitating condition and once, to cope with fear, silence is learnt, it is difficult to unlearn, especially when it continues into adulthood. My school days were certainly not the best years of my life – in fact – they probably were the worst.

And Kerrie, who was mute for the entirety of her high school life, suggests that, educationally speaking, she had the potential to have done better.

I remember being ignored a lot of the time as though I was invisible. I used to cry a lot at school. The teachers would send me to sit in the sick room as they thought I was not very well. I would usually end up going home. I cried because I was so unhappy and found it difficult to cope. I managed to get through the four years and took my GCSE exams. I didn't do as well as I was capable of. I could have done a lot better.

I believe that any child who experiences SM at school, and does not receive appropriate support, does exceptionally well to achieve examination results at all.

Work experience

Work experience can be challenging to children with SM. Yet, it can also provide an opportunity to push one's personal boundaries. Danielle, who changed school environments to overcome SM, returned to the original environment where she had been selectively mute to do her work experience, challenging herself to speak in an environment where she previously had not been able.

During my first year in sixth form, aged 17, I had to complete a week of work experience. I decided to use this as an excuse to return to my old school and face the demons that still haunted me. The first hour or so that I was back in my old school was the most nerve-wracking hour of my life but, after that, I started to feel more at home. I slowly started to see a lot of the friends that I had left behind, the big difference this time was that I was the one doing the talking. I also got to spend some time catching up with some of the teachers who supported me during my time in the school. This was definitely the hardest thing I've ever done but, without doubt, it was also the best thing I've ever done. My time in comprehensive school presented me with a lot of SM-related challenges that no child should have to go through. However, there was a light at the end of the tunnel, I just had to keep striving to reach it.

Tessa found work experience too much of a challenge and couldn't complete it. Nonetheless she still feels that work experience gave her a push to speak more.

In year 10, we had to do one week of work experience. This was very daunting for me, having to go in to a strange workplace on my own, and be expected to speak. I didn't complete my work experience, as it was far too hard for me. I tried hard to speak, and managed to get through the first day. On the second day, however, I was put in the very uncomfortable position of being in front of a group of people demonstrating. I am sure that, for most people, this is horrible, but for me it was too far. I left work experience, the confidence I had built up gone. However, work experience has given me the push that I need to try to make myself more confident and speak more whenever I can.

CHAPTER 6

Parents' Experiences of High School and Home-Schooling

Ann, Bronwen and Dawn (parents)

The previous chapter included experiences of SM in high school from a first-hand experience. In this chapter, three parents – Ann, Bronwen and Dawn – write candidly about their children's experiences of high school. Dawn made the decision, through necessity, to home-school.

ANN'S STORY

If you ask my selectively mute daughter about her years in high school, she will roll her eyes and moan. If you ask me about her high school years, I will have the same reaction. Just dealing with the school and the state agencies that were supposed to be helping her transition to life beyond high school was beyond stressful.

If you want to stump every education professional that you encounter just mention Selective Mutism and ask what they plan on doing to accommodate your child. You will be looked on as though you have three heads. But in defence of these teachers, psychologists and social workers, there was not and there still is not enough information about this disorder for them to fully understand the scope of the problem, let alone attempt to address the needs of your child.

Due to SM and an auditory processing deficit, our daughter, Brooke, received special education services all through her school years. Because she would not speak, it affected her academically.

If she didn't understand something, she was not able to speak up to the teacher to have her/him explain it to her. Instead, she just blindly went ahead with whatever task was put in front of her, failing miserably. It was a vicious cycle with no end in sight.

In high school she was placed in a self-contained class, which I was originally quite opposed to. Once you have your child placed in a self-contained classroom you pretty much know that they are not going to have the 'normal' experiences of regular students. These children are segregated, and as much as the special ed. board wants you to believe that they are part of the general school population, they are not. The regular ed. students definitely look at them differently, they are labelled, and there is no way around it. Our daughter was known in school as 'the girl who didn't talk'. By the time she entered high school, everyone pretty much knew her situation and didn't bother with her. Although she was never bullied or teased, which I was always grateful for, she led a sort of invisible existence in school, especially in high school. Most of the cliques that were formed in middle school flowed into the high school years and Brooke was not included in any of them.

She would rarely complain to me about not having many friends but I knew deep down it bothered her. She went to school every single day, rarely missing a day and just accepted her life as it was. She knew she was different and secretly wished she could be like the 'normal girls' who spoke up loudly with their outgoing, bubbly personalities.

There were a few times when she would be in her bed at night where she would be looking very sad, only to burst into tears of pain as to why she was born this way. Why did she have to be the way she was? Why couldn't she be like the other girls in school who seemed so perfect to her, simply because they were able to speak? My heart would ache for her.

Brooke's only friends were those that were in her class. And out of the six, there were only one or two whom she would see outside school periodically. In the afternoons, she went to Boces – a continuing education trade school – to train to be a cosmetologist – a career definitely not suited for one with SM. But this was her dream, so I supported her in any way I could. Brooke had selected a career that is based on being highly social and communicative. Yes, you need talent and a natural gift for styling hair, but I've learned through Brooke's post high school years that one's skill at socializing can trump any talent you may have.

I have experienced great pain as a mother having to watch my daughter being left out of social situations and not having the same experiences as other teens her age. Her years in high school made me face the harsh reality of our family's situation, for SM not only affects your child's relationships, but it affects your own relationships as well. I found that other parents couldn't relate to what my husband and I were experiencing with our daughter, nor could we relate to their experiences. I felt alienated and alone, not being able to talk with other parents about my daughter's problem. No one understood, because no one had ever heard of this horrible disorder.

If my child had had autism, Asperger Syndrome, or ADHD I would have at least had some sort of support system, as those disorders are more talked about. The diagnosis of SM was and still is relatively unheard of, which makes it difficult to find people who you can share your experiences with. It was painful to listen to mothers talking about their daughters' busy social lives, the dating, the parties etc. and they in turn, not having any interest whatsoever in my daughter's struggles. I had lost friendships because of this as well as straining family relationships. The few friendships I had formed with other mothers when Brooke was in her elementary school years had begun to unravel in the middle school/high school transition. Their daughters were moving on in their lives, and leaving Brooke behind. Not normally one to beg, I began suggesting to my 'friends' that it would be a great help to Brooke and myself if their daughters could include her once in a while in a trip to a movie or the mall. I understood that these girls were more advanced and maturing faster than Brooke and had begun to form new friendships, but I wasn't asking for a daily invitation, just an occasional invite, even if it were every other month. But the invites never came, my 'friends' suddenly stopped calling me and it was then that I realized that these women were not true friends at all, but just passing acquaintances who at one time shared common ground with me. It seemed as though our daughters' friendships were the basis of our friendships, and once their friendships ended, so did ours. The real problem was explaining to Brooke why her friends dropped her. SM was ultimately the reason.

But for the occasional day out to the mall or movies with her one friend, Brooke led a predominately quiet, solitary life during her high school years. I had become my daughter's best friend – spending weekends with her, taking her to the mall, the movies, and the beach – my husband taking her to concerts. We didn't want her to miss out on these experiences just because she didn't have friends, so we took the place of them. But there is something about sharing those experiences with a friend that is so special and to this day, my heart aches for her for missing out on that part of her life.

Through all those high school years, she managed to keep a smile on her face. And even now, with the constant rejections she faces in acquiring a job, she somehow keeps her chin up. I found that humour eases her anxiety and helps her cope with her problems. People don't realize how brave one must be to live with this disorder. To be afraid to hear your own voice, and at the same time wanting so desperately to be heard, must be sheer torture. Brooke's determination amazes me.

I always believe that there is hope as long as you persevere. We, as parents, need to be advocates for our children, because we, above anyone else, know their true limitations. I was told Brooke would never function in a regular school. She has. I was told she would never receive her high school diploma. She has. I was told that she would never be able to complete an adult cosmetology course, let alone receive her state license. She accomplished both. I was told that her inhibitions would prevent her from learning how to drive. She has learned how to drive and has her driver's license. I was told that not only would she never be able to work in a salon – her chosen profession – but probably would never be able to work at all. She continues to struggle in this area, but we must always remember that nothing she has accomplished has come easy for her.

It took many baby steps for her to reach all of these goals, so the trek must continue – no matter how many steps it takes to get there!

BRONWEN'S STORY

Secondary school provided the fresh opportunity Haydn needed. All the children had to fill out a form in their final year at primary school stating three people from their class they wanted in their new tutor group at secondary school. This would then be considered as part of the allocation of pupils into tutor groups. While well liked at school, Haydn had struggled to make significant friendships at primary school.

One friend Haydn had spoken to outside school was placed in his tutor group and this was a safe choice but generally he preferred to have a fresh start and not be with those from his primary class or year group. School struggled with this, but Haydn was adamant it was a fresh start and this was the best approach.

At secondary school Haydn found it was much more acceptable for individuals to be allowed to use their individual strengths. For example, at the year 6 leaver's production it was unusual to be on the production side and not a member of the cast. However, at secondary school it was actively encouraged and accepted that the roles of producer, cameraman and sound technician were equally as important.

Haydn will enjoy and appreciate amusing events in class and will often recount his day on arrival home from school but he also goes to great lengths not to get involved in difficult situations. This is evident when friends have fallen out with each other and he will always remain impartial.

Haydn has insight into his SM and I am told he has a strong presence within his tutor group, despite not speaking. At primary the girls often fussed and mothered him a little bit for not speaking but there is no evidence of this at secondary school. Other children his age acknowledge us when we are out walking even though they know they will only get a non-verbal response from Haydn.

Haydn's secondary school refers to his SM as 'Haydn's communication difficulties'. This is how his class interpret it as well, and this phrase sits comfortably for Haydn. I can only recall one incident where Haydn got into difficulties and a supply teacher was in attendance. The teacher said, three times, 'If you don't answer the question you will have to wait outside the class.' One of the boys in his class spoke and said 'Sir, Haydn doesn't say much.' This boy then got into trouble for speaking. However, the boy went to student support after the lesson and the issue was resolved. I was informed by telephone and given an apology. I don't feel one incident in four years gives me grounds to complain. The issue here is how Haydn managed the situation and that he did reasonably well, as a 12-year-old, and I feel confident that, at 14, he would handle it even better now. My response was clear: Haydn has to manage these situations and to be fair, in his own way, he did. There was no evidence of reactive behaviour in the classroom and Haydn will be faced with a lifetime of scenarios such as these. Interestingly, Haydn was given a laminated card in his first year of secondary school, which stated that if he felt anxious he might not feel able to speak. He always carried this with him for the first few years, but never used it.

Secondary school adopts an inclusive approach. If Haydn is unable to answer a question in class, he is expected to write the answer down. Generally this works well, without fuss from the other pupils. A wipe board or the back of the exercise book is Haydn's usual method of communicating. However, the level of comfort he has with this is variable depending on the subject, the teachers and the pupils in that particular class.

As a family we attribute much of Haydn's progress at secondary school to his increasing maturity. I can also see a shift in Haydn's confidence since completing his subject choices. I will always be amazed how Haydn managed art, drama and music at school, while also managing to continue to enjoy school. However, now he is in year 10 and has started his GCSEs, life is considerably easier for him without these subjects on his timetable. The fact these subjects are heavily reliant on expression, creativity and verbal expression with drama and music made them very challenging but he always participated.

Another challenge for Haydn is that he has had to drop German as a GCSE course. He attempted two mock oral exams and was unable to speak on either occasion, making this unrealistic, as the exam requires the oral component to be completed. He instigated these two attempts and the environment was as supportive as possible in that he chose the classroom, teacher, time of day, etc. Haydn was very disappointed to not be successful in his attempts and it was the first time that school and us, as parents, had directly challenged Haydn to speak. It is important to re-emphasize Haydn wanted to do this and thought he could achieve it and it answered many questions for him. His German teacher said it was evident how hard Haydn tried to speak and, on the second attempt, Haydn was given a question and answer sheet to read from in case there was any anxiety linked to not knowing the answers. Both school and us as parents are clear that while it gave us much insight we would not adopt this approach again.

There was a possibility he could have undertaken half a GCSE without the oral exam, but Haydn has preferred to pursue other option subject choices instead. Most importantly these tests were done just before the summer holiday and Haydn took ownership and emailed his German teacher and Special Educational Needs Co-ordinator (SENCO) to ensure his timetable was organized and he knew what he would be doing in September.

Interestingly, having successfully completed his work experience where he spoke to work colleagues including the boss, receptionist and men on the garage workshop floor as well as independently getting the bus there and back, the following week he could not speak at parents' evening. He is determined to leave school as soon as possible and get an apprenticeship. I suspect this is his best opportunity for progress because I do not believe he will be able to speak at sixth form.

DAWN'S STORY

I should start this by saying during Tom's last year at primary school we decided that if he went to secondary school, and it was no better for him – if he was still so anxious – we would take him out of school and home-school him.

Before starting, Tom had about six visits to secondary school, and a four-day course in the summer holidays just working out where everything was, getting to know a few staff members and a few children who also were felt to need a bit more help with the transition. So I don't know what could have been handled any differently to make it any easier for him. But, for him, it was the end of the life he had previously known, and the start of a downward spiral that ended in us removing him from school completely.

On our first visit we should have realized what a huge deal this was going to be for him. As we were walking around the school, he was hiding under stairwells or in doorways when he saw anyone else coming. As we walked outside, he walked as close to the buildings as possible, and around the perimeter fence commando-style – as if he was on a surveillance mission. It may seem funny to an observer, but it was definitely not funny; and a sign of just how hard he found having to mix with hundreds of people.

I had made sure that I knew the SENCO, Tom's Learning Support Assistant (LSA), parent partnership lady, speech and language therapy (SALT) – i.e. everyone Tom was going to need to make this work. All the staff from the head teacher to dinner ladies had been on a course from SALT about SM, so everyone was aware of Tom and knew not to put him under any pressure to speak. Tom knew where he had to go, who was going to take him, etc. One of Tom's biggest problems was that to actually get around school, he needed to have his LSA accompany him. If he was spoken to on his journey around school, he knew she would intervene and speak for him. He had a quiet place to go break times and lunchtimes, where it was possible for him to be completely alone if he chose. He had a key to the disabled toilet, which only one other person had, so his school were very accommodating.

Within two weeks we began having problems. Every day Tom would feel unwell with a crippling headache. He would feel sick and have aches and pains all over. He would refuse to get ready for school, getting dressed minutes before we had to get into the car to go. During that time he would call me a 'bitch' and far worse for making him go, and he would plead with me not to send him. It was horrible…

His attendance dropped very quickly to about 30 per cent. School were very quick to act. Taking advice from SALT and CAMHS, Tom started on a very gradual journey back to school. It was very slow: one hour a day at first, for a few weeks, then adding an hour until we got to lunchtime. We never got further than this, as during this time my husband and I decided that there must be more to life than sending him somewhere that made him feel so bad.

Tom would come home from school, and go in the bath for hours on end. He would chew and pick his fingernails until he had no nail left on some fingers. He would rub his skin and make scars that he would then pick until he had big holes. The effect of the anxiety was obvious to us. He would not come out of his bedroom, and he barely spoke to us. Things came to boiling point when our car broke down and, walking home, a girl from his class appeared behind us and overheard him talking to me. He never went back to school again. He just refused. He became a virtual recluse. He wouldn't come out of his room, in case I sent him to school – even if I promised I wouldn't.

We had had enough. There is more to life than school. Academically Tom already knows far more than I do. He loves information. I hope one day he will be able to take exams. There's no point even worrying about it though. If you can't leave your house, it doesn't matter if you're a genius. No one will ever know.

So that is where we are at now. Tom is 13 and home-schooled. He is definitely calmer. We have no more self-harming and he seems happier and if you ask him he says he is. He is still very reclusive. He spends most of his time alone. He talks to us when we go and talk to him, but never really begins the conversation. He only speaks if he wants to and he only goes out if he wants to. We encourage him to take baby steps forward on a daily basis as we hope that one day he will feel able to cope with everyday life outside our house, and to enjoy life a little.

Our only regret is that we didn't take him out of school sooner. If we had, when we first thought the system wasn't doing him any favours, he wouldn't have been so desperately unhappy and nowhere near as anxious as he is now. The system isn't set up to help kids like Tom.

CHAPTER 7

Becoming an Adult with Selective Mutism

Carl Sutton; Sonja, Kat, Christina, Wendy, Liz, Sophia and Kimberly

It has been rather a quest for me over the last few years to discover other adults with SM. By running a support group, called iSpeak, for adults and teenagers with SM (and their parents) and also undertaking an exploratory research study on SM in adults (Sutton, 2013) I have now encountered several hundred adults whose SM continued into adulthood, many of whom still significantly experience SM. It has benefited me emotionally and psychologically to know that I am not alone; and, when a new adult, or their relative, contacts me, this is the message that I always try to convey: they are is not alone either.

Regarding the adults that I have encountered, many are creative individuals – artists, graphic artists, and published writers. Not counting myself, I know five published writers who are adults with SM. A couple have gone a step further and become public speakers, including Beth and Rachel in Chapter 17. Helen Keen, who presented the BBC Radio 4 documentary 'Finding Your Voice' (Tzabar, 2015) became a broadcaster and well-known comedienne.

In my own case, I am a software developer. For the majority of my working life I sat silently in the corner, being creative. I was extremely good at what I did – and that fact protected me, because I never needed to ask a question.

Others work in the caring professions – a few even working with children in their early years, keeping an eye out for the silent ones in their midst.

A few are lecturers, comfortable with the functional speech required to teach in a classroom setting, much less comfortable with 'social' communication. Many others are students, struggling to stay in university. And others are students who couldn't get through university because of the social difficulties they experienced.

Many of the younger adults with SM are Not in Employment, Education or Training (they are so-called NEETs). They are entirely dependent on their parents. Many are housebound, suffering from depression, anxiety and agoraphobia as well as SM.

For young adults with SM, being mute at the Job Centre counter, being talked for by a parent, tends not to be well received to say the least. Likewise, accessing further education is, emotionally, very difficult for such young adults too. Even when they do force themselves into adult education settings, they can encounter unhelpful tutors who don't know what to make of them. For instance, I know of one young woman with SM being thrown off a flower arranging course for, of all things, 'being disruptive' – she couldn't talk and the course tutor couldn't deal with it.

Most research on SM is about young children. The life outcomes of adults with SM are disregarded, because, as a population, adults with SM are wrongly assumed not to exist. However, for me, the worst of my experience of SM was as a young adult when I was first trying to make my way independently in the world, as I described in my life story in the introduction. Thus adulthood and SM is my primary personal interest and focus.

At university, in my late teens and early 20s, I had what I felt to be insurmountable psychological problems and speech rules.

I couldn't talk about being unable to talk, hence seek help for myself because, ironically, my mutism was my deeply held secret (even though it was quite apparent). I was riven with speech rules, unable to speak to this person or that depending on whether my emotional memory interpreted them as 'threatening'. As I described in my life story in the introduction, I eventually had a nervous breakdown, the effects of which have lingered.

As an almost entirely mute PhD student I was excruciatingly isolated – living alone in a flat, wandering the streets at 23, over a hundred miles from 'home' (a home where I was entirely mute), barely able to speak to anybody. Walking into a supermarket to buy food for myself caused me to feel irrational, due to immediate stress headaches and physical pain. I felt that every door, window and life opportunity (besides education) was closed to me. The world felt like a profoundly inhospitable place, with no place for me. Every ordinary thing – the most important to me being finding a life partner – seemed unattainable.

I do not feel failed by 'the system' because I was an adolescent and young adult in an era (the 1980s and early 1990s) when there was very little awareness of SM. However, I now hear of many young adults with SM who I feel definitely are failed – despite so much more awareness of SM than in my day. Many young adults with SM had a torrid time at school and leave with few, if any, qualifications. Having left, their parents, doing their utmost to help, just can't get the support their adult children need. Neither the education system nor CAMHS get a good press among this population.

Following are seven pieces written by people who have experienced SM in adulthood. Each is very different. However, I feel each story is full of hope for the future in one way or another.

SONJA'S STORY

From my late teens I would binge drink. It enabled me to socialize. It made me feel confident and able to talk to people. It also helped to break my severe pattern of SM. In my late 20s, I would often be paralytic and pass out. In my 30s, because I was constantly getting severely physically sick, I stopped drinking. Gradually, over this time, the number of places I was able to speak outside of home increased. However, work and anything work-related remained, and still remain, the only places I have not been able to 'conquer'. And, in situations that make me feel anxious, I still freeze or find it difficult to speak. In my 30s I went to interviews drunk, or would buy one of those one-glass bottles of wine and drink it in the toilets before a meeting, just to feel calmer. I tried beta blockers for interviews and meetings for a while, but they made me feel spaced out, very cold, and I felt cut off from the passion I felt about what I was good at. I don't/can't drink alcohol at all now, I am sensitive to most types of medication and have an intolerance to some foods. I think it has probably affected my physical health generally in many ways.

I started to research SM (still called Elective Mutism then) in my desperation to find help as an adult, but everything I looked at only acknowledged that it was children who had this condition. I thought that I must be the only adult still having problems, and would have to continue to cope on my own, together with the constant fear of being exposed (finding myself in a situation where I was unable to speak), and 'revealed' as deficient, a failure. There are times when I felt I had left SM behind, and I was 'cured', but I just hadn't been in a situation for a while where I was unable to speak. Whenever it happened, I would feel confused and devastated, my confidence shattered. I believe the effects are cumulative, in that I don't really get over each event, each one is traumatising. It never occurred to me to ask for help. This was me and I was deficient – fact. Even if it had occurred to me, I would not have been able to ask; what exactly would I be asking for?

I have had problems in further education and in all the jobs I have had to varying degrees because of SM. My grades have suffered, and I have been bullied or reprimanded because sometimes I don't respond in the way that people expect or I may not respond at all. Sometimes I don't seem to be able to communicate with others about what

I'm doing, I just do it. If you don't respond, or can't respond quickly enough, and do this a number of times, people start to ignore you, or they assume you're 'slow', or you're not interested, or you're rude, or useless at your job. How do you explain? When can you explain? People just about understand that someone with a stammer needs to be given time to say something, and that someone who has an obvious disability is not also voiceless. It is hard to explain how it feels when you have become used to being ignored or excluded because of something beyond your control. Therefore, something as simple as someone not saying good morning, or greeting me at work when there is an obvious opportunity to do this, will have an adverse effect on my anxiety levels that day. This has made me acutely sensitive to others' feelings, so if I feel that someone is being excluded or left out of a conversation I will find a way to include them.

I have been lucky to have a skill/talent that I have always excelled at. After doing many different jobs, some related to my skill and some not, I am now 'successful' in the fact that I earn a living from a profession in which those with professional/educated parents and privileged backgrounds are the majority. However, I have not been able to further my profession in the way I have wanted to. I am unable to 'present' to other professionals in my field, or network, or attend an interview without suffering severe and disabling anxiety. In the field that I work you have to network or you don't 'get on', no matter how good your work is.

I have been invited to talk about my work and to be on panels with other professionals at conferences, but I have had to turn these opportunities down and not be able to explain why. In the end people stop asking. I have applied for commissions and have been shortlisted, but I can't communicate well/at all at the interview stage. However, my work has taken a different direction because of it, and I get enormous satisfaction from this. I could not have achieved what I have done without the support of my long-term partner, who has been my 'guide', and counsellor, and all the good things that a life partner should be.

When I look back at what I have achieved despite SM I often feel as if it was someone else, not me. So much of my life has been dominated by a sense of failure because of SM, and constantly trying to cover this up/hide it, so that I would not be seen as inadequate, or exposed as a fraud. On job applications, I have answered the question 'good communication skills' affirmatively (because I am very good at communicating in some contexts) but how do you explain SM on a job application? I feel I have lied, and I work under the threat of being exposed as a fraud or a liar, because of SM. There are a whole range of situations at work where I have difficulty, particularly when there is an 'expectation' to speak – formal situations mainly, anything performance related, authority figures, group situations if the majority of people are new to me and I have not spoken to them before, and/or crucially, if someone is present who has witnessed my failure to speak in the past. Presentations per se are almost impossible and, sometimes, so is just introducing myself.

In most situations outside home now (apart from those mentioned) I can express myself well, but this has taken me a lifetime to learn and perfect; and it makes the potential 'slip up' more difficult for me to deal with because people don't expect it. It is only very recently, finding the iSpeak site, watching videos of young people with SM on YouTube and reading other people's stories, that I have begun to accept and understand the condition, and to acknowledge and celebrate the courage, strength and determination of every child and adult with SM, and through this, finally, my own.

KAT'S STORY

When I drank, I wasn't trying to fit in or be someone else. I was being myself, and having a lot of fun doing so – until the next morning, when I would wake up drowning in guilt, self-doubt and, as I got older, a terrible hangover.

In my early 20s I worked hard, played even harder and didn't give myself a spare moment to be on my own. I was too scared, I guess, of what I might have found there.

I feel incredibly lucky to have met Simon at a time when the wheels truly were beginning to fall off for me. I was 23. I had moved from the UK to New Zealand – running as far away as I could from the person I didn't want to be. I continued to burn the candle at both ends, and was finding that meltdowns were becoming commonplace. I felt lost and confused – but somehow, Simon could see that there was more to me simmering deep within.

As I weaned myself off alcohol, I experienced eight years of intense night terrors. Several times at night I would fear for my life, Simon's life, and, later, the lives of our children. I would act out the scenario as I screamed, kicked, ran and gave myself several black eyes, bumps and bruises in the process.

It wasn't the ideal way to return to myself, but it was the only way I would allow it – unconsciously, when there were no walls of habit standing in my way. Night terrors led me to various forms of therapy and, piece-by-piece, I began to re-discover myself.

I realized that the scared little girl who couldn't talk at school was still there. She always had been patiently waiting for me to come back and help her to find her voice. I realized how much she had to say – and it was overwhelming as it began to fall out of my mouth in all kinds of jumbled combinations.

One day, I noticed how I felt when I wanted to say something. I noticed the burning passion within and the heart-felt need to speak. I noticed that when I spoke from that place, my voice sounded different. It sounded natural and free. It sounded like me!

I am still in the process of fully returning to the place where I speak my truth – and every part of the journey is immensely rewarding and revealing. Sometimes I notice myself in a situation where I can't speak – and I am grateful that I don't feel the need to pretend. I ride out the situation and speak as, when and if I am ready. Sometimes I notice myself slipping into my old habits, and sometimes I let myself pretend. Sometimes I stop, breathe and begin again, speaking instead – as myself.

It is an on-going process, but one which reminds me at every turn of the beauty, uniqueness and fragility of every single one of us. I feel like SM gives me a reason to become more than I think I can be – more than maybe I would be without it. For that I am grateful.

CHRISTINA'S STORY

I think that if there were more awareness of SM in adults, my life would be easier. The world would feel more adapted to my needs.

I am 39 now, and I have had SM since I was a child. When I was a child it was severe. I used to speak very fluently at home, with my family, but become absolutely mute in the presence of strangers. My lips would feel stuck together and I could make no sound at all.

I often felt physically frozen. In fact, I couldn't imagine saying a word, even if I could see exactly what to say in my mind. And I couldn't bear listening to my voice.

If I was asked a question suddenly I didn't even know what to say. I spent all my school years having just one friend. I could only talk to her when nobody else was listening. Because most girls chose not to be friends with me I was alone most playtimes. I could never ask to go to the toilet. And if someone was hurting me I couldn't make a sound to tell someone what was happening.

As an adult my actual speech difficulties are not quite so bad in some ways. However, it is harder to live with the condition as an adult because, at my age, it is expected that I can survive by myself. When I was a child I could hide this problem. Now I can't. The world is full of talkers and I feel I can't be the same as them.

Employment is my greatest hurdle. I can't find the kind of job I would like to have. This makes me think that there isn't a place in this world for me – and that I can't become who I feel I ought to be. I would like to work, but this requires me to be much more vocal than I am. While, as an adult, I can now speak with more people than I used to, there are still many days and many situations in which it is still impossible for me to say a word. I still get very anxious and I still feel physically frozen. Even on the days I can speak, I stick to short dialogues because I quickly get to the point where I don't know what else to say.

For me there is hope, however. Step by step I am getting better and better – speaking very slowly, and requesting people to allow me more time to speak, when I am struggling. I am getting better because of my persistence, because of my increasing knowledge of SM, and because of the wisdom, courage and compassion I am finding within myself. I have started to practise Nichiren Daishonin's Buddhism, which has been a great help to me. Two years ago I could barely say 'Hi!' Now I can speak with more people and I am speaking for longer.

I know that I will get there eventually. I will find the job I want, but the path is very hard because the world is not aware of SM in adults and it does not cater for us.

WENDY'S STORY

Becoming an adult was a difficult time for me. It coincided with marriage and with becoming a mother. I married very young – against all the odds really, considering how socially challenged I was. I think it is significant that the man I married was from a very different culture. English was not his first language and he had been in the UK for less than a year when I first met him. This being the case, he may not have had a clear idea of what English girls are usually like and he may not have realized how strange I was.

The only paid job that I have ever had was a Saturday job while I was still at school. On leaving school I applied for some clerical jobs. I filled out the application forms well enough to get two job interviews. But I didn't have a hope of getting any further. I was very childlike in my appearance and in the way I presented myself. My lack of confidence and lack of maturity really showed on the outside. Because I had never had normal social interaction with the outside world, I was very out of touch with social norms. Going to a job interview wearing down at heel shoes and a coat that had seen better days was not going to create a good first impression. This, coupled with my very poor social skills and lack of social experience, meant that I had no chance of getting through those interviews. My lack of interview preparation, my inarticulate, almost mumbled answers and my inability to answer questions properly meant that really they might as well have been interviewing a primary school child for the position. Unsurprisingly, there was always a letter in the next post saying they hadn't felt able to offer me the job. I realize now that they did me a kindness by not offering me a job because I wouldn't have survived in an adult work environment. I have done voluntary work at times, and because I wasn't being paid, I was accepted and even appreciated up to a point. Because I wasn't able to interact socially in these environments, I needed a practical task that I could focus on. This meant that I was willing to do some quite unpleasant cleaning tasks. Even though I dislike cleaning and have always found it difficult to keep my own home clean, doing those tasks enabled me to be in that environment. I still felt very self-conscious about my social behaviour, and imagined that other people would be talking about me behind my back. I thought they would consider me the strangest person they had ever known.

After I left school I took a one-year secretarial course, which I managed to complete. By the time I had finished the course I was already married and expecting my first child. I had very high expectations of motherhood. I hoped that it would have a 'normalising' effect on me. I thought that, being a mother, I might then feel I had something in common with other women. The reality was very different. The birth of my son was emotionally traumatic for me and it left me feeling even more alienated from other mothers. I was totally unprepared for motherhood and hadn't had a clue what to expect. I wasn't able to bond with my child; I didn't feel like a mother; and I felt completely overwhelmed by the practicalities of caring for a young baby. I had imagined that I would naturally fall into my new role as a mum, and it hadn't occurred to me that I wouldn't be able to cope. But I wasn't coping at all. In the past I had always been able to run away from things that I felt overwhelmed by, but there is no running away from the responsibility of motherhood. I didn't feel able to tell anybody how I was feeling and I became even more withdrawn. I found it more difficult to talk to people outside my very immediate family, and my SM got worse.

Perhaps the most serious consequence of growing up with SM has been the damage to my self-esteem and to the way I perceive myself as an individual. Because I'm not able to connect with other people, it is difficult for me to see myself as human. I have never felt like an adult, even though I now have adult children. This has impacted on my ability to be an effective parent. We lived with my parents until my eldest child was 19 months old, when we got a flat of our own. I thought, perhaps, I would start to feel like an adult when I moved into my own flat. But I was quickly disillusioned. Now I had the responsibility of a child, and a home as well. Everything got on top of me and I wasn't keeping up with the most basic household chores. I had two more children quite quickly, and although parenting them was never easy for me, I did bond with them in a way that, unfortunately, I hadn't with my first.

As a young mother, I took my children to a mother and toddler centre, really for their benefit. But I was so out of touch with people that I was like an alien amongst the other parents. I couldn't talk to them and I couldn't relate to them. I was excluded from their activities as if I just wasn't there. I hid behind my children as much as I could. When my children got a bit older, I depended on them to speak for me. This was especially true if I needed to get somebody's attention, for example a waiter in a restaurant, or even if I needed to communicate with their teacher at school. In this way our roles were reversed. They became the caregivers and I was like the child who needed to be looked after. I was only able to talk normally to them in private, so I behaved very differently towards them when we were out in public.

I didn't have any peer support from other mothers. They seemed like aliens to me. I couldn't talk to them and I was quite afraid of them. I still felt very much like a child, and this showed in my appearance and in the way I carried myself. Children often used to ask me 'Are you a little girl or a lady?' and I couldn't answer them. I couldn't feel equal to other parents. I thought they would be looking down on me and judging me unkindly for being so unsociable and just for being downright strange. People used to assume that I was foreign and didn't speak or understand English. So many times I have been asked which country I am from. This was very embarrassing and shaming for me. I had no way of being able to explain that I am not foreign, but I was unable talk for other reasons.

Some people spend time in therapy trying to get in touch with their 'inner child'. For me it was the opposite. I have always felt very much the child. It was only through so many years of 'looking inwards' that I have finally discovered my 'inner adult' if that makes sense. I have discovered that somewhere within myself there is quite a nurturing mother who can take care of the child. And when I really was a child, I couldn't do that for myself.

LIZ'S STORY

As a young adult, life seemed to stand still for me. This was the time when I should have been finding my way in the world and enjoying new experiences. Instead I spent most of my time clinging to my home and family.

After leaving school I was lucky enough to find a job as a clerk in a local garage but my world consisted of walking to work and facing the challenges of communication with the people around me, then returning home and spending most of my time in my room safely away from the nagging reminders that I was not like most 17-year-olds and the guilt that I found it impossible to do what was expected of me. I didn't enjoy school, but at least at school I had a few friends with whom I was comfortable talking to; they had now found other lives and friends to spend time with. I found it particularly hard to get to know people at work and would often sit in the office trying to pluck up the courage to walk to the next office and speak to someone. Sometimes I tried, sometimes I failed and sat alone – but when I tried I was always awkward, and it showed. I was terrified when I found that one of my tasks would be ad hoc switchboard duties and I never got used to the task – the fear didn't recede – in fact years later when I was given the same duties in another job, the fear and dread returned.

Every day presented a challenge that seemed insurmountable – talking to people, asking questions even just saying how I was feeling filled me with dread. Talking spontaneously was not something I could do – it always took a lot of conscious effort and bravery on my part. I suffered from bad headaches and a lack of energy, which now I feel sure was due to the anxiety I was experiencing. I believe that I was depressed. Going out became an ordeal for me. Even speaking to a shop assistant or a bus driver scared me. A lot of people have phobias – some people are afraid of spiders or snakes but when you are afraid of being expected to speak, when you worry every morning and dread each day that might bring you into contact with this expectation, and exposure to this fear never makes it any less daunting, you begin to imagine how debilitating it can be.

My parents were worried about me. My father tried to push me out of my comfort zone and remind me how I was wasting my life. But this only made me more afraid and determined to hang on to the safety of my silence and served to confirm my own idea that I was not good enough. Without words I couldn't influence my life, I was never at ease in any social or working situation, and in fact there were times when I actually physically trembled with fear.

I hadn't made any real friends at work in the three years I was there and my life was stagnating. I summoned the courage to get through an interview and secure a new job that was away from the village where I lived and would, I hoped, broaden my horizons.

Starting a new job created a lot of anxiety, as it does for most people, but after some time I found that my new work colleagues were friendly and welcoming and I felt that I had made an important step into being more sociable. I also caught up with old school friends who I occasionally went out with in the evenings. The biggest element that brought me out of my shell was humour, and this is what helped me relax and even join in with conversations.

But then I experienced the most tragic set back in my life. Just before my 20th birthday I received a phone call at work. My mother had been involved in a road accident and had been taken to hospital. She survived for three months then sadly passed away. My mother had always been the parent who was on my side, who understood my fears and protected me. I no longer had this safety net. My father and I were ill-fitted companions. In our loss we did little to comfort one another as we both found it difficult to express our feelings. My father grew frustrated with my timid behaviour. He tried to push me to be more sociable and I resented this. He did what he thought was the best for me but it was just making me more fearful. I just needed someone to accept me and tell me I was okay. I lived with my father for the following eight years. I always thought in time I would gain confidence and life would get easier but my progress was very slow. My young adult life passed me by.

Sometimes I made huge leaps in my confidence in speaking to people. I even travelled abroad with a friend but it was ironic that I could come back home from a trip aboard and still be afraid to walk down the road to the shops where I lived. I think some of the problem was that I had developed the habit of overthinking situations rather than just acting spontaneously – the anxiety set in before the action.

It took me a very long time to battle through SM as it became an ingrained behaviour but I am now a happy and optimistic person. There are still things that I find difficult, but they are not insurmountable and I am so pleased that children are now gradually getting the help that I so desperately needed when I was young. No child should grow up unhappy and in an almost constant state of fear.

SOPHIA'S STORY

I am naive where men are concerned and I find it difficult to accept that anybody could be interested in me romantically. Growing up with SM has had a devastating effect on my self-image. I don't even feel human enough to be acceptable to another human being. If I feel attracted to somebody I wouldn't dare let them know. The other person would always have to approach me. I am especially self-conscious about speaking to or in front of somebody who I'm attracted to; I don't like the way I sound and don't want to make a bad impression.

If the partner doesn't know about SM it can cause serious misunderstandings in a relationship. I couldn't explain my condition to my husband because I didn't know about Asperger Syndrome then and I didn't know about SM either. I wasn't diagnosed with anything, and depression was the best explanation I could come up with. I just knew that I was really struggling and that I wasn't coping with any aspect of my life. For a long time my husband seemed to think my behaviour was intended as a personal insult directed against him. That was not the case, but if it had been then surely I would have had normal social functioning with other people. Why would I have withdrawn from the world just to get at him?

By the time I met my second partner I had been diagnosed with AS and I had self-diagnosed with SM, so I could offer some kind of explanation for my behaviour. We have definitely had our moments because it was a very difficult concept for him to understand and I needed to explain it to him more than once. But at least he got to know that when I didn't speak it wasn't because I was mad at him or because I didn't care for him. When I first got together with him I could be physically affectionate and demonstrative with him but I could barely talk to him. If I hadn't been able to explain my condition to him I don't think we would have stood a chance. The behaviour of somebody with SM can be baffling, and can seem very hurtful to a partner who may never have come across this condition before. I never mean to be hurtful. I wish I could simulate for other people what it feels like to be in company and not be able to speak. I know that at times my partner has felt alone and possibly quite lonely in my company.

Even if the partner does eventually come to understand and accept me, family members, friends and acquaintances probably will not. It isn't just communication with the partner that can be problematic. I'm not the sort of girl that a man could take home to meet his mum; I wouldn't be able to talk to her. Luckily I never had to meet the in-laws, but if somebody with SM cannot speak to their partner's family members it's going to be seen as a choice not to speak to them, and that can cause such a lot of conflict all round.

My also having Asperger Syndrome does complicate matters somewhat. In the most comfortable of situations I still can't do small talk. I can talk most easily when I've got something deep and meaningful to say. But nobody can keep up deep and meaningful conversation all the time; and I am not able to 'pad it out' with the spontaneous chat that most people do so easily. This means that even with a romantic partner my SM still rears its ugly head. There will often be uncomfortable silences between us, just as with anybody else; and I can't use my voice to break that silence. I am very dependent on the other person to lead the conversation and to do the talking.

I think anybody who can weather a relationship with me must be an exceptional person and possibly not quite typical themselves. They are the kind of beautiful individual who deserves so much better than a partner who cannot interact with them half the time.

KIMBERLY'S STORY

Social phobia is a fear of interacting with people. It's so anxiety-driven that it makes a person self-conscious about everything. Agoraphobia is an irrational fear of crowded or public places. Although some people do have a cocktail of conditions, I have neither of these two problems. I have SM. It's an inability to speak to some people and in some settings. I've heard accounts of people who've 'outgrown' it. I have 'improved' since I was a child, but it's still there. It's my normal state of being. Silence is as natural to me as breathing. When I do speak, I often hear this, 'She really can talk?' Suddenly I'm a novelty.

When I was in my 20s, I went through a phase of trying to 'break through' my condition. I accepted invitations and enjoyed them in my way. There must be an internal acceptance of myself inside me that doesn't judge me, so when I hear things like this I'm always surprised:

'Do you smoke?' one aunt asked. 'Do you swear? Drive? Tell bawdy jokes?' No to all! She turned to my mother and remarked, 'She hasn't changed one bit. She always was *special*, wasn't she?' A cousin tried to engage me in conversation but I was too far gone by then. Finally she turned to my mother and said, 'She'll always be that way, won't she?'

I kept trying. What did special really mean? I didn't want to be perceived that way. People inside my close one-on-one circle knew I was funny, intelligent and kind. I continued to grow into a married mother of children, I found employment and developed hobbies, and I kept doing things outside my comfort level.

When I was 26, I looked out the window and saw some boy stomping my eight-year-old son to the ground. I walked to that boy's house and yelled down the neighbourhood, in his defence. I WAS LOUD! Another success.

When my husband got ALS (Lou Gehrig's disease) in 2000, it was at a time I was finally ready to brave college. I chose being his sole care provider instead (for the following five years) until his demise in 2005, and I put education on hold. After a few years of caring for him, I started dressing in mime around the house. I ordered the best makeup online, had it delivered to the house, and found a striped shirt and suspenders. Topped with a velvet hat or a black beret, my look was complete.

I told myself I was helping with my son's girlfriend's RIT assignment. She needed a model for her photography homework, and in between full-time husband care, preparing meals, caring for kids, laundry, and all the rest, I would pose for her pictures. But after her assignments were complete, I felt I didn't mind feeding my husband through his feeding tube while dressed as a mime. I didn't mind walking by the gathering of young teens and my son, down in the basement (dressed in full mime) as I did laundry. Funny thing is, because I was so naturally quiet and quirky, no one remarked on my appearance. Mimes aren't expected to speak, after all. They either annoy the hell out of people or amuse them. Best of all they're mute and I relate to that! Miming appealed to my creative side and to my core self.

In 2006 I participated in my first art show. There was a wine and cheese get together for the artists. Potential customers congregated in the small room, mingling with us. Imagine my horror when we artists lined up and had to answer questions about our paintings! The question directed to me: 'What's the favourite painting you've done?' I answered, 'It's called Baby in Chaos but I didn't bring it. It's home.' People laughed. Someone then asked me how long I'd been painting. Ah, I could get away with a mere couple of words: 'Since 1990'. Satisfied, the crowd moved on to the next artist. I didn't elaborate. My voice shook. But... I SURVIVED!

That same year, I was asked to be part of a 'focus group' for disabled people, because I'm a person diagnosed with Asperger's in addition to SM. I sat around a table at a local college with a dozen people with various disabilities (post-traumatic stress disorders (PTSD), multiple sclerosis (MS), etc.) Each of us in turn spoke into a microphone, answering questions about transportation and similar issues we faced. We were on closed circuit TV. I contributed my thoughts with much anxiety and no poise, but I did it!

I wrote a book about the experience of communication impairment and ALS. I found an agent in 2011. It was published. My peer – author friend Donna Williams – says that I 'succeeded where many other nondisabled people would've crumbled'. ALS stole my husband's voice. Ironically for five years I became his voice when it mattered – to doctors, nurses, family I could decipher his garble. I'm a great listener. I made a great interpreter and, overall, I'm pretty proud of myself!

CHAPTER 8

Bullying and Selective Mutism

Cheryl Forrester; Mandy and Dawn (parents);
Kimberly, Nicky, Danielle, Wendy and Vivienne

I, myself, was bullied extensively throughout my childhood, and, on occasions, as an adult. In my opinion, the school I went to promoted a culture of bullying against children by both children and teachers. Bullying took away my childhood, and left me feeling, as a child, that I wished I had never been born. Fortunately I don't feel like this now. I learned to protect myself, because the school system was not doing anything to protect me, by growing my fingernails very long and scratching my perpetrators before they physically or verbally attacked me.

I didn't have SM. However, from experience, I can say that bullying can be very damaging to a child's self-esteem and, potentially, future prospects in life. In my own case I managed to use my personal experience in a positive way. My own experience of bullying has contributed to my being very intolerant of injustice, which is something that I took forward with me into my career as a social worker, working with a variety of client groups including people with disabilities and the elderly.

Writing from my own experience, children who are bullied need effective support from education providers, family members, and so on. It should be realized, however, that children with SM may find it entirely impossible to say to a teacher, 'I am being bullied,' not least because the teacher may be one of many people they are phobic of speaking to.

SELECTIVE MUTISM IN OUR OWN WORDS

Likewise, admitting bullying to a parent would cause most parents to address the issue by approaching the child's teachers at school (something, of course, they ought to do). A child with SM, who experiences exactly the same fear of the repercussions of reporting their bullies as every other bullied child, can, additionally, be afraid of spotlighting, hence challenging their own speech phobia even more.

I personally define bullying as the erosion or disregard of the human rights of the person who is being subject to bullying by an individual bully, group or institution – such human rights as being able to go about the day without fear or harassment, and having the freedom and opportunity to communicate. Bullying often leads to a sense of acute isolation. Even without SM one of the things that bullying affects is, indeed, communication. From experience: when every word one might say could be used against you by a bully, then it's natural that you keep your thoughts and feelings close to your chest. This is a classic safety behaviour. It thus does not surprise me that, in many cases, SM is worsened or triggered by bullying. Bullying is a violation of the basic human rights we are all entitled to enjoy, such as feeling respected, having dignity, and having the freedom and confidence to communicate.

The effects of bullying can leave a person feeling emotionally traumatized – sometimes for years to follow. It can happen to anyone. A person subject to bullying may not even have an individual difference such as SM, or a cultural difference or similar. Bullies may use 'difference' to justify their inappropriate behaviour. However, the truth is there can be no justification or rational argument to bully anyone.

As an example, Mandy writes about her son, Aaron, whose Selective Mutism caused him to be a target for bullying at school:

> When Aaron went to comprehensive school he was in a class with only one other child from his primary school. He didn't like answering questions and teachers would always

push for this. Apparently from what he told me this made him more of a target for being bullied. He stayed quiet to try and remain unnoticed. He was kept down academically because he wouldn't speak in class, even though his exam results showed he should have been in a higher form. In his second year the bullying became intolerable. He didn't want to go to school he was so distressed.

It goes without saying that bullying is never the fault of the person being subjected to it. And concerning difference, as human beings we all possess some degree of difference. We are, each of us, unique. It could be argued that only through embracing difference and uniqueness can we truly acknowledge ourselves, and the uniqueness of others. In terms of valuing difference and diversity there is a clear argument for focusing on the positive contributions people with SM can make towards the school environment (because they can be kind, compassionate individuals who, simply, can't speak) and subsequently society as a whole.

Sadly, of course, bullying can take place within the family home too. When this is the case it needs to be addressed effectively by the family, as nobody benefits when they have a bully in their midst. In some instances families may need professional help if specific patterns of relating within the family have become problematic.

Kimberly writes about her own experience of bullying at school, describing the specific difficulties she experienced when she was a child with SM:

'The squeaky wheel gets the grease,' right? If you're loud you get plenty of attention. But the same can be said for being the opposite. Being quiet puts you under a microscope. People study you and try to figure out what makes you tick.

My earliest memory of bullying took the form of manipulation in third grade. A student beside me demanded I let him copy all my work. He'd whisper things to me like, 'put your fuckin' paper so I can see it, retard.' I was intimidated and did as I was told. I was angry inside, but I stuffed it down.

In fifth grade, a girl whom I'll call Holly invented reasons to walk by my seat so she could give me a swift kick with her sharp black and white dress shoes as she sashayed up the aisle, and then again when she returned to her seat. She 'needed' to throw away a paper in the waste can, or sharpen her pencil, or ask a question at the teacher's desk. My mother noticed the purple blotches on my right leg. I was worried she wouldn't believe my practised story that I was clumsy, that I fell at recess a lot. So rather than telling her about Holly and the huge smile she aimed right at me when she kicked me, I started crossing my legs and hanging my left leg out into the aisle. This way, both legs would get kicked evenly.

I had a blank expression. I sometimes nodded, sometimes answered monosyllabically when spoken to. My own voice, the sound of it stirring the air, scared the hell out of me. On another occasion, I remember being at a school assembly in the gymnasium. My mood was light. No talking expected here. Janet was sitting behind me on the wooden bleachers. Suddenly she punched me with all her might across the upper arm. Tears stung my eyes; my mouth fell open. I turned to see her grinning face. I couldn't cry out. A hard knot formed in my arm that lasted a very long time. I cried myself to sleep at night. I wore long sleeves during the day to hide the purple lump. I was certain I deserved this somehow. I must've done something to provoke her? What had I done?

NOTHING.

I had been myself.

Part of being me meant being selectively mute.

I was trapped in a silent place.

I was guilty of being quiet.

There was one boy who liked to call me retard; another one preferred the word scumbag; two separate girls fancied the word bitch as in, 'are you gonna be a scared little bitch your whole life?' One girl called me 'scared little rabbit', which wasn't as bad as hearing the other names. Words hurt! But trying to decide what I had done to deserve those descriptions – that hurt more because I could never be any other way.

Because children with SM generally can't answer back when they are bullied, and are even less likely to report their bullies than other children, it can make them an easy target. As an example, writing about her son, Tom, Dawn writes:

Over the years Tom had many incidents at school: for instance, being pushed into a big tyre in the playground, then sat on by four other pupils, unable to shout or cry, just lying there only to be rescued by the dinner lady when she saw.

Likewise, because children with SM can't easily defend themselves, this can be taken advantage of in terms of getting a child in trouble with teachers or other staff. Nicky writes:

I was misunderstood by the teachers and bullied by the other children. I spent playtimes on my own – and I was led to believe that I was weird. One girl I disliked the most in my class bullied me. She once, at playtime, lied to the dinner ladies, accusing me of hitting her. Even though I kept shaking my head every time she went up to them to tell the same lie, they still sent me to the headmaster's office because I couldn't speak to defend myself. I was very upset being accused of something I didn't do. What I find most frustrating about this memory is that the dinner ladies could plainly see that I hadn't hit her!

The data does not exist to say whether children with SM are more or less likely to be bullied in the school environment. So the sensible position to take, until more accurate information is available, is to say they are equally likely to be bullied. However, because children with SM may already find school intolerable, even before they are bullied, they are more likely to become (as some authorities deem them) 'emotionally-based school refusers' and to need to abandon school, the full burden of their education provision via home-schooling, for instance, then falling on their parents.

Danielle writes about several experiences of bullying at school. In Danielle's case her inability to speak at school was one of the things she was picked on for.

> *Although I settled fairly well into the school, it was not long before the first of many problems started. Within my first few weeks, a girl a couple of years older than myself took a dislike to me. She used my SM to her advantage and intimidated me every time I passed her in the corridor or saw her in the canteen. She would push me into walls and shut doors on my fingers, using the fact that she was so much bigger to her advantage, but a few cuts and bruises didn't bother me as much as the verbal abuse she would often throw at me.*

> *I faced another, much longer, episode of bullying during years 8 and 9, this time by a girl in the same year as me. This was never physical, only verbal, but to me that was far worse. I would be waiting to go into a classroom, always with my group of friends around me, and she would intimidate me and talk about my SM, saying things like 'How can you be friends with her? She doesn't even speak.' Although we were not in the same class, we used to have PE lessons together, and so the bullying episodes used to happen frequently in the changing rooms before the lesson, to the extent that at times, I used to be too scared to take part, feigning an illness so that I could avoid the changing rooms.*

Whenever I saw her around the school, a comment was always made about my SM, making me feel more and more different and isolated from everyone else. Again, had I been able to retaliate verbally, I doubt that this would have happened at all, highlighting the problems that SM can cause.

Likewise, Kimberly was specifically picked on because she couldn't speak:

I had crying jags and created diversions in the mornings, to the extent that I would miss my bus. I was intentionally absent on every day that I knew I had to be vocal at school. Sometimes I got on the bus and simply didn't go in to the school when I got off of it. I hid out until it was time to get back on the bus. I called this 'self-preservation'. It was classic avoidance behaviour and I excelled at it!

One day some boys held up signs for me to see as I sat on my bus seat: 'Are you deaf? Mute? Or just dumb?' Soon they wrote signs every day. Always the signs had a mean new twist on me being mute. I stared straight ahead. Mute. Friendless. I would drop out on my 16th birthday. Not soon enough. Shame. I was so bright. Emotionally I forgive, but I don't forget my bullies.

Wendy writes about bullying serving to make her feel even more alienated than before:

The other girls just couldn't understand my extremely withdrawn social behaviour, and it made me unpopular, and a target for bullying. While it was a rather genteel kind of environment where physical violence and bullying of a physical nature didn't really happen, there were some quite unpleasant girls in my class and I was a target for practical jokes, mockery, and for generally humiliating treatment. On one occasion I heard a girl from another year group say, 'There's that mad girl!' Looking round, there was nobody else there: she meant me. Another time I found a seat in assembly and when I sat down, the girl whom I had 'dared' to sit down next to exclaimed 'Oh no!' and she and the whole group she was with – quite a few of them – all got up and moved because I had sat down by them.

Bullying can appear to be sanctioned by support staff or teachers, or even perpetrated by teachers. Describing a specific teacher, Vivienne writes:

I was called a 'retard' by the other kids in my class and couldn't go out to play at home because of this. The teacher concerned described me to my parents as a 'very slow learner'. She frequently conversed with the other children about me. She also told my mother that I would never be able to cope with maths. In fact, I later obtained my maths 'O' Level by studying a 'Teach Yourself Maths' book and enrolling for the exam at my local further education college.

The class sometimes played rounders during PE lessons. I either used to be a fielder in the background or stand at the back of the queue to bat, so that I rarely got a turn. However, on one occasion, the teacher suddenly shouted 'Stop, stay where you are!' She ordered everyone to take up the position they were standing nearest to. I happened to be walking past the first base. Everyone took up their positions.

She pointed to me and said to the rest of the class 'Well I am not having her on first base, she is too stupid!' She shouted, 'Who wants to replace her?' – and several hands went up. I was sent to the back of the field, where I would have gone in the first place, if she had not shouted, 'Stop!'

In specific relation to Selective Mutism, Danielle writes about a particular teacher who chose to try to humiliate her due to her SM:

I also faced verbal abuse from some of my teachers. When I moved into year 9, one teacher in particular took a strong dislike to me and would often make comments about my SM to the class, singling me out and embarrassing me, to the extent that I would dread going to school if I had a lesson with him that day. He even told me once not to bother turning up for my GCSE exam, as I would never pass it.

In another instance, supply teachers who had no awareness or understanding of her SM would inadvertently bully Danielle:

Supply teachers were also a great fear of mine during my time in comprehensive school, due to the fact that more often than not they were not aware of my SM and thought I was deliberately being insolent. I was often asked if I thought I was being funny or clever by not verbally answering to the register, even though my hand was always raised when my name was called. My friends frequently had to stand up for me during lessons with supply teachers, even though this was not their place, as the teachers should have been informed in advance.

To finish this chapter, Vivienne provides specific recommendations for parents of children with SM in relation to bullying in the school environment in the below story:

VIVIENNE'S STORY

I am both an SM sufferer and the parent of an SM daughter (now adult) who was educated both at home and within the state school system. I believe that a fine line exists between deliberate bullying and suffering caused by intransigent and ignorant behaviour towards those that have SM. I have based my ideas on both my own school experiences and the measures that were employed to support my daughter in school.

Bullying could be defined by an imbalance of power and includes actions such as making threats, spreading rumours, attacking someone physically or verbally, and excluding someone from a group on purpose.

A person who can't speak in school or college and is surrounded by those who can is at a definite disadvantage. Consequently a power imbalance automatically exists, unless measures are put in place to redress this.

Frequently, pressure may be exerted on the individual inadvertently as teachers or lecturers may lack awareness of SM and may not know how to interact with the sufferer. It is therefore best practice to produce an Individual Education Plan (IEP). Note that when dealing with older children and adolescents, permission should always be sought first and the content of the IEP agreed by them. Whenever an individual with SM starts a school or college an IEP should state clearly to all staff what to expect and how to react (together with any additional SEN requirements). A line of communication should be set up between the parent/guardian and the SENCO so that if issues of pressure or bullying arise, they are dealt with promptly. In addition, an in-school/college mentor may be needed. Having such a plan in place should reassure the individual that their needs will be met and that they will be 'safe' in school.

SM individuals are particularly sensitive to being pressurized to speak. This is not normally regarded as bullying and may be done unintentionally – for instance, by openly asking the individual to respond verbally to a question in front of classmates. Because SM may be regarded as a speech phobia, such demands can be traumatic for the sufferer, however unintentional the request is. That said, demands to speak can be pernicious in nature. I have personally known teachers to make spiteful remarks, resort to name-calling and other provocative behaviour, in the belief that if they provoke the individual enough, they will become so angry that they will be incited to speak. This is bullying! In either situation the parent/guardian should contact the SENCO immediately!

It is very easy for an SM individual to become excluded from activities and interaction with other children both in the classroom and in the playground. Lack of intervention, due to intransigence or neglect on the part of staff, coupled with the SM sufferer's absolute inability to initiate, when left out, creates a recipe for exclusion. Deliberate social exclusion is a form of bullying. Occasionally an individual may take the view that if a child refuses to talk to them, then they won't talk to the child. This is bullying. More often there is ignorance regarding how to best communicate. Although 'no pressure to speak' is a golden rule, there are caveats. It is imperative that other means of communication are always possible. For the SM individual this could be: pointing, nodding, sharing, smiling, using word or picture cards, whiteboards, text-to-speech software or using agreed signals. For instance, a pencil case placed on the front of the desk could mean, 'I need help.' Even if the individual fails to communicate, it is vital that teachers and peers communicate with them. If two-way communication is not facilitated then social exclusion occurs. Generally, SM individuals can interact well with others once the anxiety barrier is overcome. This places a responsibility on those who work with SM individuals to make sure they are genuinely valued and integrated.

It is known that as SM affected individuals begin to recover their functional speech, assertive speaking is the last form of speech to develop (that is, if it develops at all). Although the individual may appear to be speaking freely, speech is usually compliant in nature – such as reading to the teacher, answering questions, participating in the school play, interacting with peers in the playground and even doing presentations. To the uninitiated, the individual may seem to have fully recovered from SM, however this may be far from true. The ability to initiate assertive speech is likely to be missing. SM individuals may find it hard to defend themselves using statements such as: 'No, I don't want to take part in this.' 'Don't do that!' 'It was actually N who started the fight; I was not involved.' This may leave individuals lacking verbal control and influence over situations and can leave them vulnerable to bullying; or at the very least being ignored, excluded and not getting their views heard. Sadly this is not well recognized. Again, this must be made clear in the IEP. For an individual who is in the process of recovering from SM, the onus should be on the teacher to facilitate opportunities for the person to get their views, opinions, objections or simply their side of the story across. Teachers should be mindful that initiating conversation may still prove difficult (for some impossible) without being given a specific opportunity (or permission) to speak, if they need to, but without pressure.

Because SM children can't speak up for themselves, I have known situations where teachers have asked one or more children to look after an SM child. This creates an instant power imbalance and may lead to controlling behaviour. Furthermore, by inference, it may leave the SM child feeling more vulnerable than others. It is important that all groups or partnerships between SM and non-SM children are set up on an equal footing (friends looking out for one another) to discourage power imbalances and therefore negate the risk of bullying.

When SM individuals freeze they are often described as totally devoid of facial expression. This can make them stand out as different. Fixed facial expressions may be misread. A personal friend once reminisced about a girl from her school days. She explained that this girl rarely ever spoke, and when she did, it was in a whispered voice, to answer the register. The girl had a frozen, fixed facial expression, which the teacher interpreted as a smirk – and as a consequence kept picking on her. I could identify strongly with this, as in infant school I recalled a teacher shouted at me, telling me to take that stupid smirk off my face. I was so totally frozen that I couldn't move my face muscles, so the situation escalated. To avoid the possibility of bullying due to misinterpretation, freezing (including frozen facial expressions) should be highlighted in the child's IEP as a symptom of anxiety that should not be confronted under any circumstances.

In a positive, understanding environment, most SM sufferers integrate well within school. It should not be assumed that they would automatically be a target for bullying; however, vigilance is required as an individual may not be able to inform staff if they are threatened or hurt. A good support network together with a robust anti-bullying policy, operated by the school or college, should greatly reduce the risk of bullying.

CHAPTER 9

Mutism, Family Relationships and the Home Environment

Carl Sutton; Mandy, Janice and Dawn (parents); Cheryl Forrester and Sarah (Carl's wife and daughter); Kimberly, Vivienne, and Jane

If one were to look at the majority of the literature on SM, besides a few individual case studies (e.g. Motavelli, 1995), it can appear that SM is entirely a school-based anxiety disorder. The truth, of course, is rather different – especially for adults with SM. They don't go to school after all.

Many children and young adults with SM can't talk to strangers or people in authority such as doctors or dentists. In fact, many can't talk outside the home environment at all. As such, the school environment (or rather the teachers and other children in it) is only one situation in which muteness is triggered. Most also can't speak when trigger individuals (e.g. strangers or seldom-seen relatives) enter their home environment, thus muteness very often encroaches on their home life. Other triggers for muteness can be: the proximity of grandparents, aunts, uncles, cousins, existing family members such as parents and siblings, or new family members such as stepparents or partners/boyfriends/girlfriends of any existing family member.

For children with SM, the incorporation of a stepparent or new partner in the family home can be a particular challenge. Writing about her son, Aaron, Mandy recalls:

SELECTIVE MUTISM IN OUR OWN WORDS

> *I met my husband when Aaron was ten and they got on
> really well: we went out as a family, did the usual family
> things. But during his last few weeks at school he talked
> less. Over the next ten years he spoke less and less to family
> until the only person he could talk to was me.*

Between 14 and 23, I was entirely mute in my home
environment. While my circumstances were very different from
Aaron's – as I demonstrated in my life story in the introduction
– one primary reason, at that age, for my mutism was the
presence of my stepfather. Visitors to the house – particularly
my stepfather's relatives, who I didn't know – would accuse me
of being very rude. Even as a young adult, I was limited to very
rudimentary sign language and facial expressions. I became a
mime. I would use my two index fingers to make a sign for 'tea'
when asked what I wanted to drink, for instance. And I would
make a swimming gesture to say that I was going for a bath.

Some young adults with SM become mute everywhere,
including in their home environment. Janice writes about her
son, Owain:

> *During his 'A' Level course I worried that Owain seemed
> very tired – he would often go to bed straight after dinner.
> I took him to the doctor, who I remember commented on
> his lack of eye contact – but at the time I didn't pick up on
> this. I said something along the lines of 'aren't all teenage
> lads like that?' The doctor only suggested making sure he
> had healthy meals and 'seeing how things went'. Perhaps
> an opportunity missed, but I still don't think there was any
> way we could have foreseen the future.*
>
>   *Owain was very close to his brother and sister. Susan
> is only 18 months older, and was always good at talking
> him round when he was feeling stubborn. He looked up
> to his big brother as something of a hero. Anything David
> liked, Owain would also like, be it books, games, television
> programmes or whatever. Sadly neither of them is able to*

break into his very private world now, and both feel the frustration of that as keenly as his dad and I.

As a mum I tend to torture myself with questions about whether I could have spotted signs earlier, or even now say or do something that will bring my funny, loving, quirky, individual son back to full participation in the family. I wonder if I was too old when he was born, or if I did something wrong, or didn't pay him enough attention when he was growing up. But, in truth, I simply have no idea what he thinks, or how he feels these days. He seems content in his own world, and at least is safe and clean and comfortable, which is the best we can do for him for right now.

Mutism in the home environment is something that has trailed me into middle age (never mind adulthood) despite my gradually eradicating SM in most other areas of my life. I am not the only person in existence with this or perhaps any pattern of speech difficulty. For instance, I have a fear that I will be unable to speak to any grandchildren (should they happen) before I die, in much the same way that I couldn't speak to my grandparents before they died. There is an element of self-fulfilling prophecy in this of course. Demonstrating that no emotion, fear or circumstance is entirely unique in this world however, a grandfather wrote to me to say he will continue to ostracize himself from his grandchildren until the day he can speak to them. Speech rules when they last so long are, actually, very limiting and very sad.

In my own case, my speech rules have led to unpleasant family dynamics in the past (arguments between my mother and stepfather, who are both now deceased, for instance) and they can still be harmful in the here and now. I am still riven with situational anxiety and I acknowledge the difficulties others have and have had with my behaviour by including them. First, Cheryl (my wife) writes about the difficulties it has caused in my not being able to speak to her mother who, sadly, passed away while we were putting this book together:

> *I have a happy marriage with my life partner, Carl. Yet his SM has, at times, led to challenges within our extended family. Carl often found it impossible to express himself in front of my late parents, and would sometimes sit there, unable to say anything – or disappear into the study. In particular, my mother was an extremely sociable, verbally expressive woman. Carl would not have been the natural choice for a son-in-law for her; yet, in the end, it is fair to say they both had a better understanding of each other.*

I am the first to acknowledge the difficulties that arise from my SM. One outcome of SM can, in fact, be divorce. By way of example, a young woman with SM wrote to me to say that because she couldn't speak to her in-laws, her husband divorced her.

From a further angle, Sarah, my daughter, writes about the negatives and positives of having a parent with SM:

> *You can't live with someone with SM without it changing you and your outlook on relationships. People with SM are largely misunderstood, due to a lack of awareness of the condition. People often mistake my dad's awkwardness for rudeness. Although my dad's teens and early 20s were the period in his life when SM had the strongest hold on him, the effects of this period in his life have rippled into later stages of his adult life, and subsequently into my mum's and mine.*
>
> *Due to SM affecting him at an age so socially important, I believe it has moulded many of the traits that have become central to his personality as an adult. Although he is no longer fully mute, some situations, particularly demanding or new ones, cause him great anxiety. Often he can't explore new things, even if he wants/needs to.*

He would rather miss out than go outside his diminished comfort zone.

As a small child, I had no understanding of SM. However, I always knew my dad was dissimilar to the parents of friends at school. Many parents relish getting to know the parents of their child's friends, bond over shared school issues, and use them as a boasting outlet for their child's accomplishments. Instead I could tell it made him profoundly uncomfortable. When younger, I didn't understand this. It puzzled me. A man who talked freely, and laughed and smiled with mum and me, could only manage the merest nod or an uncomfortable shuffle away. It used to make me frustrated. I knew he had the ability to talk freely, and people often passed him off just as rude or standoffish. Why was he being so difficult? Why couldn't he just act like everyone else's dad?

As I became older, in some ways I began to relish being one of the inner circle – one of the few people my dad actually could talk to. I felt angry towards others for their treatment of him. Had they ever thought maybe there's more to this? My dad is an intelligent man; and as well as being intelligent, he has a strong wit, and a very quick and sarcastic sense of humour. Not that you would imagine it if you were to meet him. I have found myself explaining his behaviour on multiple occasions, in defence of him, and to prevent the wrong assumptions being made. Part of me now feels like there should be no reason for having to explain someone else's actions. If they make assumptions, it's their own ignorance. On the other hand, is it not better to educate?

Personally, I feel knowing someone with a condition such as SM has made me more open-minded. It's made me more patient and willing to invest time in people who maybe others are often too quick to judge and cast off. It has also made me consider what the key characteristics are to a successful relationship. SM sufferers talk to those they trust, who support them, who take the time and effort to not judge but understand them. Shouldn't everyone base all meaningful relationships on these characteristics anyway?

Following are the personal experiences of three people writing from different angles about mutism in the home environment. First of all, Dawn writes about her son's mutism at home, and the upset that this tends to cause with grandparents. Next, Kimberly writes about her own mutism at home. Vivienne concludes the chapter with her own experience, being unable to speak when her stepfather joined the family home.

DAWN'S STORY

You would think that family members would get that they mustn't take it personally when Tom doesn't speak to them but they don't, despite trying to tell them about SM and how he just can't speak to them. It is still an issue for us.

Tom can't speak to any family members apart from his parents, brothers and sisters, nieces and nephews. His nan, granddad, aunties and uncles are still people he can't speak to. He retreats to his room when they visit. Over the years this has caused huge upset. His nan and granddad in particular take huge offence at his not speaking to them and barely acknowledging their presence. They think, after 13 years, he should speak to them no matter how many times it is explained to them. It's like they think he is just doing it to be rude. So now we are at the point that he doesn't choose to visit them and they only come to our house once a month or so. It's just easier that way – they are never going to get it.

He also has an aunt who, when he last met her at a family gathering, reduced him to tears. She spent 15 minutes badgering Tom to tell her what the book he was reading was about. Tom takes a book everywhere with him; it's like the barrier between him and the world. When he didn't reply she got very loud and abrupt with him telling him he was rude and so forth. I found Tom sobbing. I wish I had been there. I would have told her what for – it was so wrong!

I think most of our relations just think Tom is strange. There is no understanding of SM among them. I am sure they all think we should force him to speak, or take something away from him until he does.

With his close family, Tom is funny, loud, often rude and sometimes outrageous. He talks freely with us, often not thinking about our feelings (that's his Asperger's). He has a great sense of humour that only we see. He is so clever it's scary – all that knowledge in one brain! He loves us knowing what he knows. It must be so difficult when he is in a situation where he can't speak. He must have a battle in his head between the non-talking part of him and the part that wants to talk. I find it very sad.

One of the only other people Tom talks to outside the home is my daughter's friend. He has cerebral palsy and has some speech issues. Tom talks to him freely, maybe because he knows he won't be judged. He is not as anxious around him. We have tried having friends over from school – when he was younger – and he usually would end up sitting under the table reading a book, his defence from the world, leaving his brother to talk to the friend. We don't do that anymore. It just makes him anxious and he retreats from us, so there is nothing to be gained.

KIMBERLY'S STORY

I was born in 1964, to a woman who couldn't keep me, so I was adopted by a couple in Connecticut where I was a cherished only child. My father was short, balding, and outgoing. I was tall, with thick hair prone to tangling, and introverted. My mother was blonde, upbeat, and quick to laugh. I had black hair, was quiet, and had trouble expressing emotion.

There were a few people I could talk to in my life outside of school. There was a girl next door but I could rarely speak if her mother was around. There was a cousin my age who had three siblings, but I was vocally constipated if their father was present or if they had company visiting. I could answer adults monosyllabically. But, honestly, some relatives to this day haven't heard my voice yet.

It was especially frustrating when my voice disappeared around my parents. I recall wanting to visit my cousins one evening. It was what I wanted but I couldn't say it. I wrote a note: 'Can we visit my cousins?' But I couldn't hand either of them the note. My mother was crocheting in her armchair. My father was on the couch. The sound of the parakeets in their cage and the TV show he was watching felt boring. I stood in a shadow in the hall just outside the bedroom with my note attached to a clothespin. I threw it in the middle of the living room floor.

Impossibly, neither of them looked up! Desperate, I wrote a new note, attached it to another clothespin and threw it. I repeated the process. My pile of clothespin notes drew the attention of my dog and also my father who eventually yelled, 'Stop throwing things!' I gathered my clothespins, threw them away, and cried myself to sleep.

Where did the words go that were never expressed? I was a note in a corked up bottle... drifting.

My parents tried to help me mingle with other kids. Still I didn't speak. I was in Brownies, Girl Scouts, 4-H, Catechism, and I marched in parades, waving from floats. They brought me to visit their friends who had two little boys. I was seven. The parents laughed and played card games in the kitchen. I sat on the carpet in the boys' room where they put their hands in front of my eyes and made sounds next to my ears. Eliciting no response, they shoved me in a closet where I remained until they heard the parents approaching. They pulled me out just in time. We went there often after that because, 'It went so well! Kimmy has new friends.'

One day that year, a boy of 15 was visiting my cousins. He tied me up, gagged me, sat on my back and tried to kiss me. Really, he never needed to use the gag. I was the perfect victim. If my mother hadn't walked by that bedroom and seen me, I don't know how far it would've gone. I had ugly red twine marks around my wrists for hours afterward.

I wrote a note to My Child Self. Here it is, in part:

Dear Child Self, you will experience overwhelming fears, tragic losses, indignities and confusion. The others your age seem to know what to do, what to say and how to bond with others. Often you can't get the words out because they stick in your throat like the biggest lump. You cringe when people say, 'she's so shy,' because you know you are not shy. The word 'shy' minimizes something more serious. What you can't know is that your senses are on high. If you could see your brain, you'd see it may look like other brains but the way it takes in information, makes sense of the information, and manages output is vastly different.

You have serious meltdowns. Sometimes you feel as if you can't even communicate to your own parents. You must know this: Many times your thoughts, feelings, and ideas go unexpressed, but they are valid!

Guess what, Child Self? You aren't alone. All this time that you've struggled, there are others who are just like you! One day you'll know true peers who understand. You'll find belonging with them such as you have never known. This I promise.

Keep journaling! One day people will read what you have to say. Keep creating! You can lose yourself for hours – just drawing. One day you'll show your paintings in galleries and you will sell them! All human beings have ways to de-stress and, for you, that is Art. Write what you can't say aloud; save those journals.

You'll write books!

And be easy on your young self. So much of what happens is a learning experience even though it is often painful. Trust me, when I say, 'Your Art will sustain you. It will always be your safe footbridge over churning waters.'

Express yourself on the written page. The things you think about are important. You are stronger than you think. You try so hard to do what others take for granted. This is called perseverance and bravery. It makes you a resilient person, just like that silly toy you have: the blow-up wobbly clown that keeps getting back up every time you push or punch it.

Take pleasure in your own company because one day others will. I promise. So draw! Make Christmas ornaments from cinnamon sticks, glue and sparklies! Spread peanut butter on pinecones and watch squirrels come for them. Write! These outlets will carry you all your life.

VIVIENNE'S STORY

My parents split up when I was a baby and I was unaware of my father's existence. I lived with my mother and grandfather.

I was always regarded as a shy child. I can remember hiding behind my grandfather's back to avoid eye contact with strangers (especially men) as this tended to startle me and cause me to blush!

I started kindergarten class at the age of four. I suffered badly with separation anxiety and used to get upset when my mother left. However, the teacher insisted that I soon settled once she was gone. This was far from true. I can remember feeling absolutely terrified at kindergarten. I didn't adapt well to transitions such as: playtime; getting ready for PE; or going up on stage to rehearse for the school play; and used to get panic stricken. Another little girl became my friend and started to look after me. I don't think that I spoke at school, apart from whispering to that little girl. The school never expressed concern about my behaviour, because they just thought that I was very shy. Consequently my mother was unaware of my problems. To all intents and purposes I seemed like a normal child, as (like many other SM children) I was very chatty at home.

Things changed suddenly when my mother began dating. It quickly became obvious that I neither spoke to nor made eye contact with her new dating partner. In fact I didn't speak at all when he was around. My mother's relationship had quickly deepened with him, so she was anxious for us to bond, but the opposite seemed to be happening. Friends told my mother that I was silent because I resented sharing her with anyone else. My mother blamed my grandfather for being over-indulgent with me. My grandfather denied that this was the cause of my strange behaviour. He continually played down the extent of the problem, and many arguments ensued between them.

My mother's new dating partner worked in England and only visited us when he had time off work, so we didn't see that much of him. Despite this, my mother began to have doubts that the relationship would work, as she regarded my apparent hostility towards him as a real threat. However, my grandfather believed that I was young enough to start a new life and would quickly settle and forget about my previous life in Belfast, especially if no one mentioned it.

My mother and her partner announced their engagement, and they, together with my grandfather and I, went out for a celebratory meal. The restaurant table was a small square one. Looking back, I realize that the close proximity of my mother's partner would have been anxiety provoking for me. I can remember feeling apprehensive during the meal, and didn't eat my food. When we got home, my mother asked me why I didn't like her partner. I had avoided eye contact during the meal and had not spoken. This confused me. My behaviour was not premeditated but simply an instinctive reaction to anxiety. I was not yet that aware of my own behaviour, and had not thought about it in terms of liking or not liking people. However, both my mother and grandfather were absolutely adamant that I didn't like him. They were adults and, to a four-year-old, adults know everything. Consequently I just went along with what they were saying. I even called him a name, and this made my grandfather laugh. But my mother was deadly serious.

My grandfather suggested that I should not attend the wedding, but should remain in Belfast until they had bought a house in England and were ready to move in. That way, he maintained, I would start my new life with a clean slate and would soon forget the past, which would not be referred to again in front of me.

After the wedding and honeymoon my mother and now stepfather came to collect me from Belfast. We caught the night ferry across to Liverpool. On the ferry, we sat in the restaurant and ordered some food. Again, I didn't speak, avoided eye contact and was reluctant to eat. After a while my stepfather left the restaurant. Once he was gone, I became more relaxed, began to eat my food and speak to my mother. My mother perceived this as divisive behaviour on my part.

Up until this point my stepfather had not played an active role in my parenting. This was to change drastically, as my mother began to withdraw in favour of him.

We moved into our new house. On the first night my mother put me to bed. However, after the first night, my stepfather assumed full parental responsibility. I suspect that he was under pressure to deal with my difficult behaviour once and for all. On the second evening, I was again reluctant to eat my food, but this time my stepfather insisted that my plate had to be cleared. This took ages and by the time I had finished, his patience was running thin. He ordered me to go to bed. I went upstairs and slowly began to get undressed.

This was the first time in my life that I had ever gone to bed on my own. I felt anxious and was missing the set bedtime routine that I had previously known. I felt unsure of what to do and wandered around upset. My stepfather came up to the bedroom and angrily confronted me. He asked why I was not in bed. I froze solid! He continued to question me, but I was frozen and couldn't engage with him. At this point he lost his temper and I was physically punished.

My relationship remained difficult with both my mother and stepfather. I did start to speak to my stepfather a little bit (usually to answer his questions) but I had little control over my voice and it always came out as a high-pitched whisper.

My stepfather had a very short fuse when dealing with me, and my mother refused to get involved when he got angry. A lack of knowledge of SM and its consequences blighted our relationships.

For me, SM in the home environment as a teenager and young adulthood was easily the worst of my own experience. I could not ask for help because, at that stage, I was unable to speak to the people one would ordinarily ask for help – my parents. My own research (Sutton, 2013) demonstrated that it is relatively uncommon for a child or young adult to be unable to speak to their parents unless they have either a difficult home environment or an element of autism (e.g. Asperger's). This is not to say they are the only two contributing factors, however, and one should never use this finding to make assumptions about the background of children or adults with SM.

Being unable to speak to extended relatives is much more common than most literature on SM would suggest. SM is not a school or education-only issue. Difficulties with extended relatives are made worse when extended relatives do not wish to understand SM and see mutism (seemingly targeted towards them) as a personal slight. Given SM is an anxiety disorder, it can easily be worsened and leave a child or young adult with SM feeling even more trapped and isolated than before when extended relatives are critical (either of the child or young adult directly or their parents) or use coercive or crude methods such as badgering a child to speak, when they are too anxious or phobic to do so.

While I do not see myself as a professional therapist, nor particularly as an advice giver, I have used my own life experience a number of times to provide guidance for parents whose older child or young adult has ceased being able to speak to them; and it has, in fact, worked. In order for any technique to work, however, the child or adult needs to wish to speak – of course. It is apparent that in virtually all cases of SM children and adults do wish to speak. As I have written a number of times in this book, SM is not wilful behaviour and has its origins in anxiety/phobia.

To begin with, the child should whisper-read to one parent and gradually increase volume (a process I undertook with my mother in my early 20s, as I wrote about in the introduction). The emphasis of reading rather than talking about any given subject is on voice rather than 'self'. The next step is for the child or adult and parent to read a play between them – this is a turn-taking communication activity and, again, the emphasis is on voice rather than 'self'. Next, the parent and child should work on functional rather than expressive speech – expressing basic needs, wishes and requests. Only finally should one try to work on expressive speech – such as a child or young adult talking about themselves at a basic level, to express emotions or feelings. In summary, the order is to work on volume first, turn-taking next, functional speech third then finally expressive speech.

In fact, I never communicated fully with my mother and stepfather (i.e. talked about things that matter, in an expressive way). I only got so far myself. I did, however, achieve full-volume functional speech, particularly while supporting my mother through severe mental illness and subsequently dementia until she, very sadly, passed away.

To conclude this chapter, Jane, who regularly support adults with as a volunteer for iSpeak, writes:

As the previous contributors to this chapter have highlighted, SM can exist in the home environment with severe consequences. Looking back on my own childhood experiences of SM, I too suffered from muteness in my home and was unable to speak freely with my closest relatives. Unlike SM children who don't stop speaking at home and are often described by their parents as 'chatterboxes', I had no place at the end of the school day to 'let it all out'. I remember being so full of excitement when the home bell rang only to find that the words wouldn't come out when I stepped through my front door. Imagine a world where, as a child, you are unable to express your thoughts, feelings, emotions and basic needs even to your mother! You are left not only in 'a prison of words' at school but also in your home.

Literature and research surrounding the effects of SM in the home environment is, as far as I am aware, virtually non-existent. However, writing from my personal experience and looking into the experiences of others who have also been mute at home, I would highlight the impact this can have on the development of relationships. In child psychology, those first relationships in the early years are core and crucial to child development and further relationships in adulthood. My adult relationships have certainly been affected by SM in my home environment – a fact I realized during recovery from SM in my 40s.

Recovery is possible, as I have found. Now able to speak freely in most situations I have also developed new and exciting relationships for the first time in my life.

CHAPTER 10

Those Who Spoke for Me

Carl Sutton; Alberta (parent); Wendy

Most children with SM have at least one spokesperson who speaks for them in situations where they cannot speak for themselves. In the home environment it may be a parent or sibling, and in the school environment it may be a school friend or sibling. In this chapter, Alberta writes about all the people who have spoken for her daughter, Lorraine; and Wendy writes about having been spoken for as a child. Of course, it is entirely natural for a parent to tend to speak for and protect a child who is anxious in given situations and, equally, other children can sometimes tend to become natural protectors of children who cannot speak for themselves.

There is a subtle difference between acting as a spokesperson for a child or young adult with SM and rendering them invisible by assuming one knows what they wish to say. It is obvious in the text that follows that Alberta has the balance right as a parent. While she talks for Lorraine when necessary and lauds those who have also assisted her daughter in the past, she also recognizes that her daughter has a voice, a strong voice even, in the way that her daughter writes and communicates in other ways.

The balance can be very difficult to achieve however, as Wendy subsequently writes. For Wendy, now an adult with SM, her mother's talking for her has caused her to feel disabled, communication-wise, in adulthood.

ALBERTA'S STORY

'Why doesn't she say something?', 'What's wrong with you?', 'Oh, you're only not speaking to get everyone's attention'. These are some of the more common comments made to me and my daughter over the years. I feel her frustration on hearing them because, try as she might, she couldn't respond. Oh, she wanted to. But she just couldn't.

When Lorraine was at primary school in her reception class she met someone who chose to make her a friend. Very often I would hear how this little girl would answer for her when others couldn't understand why my daughter didn't speak. I believe that this help from her friend encouraged my daughter to become more confident. Eventually, she began to interact with a small group of girls and together they helped each other develop socially throughout their early school days.

Alas, the old proverb 'all good times come to an end' played its way into my daughter's life. And so when she ventured out to pastures new at her newly assigned secondary school, there were major adjustments to be made. Gone were the close friendships that brought acceptance of who she was. In their place there was loneliness and misery. I feel that she became lost in the numbers of mostly well-adjusted pupils in a large school. Additionally she became isolated as her silence was misunderstood as simple shyness. I felt that if the teachers had known more about her, they would have realized that she needed a little bit of support to help her make, what was for her, this massive social adjustment.

But, on this occasion, my courageous daughter, fuelled with a simmering fire that sometimes ignites in moments of frustration and injustice, spoke for herself! So, one day when she had had enough of the references to her quietness by teachers and peers alike, she did something amazing! The little girl with no voice at the grand age of 12 shouted – through the medium of a pen – that she needed to be heard. And heard she was!

She wrote a very well-thought-out and comprehensive account of her feelings about school entitled 'The reasons why I dislike school' (Lorraine's text is included in Appendix B).

There! She was noticed. From then on everything changed. I feel that this was because the teachers became aware that this seemingly unassuming child had an intelligent and highly functional mind and a way of thinking that was articulate and highly cognitive beyond her years. They were amazed! From then on I attended several meetings. The premise of them had changed from acceptance of her silence to actively seeking how they could help her to verbally express herself.

During these meetings I met a learning mentor who wanted to help us. I know from the conversations we had that she had genuine concern for my daughter. I know this because she knew things about her that can only be gleaned from spending quality time with her. She was one of those people to whom I will always be grateful, because she showed us that she cared. She was there at every meeting that was held telling colleagues about my daughter's qualities, strengths and needs. She would also be there every morning to escort her to an inclusion room. I feel that her presence gave my daughter the courage that she needed to continue going into school as long as she was emotionally and physically able.

But, even with the invaluableness of the thoughts and actions of this individual, I eventually had to take my daughter out of school. I knew it was the best thing to do for her. So we said a very sad farewell to her learning mentor and made it on our own for a while.

After time spent at home, in an attempt at educating her ourselves, my husband came across an educational provider that helped children who, for various reasons, no longer attended mainstream schooling. I was overcome with gratitude for these people. They were dedicated individuals who worked with educationally switched-off kids in a small group setting. I could see they had a personalized approach to teaching and Lorraine was assigned to a skilful and caring teacher who became a close and endearing mentor and friend to her. I watched as the teacher was able to build up her confidence so she could eventually speak without prompting in social situations. This teacher was a godsend to us and I shall never forget how she spoke to her and for her while she was with us.

The teacher developed the art of one-sided conversation... She would continue speaking to my daughter, even when she didn't answer, and she happily accepted her initial lack of response. I marvelled at the way she treated her with respect and acceptance from the time they met and my daughter thrived during the time she was with her. But, unfortunately, that too came to an end.

Thankfully she still has, and always will have, her family. I feel that we are the ones who can sense the things more accurately and get the general gist of what our daughter needs to say, but can't.

We intervene when we see her struggling. We don't always get the things that she wants to say right. But we try and learn from previous experiences the best way of interpreting her words to others.

Even though I have had years of practice I know that I don't always say the right thing. There are many times when I have walked away from what seemed to be a supportive conversation only to be told by her that I said the wrong thing or pronounced something incorrectly. At moments like this I try and remember how it must feel to be unable to say what you want to say and how you want to say it. I have tried to put my own feelings aside during these times; and over the years I have spoken for her by translating and interpreting her thoughts and actions to other children, psychologists, teachers, retailers and friends.

We are grateful for those who have spoken for her and those who will in the future. Their contribution to her life has left its own positive invisible mark on her personality and confidence. I like to believe that with each positive verbal interaction she has, whether supported or unsupported, she will be enticed to try another. These attempts at communication may eventually entice a young vulnerable girl to one day have the courage to stand up and not depend on others to help her speak, but instead have the ability to speak for herself.

WENDY'S STORY

Most parents speak for their children when they are young, whether the child has SM or not, but my mother spoke for me for much longer than is usual. When I needed a spokesperson, it was nearly always my mother who did the talking for me.

I didn't have much interaction with my peers either in or out of school, so I didn't really have a friend to speak for me. I never wanted to seek out social interaction with anybody, so I didn't want a spokesperson to help me socialize; I was more than happy to just be left alone. Problems arose for me when other people tried to initiate social interaction with me. Far from finding this enjoyable, it felt more like a threat. It put a spotlight on my biggest problem and I felt put on the spot and under pressure to do the one thing I was least able to do – respond. I think in these situations my mother spoke for me purely out of embarrassment.

I didn't like the sound of my own name and never could bring myself to say it, so I especially hated being asked my name. Sometimes on these occasions another child would 'help out' by answering for me. One time, soon after I had started school, a teacher who didn't know me yet asked me my name and a little boy answered for me and told her my name to which the teacher replied, 'She's got a tongue, she can talk'! But of course I couldn't answer her. That same teacher later took a special interest in me.

The times when I felt I needed a spokesperson would be if I needed to communicate information to somebody. This was usually when there was a problem that I felt totally overwhelmed by, and it would often mean a potentially difficult interaction with somebody who I saw as an authority figure, for example a doctor, a teacher or even a head teacher. This kind of interaction would be difficult for most young people, but for me it felt so impossible to deal with that I just wanted my mother to take care of the situation for me while I stayed far away. I didn't feel that I could even cope with being present while my mother spoke to these people on my behalf. When I was 17 and in the sixth form at school, I had got behind with the work and everything had just got so on top of me that I felt I just couldn't face going to school any more. I was legally old enough to leave school, but knew that my decision to leave half way through the sixth form would not sit well with the headmistress. I made plenty of noise about it at home, lots of tears and hysterical tantrums, which my parents bore the brunt of on a daily basis. But discussing the problem and how I felt about it with the head teacher, or with the doctor, felt absolutely impossible; like running through fire, or like doing something that is dangerous to my life. I felt I needed my mother to speak for me like I needed air to breathe. One time when I was younger, my mother took me to see the family doctor and the doctor asked me what the problem was, rather than asking my mother. I just stared blankly. It wasn't because I didn't know what the problem was, but the idea of speaking for myself – well it had never occurred to me that I even could. Speaking felt alien to me and it also felt unsafe. It felt as if there was a physical barrier within myself preventing me from speaking; other people who have SM might understand.

I found it harder to speak to outsiders if my mother was there, or if somebody else was listening. I felt as if I was being assessed on my social performance and on my ability (or not) to speak; rather like being asked or expected to perform on stage in front of a critical audience. I'm not saying this was my mother's fault, or that she is very critical; I don't think she is. But due to my SM, and because so much fuss had been made about my not speaking, that was how it felt for me.

By the time I was a teenager, I think it had become fairly automatic for my mother to answer when somebody spoke to me. When I was 16, I went to an interview for a Saturday job in a small supermarket. My mother came along with me and, out of habit, started to answer questions that the shop manager was putting to me. He said to my mother, 'She has to stand on her own two feet!' and after that I did make some effort to answer his questions. I may not have done brilliantly, but I was able to answer for myself. All the time somebody was willing to speak for me, I was only too willing to let them. My mother said afterwards that when I was asked a question I used to look to her to answer. That shop manager offered me a Saturday job. I hated it though. I stuck at that job for a year until, as with school, I felt I could take no more of it. But of course I wasn't able to go to the manager and give him my notice; my mother had to deal with that for me.

I had no confidence to even try to advocate for myself. My being on the autism spectrum means that being verbally articulate does not come naturally to me, and I just hadn't had any practice. So as a young adult I was very disabled socially. As a parent myself, I depended very much on my children to speak for me. This was especially the case if I needed to get someone's attention, for example a waiter in a restaurant. In that way our roles were reversed, my children became the caretakers and I was like the child (the one who needed looking after).

I wish very much that instead of being spoken for, I could have been helped somehow (I'm not quite sure how) to find the confidence and the courage to learn a way of advocating for myself that works for me. The real problem arose for me when I still needed a spokesperson in middle age. At times I needed service providers to intervene to deal with difficult social situations for me. I realized then how undignified and how unhelpful it really was for me to still have people speaking for me. It is undignified because it makes me look like a very disabled person, genuinely unable to advocate for myself. I realized that being spoken for meant that I could never really grow up, I'd always feel helpless, powerless and I'd always be like a child.

I decided then that the time had come when I needed to either find a way of advocating for myself or accept the consequences of not doing so. Now though, I think perhaps the worst consequence for me would be to suffer the indignity of being spoken for.

The case studies have demonstrated the need for balance when talking for or acting as spokesperson for someone with SM. The first case study demonstrates the positive effect a parent or friend can have when they fulfil this role effectively. Alberta's support enabled her daughter to find her voice in written expression, including online. In fact, Lorraine contributes to the next chapter in her own right, about Selective Mutism and Asperger Syndrome, and clearly demonstrates her written eloquence.

More negatively, Wendy suggests that when the balance is not achieved it can lead to a disabling effect on a child/young adult, and it can cause further difficulties later in life. Wendy also contributes very candidly to the next chapter too.

CHAPTER 11

Selective Mutism and Asperger Syndrome

Carl Sutton; Bronwen, Dawn and Mark (parents);
Sonja, Wendy, Kimberly and Lorraine

In this chapter, four people with SM who also have Asperger Syndrome (AS) – Sonja, Wendy, Kimberly and Lorraine – provide their own views of having both AS and SM. Parents' views of both conditions are also given by Bronwen (writing about her son, Haydn), Dawn (writing about her son, Tom) and Mark (writing about his daughter, Nicola).

SONJA'S STORY

Over the years, in my desperation to find out more about SM I often came across information about Asperger's. Some of it fitted but other bits didn't. It was only when I came across the iSpeak website for adults with SM and participated in Carl's research (on SM in adults) that I really started to understand it more… and I began to realize that some of what I was experiencing didn't seem to come under the heading of SM.

I've always felt that I have to think around things in some way as if there is a part of my brain that's missing that other people have – it sounds mad but it's the only way I can describe it.

A number of different things coming together prompted me to ask my GP for help. I was feeling increasingly anxious and stressed at work – there was change happening in the organization, and a new manager who had a management style that I found difficult.

There had been a few instances where I had been unable to speak at important times. I had disclosed SM at work and most responses were very supportive, but there was one comment which made me realize that I needed help, and that I'd never had any real help, ever. My partner urged me to contact my GP. I had never told my GP about SM and the difficulties that I've had over a lifetime living with it.

The SM in adults study referred to a link between SM and Asperger's, and I consequently looked into this and discovered Lorna Wing and research linking SM to Asperger's particularly in women and girls, and missed or misdiagnosis because most of the assessment criteria are (stereotypically) male biased.

When I then started to read up on it, every aspect 'fitted'. What I started to read lit up memory after memory, from the depths of my awareness as a child and things that I had been puzzled and troubled by for most of my adult life. I kept telling myself that this could not be true, and was expecting to come across information that would discount it all, but instead what I was reading kept confirming it.

On this basis I saw my GP and asked to be assessed, and was eventually (it took nearly six months to get to see someone) diagnosed with an Autism Spectrum Disorder (ASD) by an NHS consultant clinical psychiatrist.

When I read *Aspergirls* (Simone, 2010) I cried with relief, and then *The Complete Guide to Asperger's Syndrome* (Attwood, 2008) my life made sense. But I am only now starting to get help and I am still learning about it.

In some ways it has made my life easier. My partner now understands, and I understand and can address aspects that have been problematic for most of my adult life. I have a perspective at last, and I have been able to get support at work and outside work, but this has been another struggle as I believe most organizations have no understanding or basic awareness of hidden disabilities, even those that have a public duty to be aware.

On the surface I've got on with my life seemingly very well – I've become a good actor... most of the time. Only my partner has witnessed the meltdowns triggered by getting too cold, or something not being in the right place, or the intense and overwhelming emotion, and confusion, after being drenched in the rain (sensory sensitivities) – but I also believe that these intense emotions come from being unable to explain/express the intense reactions that I feel, and because of being diagnosed later in life not having had the support and understanding that would have helped early on.

It is always hard for me to articulate what is making me feel stressed – to put this into words. I might be able to do this an hour, a week, a month, or a year later. I have trouble processing verbal instructions, particularly if I need to act on them. Often I try to figure out what was said – piece things together, listen for clues; this is how I have coped. For me, my struggles with communication, but particularly verbal communication, are where SM and AS merge, and I'm not sure where one begins and the other ends.

WENDY'S STORY

I was diagnosed with AS at the age of 42, after a lifetime of feeling there was 'something seriously wrong with me'. Over the years I lost count of the mental health professionals I saw and the self-help books and psychology books I dipped into in the hope of finding out why I am the way that I am. I finally found a mention of AS on the problem page of a magazine, and I was diagnosed just over two years later.

I'm sure they didn't mean to, but the diagnostic team used language which made me feel even more self-conscious about my speech. When I was seeking a diagnosis, I called the service that eventually diagnosed me and the behavioural genetics nurse whom I spoke to said that I sounded as if I do have difficulties, and that my interaction over the phone sounded typical of someone with AS. And I thought well if she can tell over the phone that I've got problems then I must sound decidedly weird to other people. In my assessment report they referred to my 'unusual monotone speech'. For somebody who is already inhibited and self-conscious about speaking, a comment like that is far from helpful. I know that it's not uncommon for people with SM to dislike their voice, or to think their speech sounds abnormal, but I do think I have particular reason to feel that way. At times I have felt there's little point in my trying to speak because nobody's going to understand me anyway. When I eventually dared to listen to a recording of myself, far from being reassured, I was horrified by what I heard.

It is difficult for me to know where AS ends and where SM begins. Learning about AS did explain some things about me that had never made sense before; and these were things that I had felt a great deal of shame over. But all the jigsaw puzzle pieces of my life did not suddenly fall into place. It wasn't that there were pieces missing, there were pieces which just didn't seem to belong anywhere. I was curious about other Aspies and I expected them to be like me. But when I met some other people with AS I realized that was not the case. I joined a UK online support group for people with AS and this group organizes meet-ups for its members. I went along to a London meet-up and came away feeling very distressed because I felt that I stood out, even amongst other Aspies, as being the most socially-disabled person there. Most of the other people there seemed so normal and they were chatting with each other just like any other group of people might do. I'm sure that if I spent a week with them, then I would see where their difficulties lie; but, on meeting them, I wouldn't have known that they had any social difficulties. I felt like the group joke and thought that other people there would see me that way too. This experience led me to question whether I had been given the right diagnosis. I understood why I had been given a diagnosis of AS rather than classic autism, but for a while I wondered whether I was, in fact, classically autistic because I had so much more difficulty with speech than other Aspies seemed to have. I can now see that I was given the correct diagnosis, and that those pieces which just didn't seem to fit anywhere are part of the SM puzzle. I am also starting to see how the two interlock with each other and how they complicate each other. I'm not sure how disabling just AS on its own would be for me; I feel that SM disables me possibly more than AS on its own ever could. Having both conditions is not by any means the cruellest hand I could have been dealt, I know that really; but sometimes it feels as though it is. I know that a lot of people with AS get by socially by having learned to mimic other people's social behaviour and so they can pass for 'normal'. I used to envy people who could do this; I'm not so sure that I still do, but having SM means that I have never been able to do this.

Another thing that makes it difficult for me to make friends, aside from the speech and communication difficulties, is that I don't feel a human-to-human connection with other people. I have often felt I haven't got a clue how to speak to another human being. I also don't find most people so interesting or so inspiring that I would feel motivated to make the necessary effort to relate to them. Occasionally I do meet somebody who I feel a strong pull towards, and I don't always know why. People with AS often develop a very intense interest in a particular subject or hobby or indeed in a particular person to the point of becoming obsessed with them. I have often had these kinds of obsessions with certain people. I think this happens because my desire to connect with someone and to be close to them is greater than my ability to achieve this. I also think it's a kind of coping strategy that I have developed quite unconsciously because I find people frightening. By becoming obsessively interested in somebody (often someone I feel quite scared of) my fascination with them overrides a lot of the fear.

I have received some useful feedback that it is social interaction rather than communication that I have difficulty with. I can speak most easily to communicate facts and information. If I am asked a question that has a definite answer and I know the answer then I don't do too badly. My SM is at its worst when somebody tries to make small talk with me. I am not able to do the usual meeting and greeting and the spontaneous chat that most people take for granted, and that is when I feel most alienated from other people. I think, for most people, trying to relate to me is too much like hard work and too far outside of their normal range of human experiences. It isn't that they don't accept any alternatives to neurotypical, they just don't realize that alternatives exist. I appreciate that I am not an easy person to get to know, but anybody who makes the effort will be getting to know a very unique, one of a kind person.

KIMBERLY'S STORY

It is said that SM is caused by: anxiety, self-esteem issues, a speech, language or hearing problem, shyness, or severe childhood trauma.

Wikipedia describes shyness as: an ego-driven fear of what other people will think of a person's behaviour resulting in the person becoming scared of doing or saying what he/she wants to, out of fear of negative reactions, criticism, rejection, opting to avoid social situations instead.

However, I would say that being labelled shy is an insult because it minimizes the seriousness of SM.

I filled over 17 diaries growing up. This served me well when I wrote my memoir *Under The Banana Moon, Living, Loving, Loss and Asperger's*. In so many ways it was easier to write about Asperger's, because it is a core part of me. It's just who I am and I embrace it. I recall doing an interview for a local newspaper when my writing was first published. The focus was Asperger's not SM (as you can see Asperger's appears in the book title). I asked the reporter not to use a negative or pathetic bent in the story. I said I didn't want it to insinuate I was a 'sufferer of a disease'. In fact, Asperger's is not a disease. My interviewer wasn't listening. The article stated that I was indeed 'suffering' from Asperger's, and the story went on to describe it as a 'disease', which, as I said, it isn't.

I don't 'suffer' for being Aspergian but there are things that make my life different from people who aren't on the spectrum. Here are a few of those things: awkward social approaches; 'flat' vocal tonality; lack of understanding of 'small talk'; limited sharing of likes, emotions, hugging, spontaneous affection; inability to understand emotion fully; all-consuming interests of study to the exclusion of all else; lack of friends; clumsiness, accident prone; not grasping rules – in my case 'rules of the road' as I'm a non-driver; isolation and declining of social invitations; NO eye contact; little understanding of 'give and take', both by reciprocating 'pleasantries' and sharing thoughts, ideas, activities; inflexibility, needing to adhere to routine; meltdowns after prolonged periods of social interaction; loving the parts more than the whole sensitivity to sound; telling all or nothing; and collecting and more collecting.

Not all people who are Aspergian (Aspie) also have SM. But sometimes an Aspie can have bi-polar, depression, dyslexia, or any other imaginable combination of things. There are many engaging, talkative, interesting, brilliant speakers who are Aspergian/autistic and bravely command huge audiences. So many people come to mind: Donna Williams, Temple Grandin, and Ari Ne'eman, to name a few. This is probably due, in part, to those speakers not having SM as a comorbid condition alongside their autism. Unlike Asperger's, when it comes to SM, let it be said I do suffer.

Back to those diaries for a moment… Not only did they help shape my book but upon re-reading them to write the book (they've since been destroyed), I learned so much about who I am. One diary entry remains vivid in my memory. It was one lone sentence written by a 13-year-old me across an entire 3" x 5" page in a small compact 'diary' which was, in essence, an autograph book with blank pages that alternated between lavender, bubble-gum pink, mint green, baby blue, ivory and goldenrod yellow. The entry, printed across a yellow page in pencil, was so heartfelt that in certain places the pencil ripped through several pages and indented the next dozen or so pages with the searing pressure of its burdensome message, which is as follows: 'If this is shyness, then SHYNESS is a DISEASE!!!!'

There were water stains on that page: fallen tears. Even then I knew that shyness was different from SM. I was still one year away from 'professional help'. I didn't have a name for SM, but I knew it felt like a disease because you can 'get over' shyness. SM strangles the throat and its mission is to keep the words stuck and unexpressed. That wreaks havoc on self-esteem, sure it does. But for me, it's not 'self-esteem issues' that caused my SM. It was the other way around entirely: my SM played unfair games with my sense of self.

Was I traumatized and rendered mute? Did I have a hearing 'issue'? Those things, as I mentioned earlier, are said to be contributing factors. Yeah, I had my share of childhood trauma: seeing someone put a gun to my grandmother's head; molestation by neighbours, etc. But the SM was ingrained long before those things came to pass. It's true I was probably born being prone to anxiety. I was also born with a 104-degree temperature and a cracked eardrum. Growing up I had numerous bouts of infections, burst eardrums, and trouble with my right ear (I have an implant now). But moreover I think SM has genetic components and is more deeply grounded in nature as opposed to nurture. For me SM is lifelong – as it appears to be for my son. I've come to this realization; however, I too (like my peers) am engaging, interesting, and even brilliant!

BUT one-on-one communication is best. There were far too many personal SM-related experiences to include in my memoir but I did write about being unable to call FIRE in a crowded room. I was the first to see a person's clothes catch fire from a candle and yet all I could do was clasp someone else on the back and point. I was in my 20s then… Why share this? Because I am not alone! I refuse to feel embarrassed or humiliated by a condition I didn't choose to have. I choose to love me just the way I am!

LORRAINE'S STORY

I almost gave up on writing this. Maybe it has something to do with my SM, but I have trouble writing about myself if I know others are going to read it. It's ironic that I run a blog. Ask me to write some advice or even just my musings and rantings on SM and I can write pages and pages, but as soon as I put myself into the picture I struggle to put pen to paper.

Anyway, I'll begin this piece of writing by introducing myself. My name is Lorraine and I'm a teenage SM sufferer. I was diagnosed with SM at the age of 15 and not only that, I also have a diagnosis of Asperger Syndrome.

'She has Asperger Syndrome.' This is my parents' explanation to an offended stranger who has tried to converse with me but has elicited no response. Not everyone knows exactly what Asperger Syndrome is but most have heard of it at least, and will a lot of the time be a little more accepting of any unusual behaviour I display from then on.

'She has Selective Mutism.' This version of the explanation will usually get a very different kind of reaction. 'What's that?' 'Never heard of it.' 'Is that some kind of made-up disorder?' etc.

The differences between the kinds of support you can receive for both is something else that bothers me. Back when I was first diagnosed I was baffled at how one little search of the Internet would turn up numerous results for support groups for individuals with autism yet finding the same for SM sufferers was (and still is) virtually impossible.

Having both conditions can be strange for all of these reasons, not to mention the fact that no one ever seems to know what to do with you. Having both can make things much more complicated than just having one or the other.

Despite this, it has always irked me when people lump SM and autism together. There are some people who seem to believe that SM doesn't actually exist and that individuals with the condition are just misdiagnosed 'autistics'. While there is no doubt in my mind that SM and autism can co-exist, I am a strong believer that they are separate conditions and should be treated as such. Having a diagnosis of both may make things more complex; however, one does not automatically equal the other.

I was well aware of my SM long before the child psychiatrist had made the announcement all those years ago. I had come across information about the condition on the Internet and knew it fitted me. At the time I didn't see it as a huge problem as I had close friends and family members who would act as my voice so I didn't pursue a diagnosis or mention it to anyone. Even after my diagnosis I was still uninterested in the SM side of things mainly because Asperger Syndrome was something completely new to me; I'd never even considered I could have something like AS. I wanted to understand so I did plenty of research and actively sought out autism-specific support, completely ignoring my SM, which is something I now regret. Maybe if I'd looked into my SM earlier I wouldn't still be battling with it now, but I digress.

It was only in recent years that I realized my problems were quite different to those of my peers with autism. I could relate to them in a lot of ways but one thing that seemed to be unique to me was my inability to speak. A lot of them experienced social anxiety and had difficulty responding when spoken to but I seemed to be the only one who often couldn't speak at all. This caused me to delve back into the world of SM.

After discussing it with my parents I was then taken to the doctors, seeking help for my SM specifically. To cut a long story short I was then referred to a mental health clinic by the doctor, but was later turned away as they believed my SM was probably just brought about by my Asperger's. I was then sent to an autism organization instead who had – no surprise – never even heard of SM and therefore had no clue what to make of me.

As I mentioned at the beginning, I run a blog. It's a space where I post things my fellow SM sufferers can relate to, information about SM to raise awareness, from time to time my own personal experiences with the condition, and I even try my hand at offering advice here and there.

Every so often I receive messages from those who are diagnosed with some kind of autism as well as SM and a large number of them seem just as confused about having both conditions as I am. They wish they could be supported with both conditions but without them being treated as one. I've even come across a few people who are diagnosed solely with autism but believe that it was a misdiagnosis and they actually have SM.

On the whole, having SM is challenging. Having Asperger Syndrome is challenging. Having both conditions is also challenging but I'm getting along somehow with the support of my family, friends and peers.

BRONWEN'S STORY

Haydn was eventually given a diagnosis of 'Asperger's with high levels of anxiety, which manifest in SM.' The paediatrician involved sought a second opinion and it was the Childhood and Adolescent Mental Health Service (CAMHS) who finally gave us Haydn's formal diagnosis.

As a parent it took me a long while to digest this information. As a health care professional I am used to being involved in complex and difficult conversations but this was difficult information to hear. The label did enable us to get a statement of special educational needs and this enabled Haydn to get used to extra support after the Christmas holidays in his last year of primary education. It felt a bit like 'supervision' at primary school but this has been crucial in secondary education and has been used mainly to promote inclusion and support where needed as well as some mentor time. However, it was very important to my son not to miss any lessons as he becomes concerned at missing key information and asking for that information at another time was clearly not an option for him. Therefore, he was resistant to much of this.

Haydn's Asperger's is most evident through his restrictive diet – he is a self-imposed vegetarian from birth. As a baby he hated hot food and still eats a very limited diet and only drinks water. Difficulties socializing would be the other obvious difficulty, which fits his diagnosis.

At the point we were trying to get an official diagnosis for Haydn I remember every time there was a visitor in the classroom he would automatically assume they were there to assess him. He would find this completely exhausting and feel over-scrutinized and analyzed. In reality, of course, many of these visitors were completely unrelated to Haydn. However, many healthcare professionals floated through his life over a period of years and I appreciate how he gained this perspective. He would always be very compliant but never contributed much at many of these appointments, always looked very uncomfortable and resented them massively.

Asperger's does not sit comfortably for Haydn. It covers such a wide variety of presentations and, in our case, the demon in our life is SM, which feels like a by-product of his Asperger's.

Nervous mannerisms also cause an immeasurable amount of distress. Haydn tries hard to control them with variable levels of success and they are so visible to the outside world. They stay for variable amounts of time and present in different ways such as touching things twice, shaking his head twice as a nervous tic, a hand tremor or more recently a shoulder shudder which has not resolved after a lengthy amount of time. We are currently awaiting a neurological review regarding this; previously Haydn could train himself to stop through holding his wrists or the back of the neck. However, with a shoulder shudder he has no way of controlling this physically. It feels less habitual and more ingrained than previous nervous traits and I felt obliged to fight hard to get a neurological medical review regarding this.

My biggest frustration is I have never managed to meet another family with a teenager in a similar situation to Haydn. When I have asked at appointments I am challenged regarding the benefits and also have been told on numerous occasions that many children are not managing in the same way as Haydn. I am told they have SM for different reasons and are not socially able to have the same level of friendship as Haydn. I have also been told their parents are struggling socially and would not be able to meet up. I have been to autism support groups and lots of conversations are linked to the behavioural challenges of these children but for us the main challenge is that Haydn does not manage to speak in certain situations.

There is great inconsistency with speech for Haydn. He will speak to me at parents' evening but then not be able to talk when we are with the teachers. He is in year 10 and doing the first year of his GCSEs but we have had to accept he will not do German, as there is an oral component to the exam. We explored alternative approaches but the oral exam is necessary currently. Having not managed to speak at secondary school there have been occasional windows of hope (laughing in an English lesson on two occasions, talking quietly in the corridor with a friend in year 7, the first year at secondary school). Most recently there has also been a further small breakthrough. Haydn has always struggled with communicating by telephone as he can't see the facial expressions involved, hence 'Facetiming' cousins has been a massive achievement and works well. In school recently Haydn managed to speak about 50 words very quietly with his back turned away from a teaching assistant he is very comfortable with. I mention this because it contradicts all previous preferred progress, so I say to any parents just keep trying different approaches to the ones you would expect to work.

DAWN'S STORY

For Tom I think that having a dual diagnosis has always created problems. Getting ANY diagnosis took many years of constantly asking school, our GP, and anyone I could think of.

Tom was finally diagnosed with Asperger's when he was about nine. He was diagnosed despite my repeatedly querying his behaviour with other professionals, by a very good audiology consultant who was treating him for a growth in his ear. She listened – the first doctor ever I think – and could see that this child who was hand wringing, couldn't look her in the eye, definitely couldn't speak, had more than a few issues going on and wasn't just shy. She referred Tom to the Communication Disorder Clinic. The one and only time we went there he was diagnosed with Asperger's. At the time this was great, because we had spent years wondering what was wrong. Having something to research seemed like a step forward. Tom was also referred to CAMHS where he saw (and still sees) a psychiatrist. He began Cognitive Behaviour Therapy (CBT) – which always seemed to me to be the strangest type of therapy to give someone who doesn't communicate at all. I have spent hours in a room with Tom and his therapist, with Tom hidden underneath his coat because he couldn't bear to engage in any way. I did lots of talking for him, and about him, which at times upset him. He didn't want the world to know about his life and his problems. We engaged in this for over two years. When the CBT therapist left it was decided – thankfully – not to get him a new therapist, as his progression was painful to see. He could barely whisper a yes no answer after two years of being told it was his choice to speak or not. It was pointless.

Tom's Asperger's presented in a number of ways. He was very obsessive, be that collecting Dr Who trading cards (we had the entire collection), to going through them and ordering them constantly, to how he had his possessions in his room arranged. He couldn't cope with failure – either academically or personally – and rather than fail he just couldn't try. He was and still is very straight and brutally honest. He has no empathy for anyone else at all – be that how clever someone is or how ill. It just doesn't register that he should care.

He has many sensory issues. Ever since day one he has never liked to wear clothes. As a school child the first thing he would do when he got home would be to strip off and wrap himself in a blanket. Now he is older this is a bit more problematic for obvious reasons. He doesn't like the feeling of different materials. He says they feel like they are scratching him, and labels are a definite no-no. He also doesn't like lots of different types of food and can't bear even to be in the same room as a blackcurrant drink! Regarding being sociable, most of the time Tom wouldn't care if everyone else on earth just disappeared and there was only him. At junior school he couldn't talk to any of his peers and he couldn't talk to any of his teachers either. He existed in a silent world all day. He couldn't use the toilet anywhere outside our home. And, even in our home, I have to wipe the toilet for him before he can use it. He has a phobia about germs. He has his own cutlery, cups etc. and can't bear to see his cup anywhere near someone else. He can't touch handles. He either has to cover his hand or uses his feet. He was very recently diagnosed with OCD because he wouldn't come out of his room when his nephew stayed at our house as he thought he contaminated the house.

Despite all these other issues, his non-speaking has always been his biggest problem. He would physically recoil when he was put under any pressure to speak. I always felt it was more than Asperger's, and the more research I did the more I believed this.

After threatening to withdraw him from school in year 6 as he was so unhappy (he'd pull his nails off in class, pick himself until he had big scabs, he was just so miserable) his school got him an appointment with an educational psychologist for the first time and also referred him back to speech and language therapy (SALT). They both very quickly diagnosed him as having SM, and immediately a different plan of action was put in place for him, removing the pressure from him to speak. The years of trying to coerce him into speaking finished. He was very quickly given things like a card to get out of lessons. At lunchtime he was found somewhere quiet to retreat to. They were small things but they helped him know that the staff understood that he couldn't speak to them, taking the pressure off him.

Unfortunately for Tom it all came a bit late. His SM is so entrenched now I believe he has social phobia as well. In Tom's world if he never had to go outside our house or if we could just make everyone disappear so that there was only us it would be ideal.

I believe that the late diagnoses of both Asperger's and SM had a huge part to play in how he is. Now, nearly 13 and a young man, when he can't or won't do something because it makes him anxious, he just refuses. This is no matter what amount of discussion is had with him. We can neither persuade nor bribe him. He is so set in his ways he just can't do it. It would have been so much easier with a five or six-year-old without the life experience or willpower he has. If only somebody had ever listened or taken his non-speaking more seriously.

MARK'S STORY

Our daughter was assessed in our home environment via the Autistic Diagnostic Observation Schedule (ADOS), and also at college, by two health care professionals (HCPs).

As a parent having a child with a dual diagnosis of SM and Asperger Syndrome throws up many questions with very few answers, such as when does SM become Asperger's, or would Asperger's be the primary diagnosis over SM?

Girls are adept at camouflaging or masking social uncertainties. The only obvious displayed characteristics quite often are the core presentations: dislikes direct questioning, looks awkward and ridged, and dislikes being touched. These are classic signs of both AS and SM that almost certainty meet the diagnostic criteria for both disorders. Being amongst children suspected as having AS for an extended period of time I believe is the best way of evaluating and monitoring potential AS candidates using baseline assessment criteria. This could involve many weeks of monitoring in different settings. While I appreciate this might be difficult to commission for healthcare professionals, surely this is a paradigm that would be more accurate as opposed to a tick box assessment (ADOS).

I, myself, worked at a local autism charity as a volunteer to gain knowledge and understanding of Asperger Syndrome around the same time our daughter received her diagnosis. After working there as facilitator for quite some time I realized that most of the people with an ASD were relaxed in their environment and, at times, I found it challenging to make a distinction between those with AS and everyone else. Other times I was able to draw similarities between our daughter's SM and AS. The only constants I could observe in those with AS were the lack of a social flexibility of thought in some situations. I don't believe this to be the case in SM. Dim the spotlight and SM sufferers will begin to function. I was convinced that our daughter had been incorrectly diagnosed. Remove the expectancy

SELECTIVE MUTISM IN OUR OWN WORDS

to speak for SM sufferers in a non-threatening environment and you remove the anxiety.

With some experts believing that SM is variant of AS, and seemingly an absence of a cut-off point in the criteria for SM, surely this will only lead to misdiagnosis. That's not to say that some SM sufferers don't have an accurate diagnosis of both disorders. It also has to be said that SM sufferers who are fully recovered, or are in partial remission, if they were to undertake an ADOS assessment during this period of recovery I doubt very much that they would come within a country mile of meeting the AS criteria. Until there is a more determined willingness from the NHS and regional trusts to implement a multi-structured approach and finally recognize that SM is not rare then we will always have this revolving door of conjecture and refutation of SM vs. AS.

Asperger Syndrome is a much more widely known condition, particularly in adults, than Selective Mutism. As such, services and local support groups are available for AS in some areas of the UK, whereas in contrast, there are scant services for SM. Based on parent reports to iSpeak, services for AS tend not to cater for people with SM, even though the two conditions commonly exist together.

Many adults and adolescents with AS learn to accept it as an intrinsic or positive part of their identity, though late diagnosis of AS can be a very difficult emotional adjustment.

In contrast, based upon my own experience, and that of many adults, SM can be very difficult to accept. Rather, it is usually seen as something to escape, a source of suffering, and a source of feeling profoundly different, isolated and alienated. Self-acceptance is particularly difficult for adults with SM because virtually all information available on Selective Mutism relates to young children. To some extent they (as I have myself) feel disinherited from their own condition due to the lack of acknowledgement of their existence.

While I personally have achieved a good deal of self-acceptance regarding my speech behaviour, it was taken me until my 40s to do so and this, for me, is without the added complications of having AS as well.

CHAPTER 12

Selective Mutism and Learning Difficulties

Ann (parent)

When your child has two problems stacked against them such as the case of SM co-existing with a learning disability, it is difficult in determining which issue should be addressed first.

Brooke was diagnosed with SM in her first year of elementary school. Soon after, her teachers noticed she was not able to keep up with the work assigned to her. Vocal as well as written instructions were not being followed and Brooke would have to look to other students for clues as to what to do next. I was still trying to accept the fact that my daughter had SM; now we had to face another challenge – a possible learning disorder. At first, I didn't accept what was being said to me. I was completely in denial. I believe that most parents go through this stage when first hearing about their child's deficits. You just don't want to believe that your child, who you believe to be so perfect, and who you have so many aspirations for, may have a problem that may affect them for the rest of their life. I have been told that denial is the first step toward acceptance. I wholeheartedly believe this to be true. The denial acts as a cushion and eases you slowly and steadily towards the realization that your child isn't perfect and does indeed have a problem. It is only when you find acceptance that you can truly begin to help your child.

When Brooke was very young, I would say about three or so, she had a great interest in books. She loved to be read to and was always eager to attempt reading by herself. She was also very creative and artistic. Her drawing skills were above average for her age and her penmanship skills were excellent. I honestly didn't notice anything at home that would have suggested a learning problem. She followed directions that I gave her, and she appeared to be doing what every other child her age was doing. It wasn't until she entered school that the problem was discovered. Very early on, in her preschool/kindergarten years, her teachers would tell me how unresponsive Brooke was in the classroom and how she didn't appear to understand the simplest of instructions. While the other children would get out their school supplies from their backpacks and take out the requested items to begin a task, Brooke would just sit there and wait until the teacher prompted her on what to do. I had believed that this had something to do with the SM – that perhaps she was so overridden with anxiety, and that it somehow caused her to totally block out her surroundings and drift off into her own little world. That would explain the dazed look that the teachers had said was always plastered on her face.

The truth was that Brooke did have a learning disorder. But due to the SM, it was difficult to assess her skills. After a requested neuropsychological exam by the school district, in addition to tests administered by an audiologist, a diagnosis of an auditory processing deficit was determined. What this meant was that Brooke's brain was not processing information in the same way that a 'normal' brain would. When there is a problem with auditory processing, the ears and brain don't fully co-ordinate, resulting in misinterpretation of sounds, especially the sounds composing speech. I then realized that all of those wonderful Disney movies, which Brooke would watch over and over again, were only being watched for the music and the visuals. The same could be said for all of her favourite books, she loved looking at the illustrations – the visuals. Her misinterpretation of sounds made it very difficult for her to follow lengthy conversations, especially if they were amongst several people. And although she could read practically anything put in front of her, she couldn't process the written material to her brain. Stories would have to be broken down into paragraphs, and ultimately sentences in order for her to understand. And even with those modifications, she still struggled. Because of this problem, she did poorly in all subjects. Every subject required her to process reading material or oral instructions – how would she be able to do well in her subjects when she couldn't understand the instructions?

The auditory processing problem, co-existing with the SM was a rough combination. The SM exacerbated the auditory processing deficit and vice versa. Brooke was lost, and at the tender age of five, already began to feel different than the other children. She not only had this horrible disorder that impeded her ability to speak, but now she had to face constant academic struggles. And I was introduced to the wonderful world of special education, where parent-teacher conferences took on a whole new meaning.

Parents need to have a say in their child's education plan and that is why there are CSE (Committee on Special Education) meetings at the beginning of each school year. Parents and teachers need to work together in order to help the child reach their full potential. Parents and teachers need to listen to each other and respect each other's opinions. Teachers know what is going on in the classroom, and parents need to be able to listen to them with impartiality. In addition, teachers need to listen to parents with an open mind and understand that they live with these children and know things about these children that they will never know. I have been in too many meetings where I have become defensive of my daughter, only because I felt that I was not being listened to. I am sure that I came across as another typical parent in denial. But that assumption couldn't have been further from the truth. I knew my daughter had a problem, and I also knew that the school professionals were not handling the problem in a sufficient and productive manner. Did I know what they should have been doing? Not exactly, but I did know that what they were doing was not improving the situation in any way. When I saw that my opinions were basically being cast aside (because after all, they were the professionals, I was just an emotional parent) I would begin to lose my composure.

A parent's input is equally as important as a teacher's input, and if both sides are not respected, it is the child who will suffer. I had been to one parent-teacher meeting in particular, where I was told that I would never know what it would be like to be a successful parent, being that my one and only child had these deficits. I would never experience the feeling of pride in seeing one's child graduate college and go off to establish a successful career. 'It is a pity,' she told me. What in the world could this teacher have been thinking to make such a statement to a parent? I was so dumbfounded that I couldn't even speak, let alone think of a response to her comment. Unfortunately, she was one of many educators who felt the need to voice their personal opinions on our situation. The insensitivity of some of these teachers was beyond words. Brooke's very first teacher, her preschool teacher, had told me that I shouldn't expect too much from my child. She would never be popular. She would never be a cheerleader or the class president, so I just better come to terms with all of that. There was another conference where I was told to take my daughter out of the public school system and place her in a program for severely developmentally-disabled children – this coming from a middle school teacher who insisted that my daughter couldn't hold a pencil. If there was one area where Brooke had always excelled, it was her handwriting and drawing skills. I was supposed to trust the judgement of these professionals?

It is vital to have a strong support system in order for your child to flourish in the special ed. system. Among that support system should be a competent psychologist who has experience in young children and anxiety disorders. Unfortunately, I was not able to find such a psychologist for Brooke in her school years. It was only recently that I have found a wonderful therapist for Brooke, one who specializes in SM. Oh, how I wish I had her support in those CSE meetings. It would have made a world of difference.

In the matter of SM and learning disorders, I believe that too much focus is placed on what the child can't do. I can honestly say that in every single meeting I have ever been involved with, whether it was a CSE meeting or an ordinary parent-teacher conference, too much time was spent on what my daughter was incapable of doing, instead of focusing on what she was capable of. What are the child's strengths?

Every child has strengths. I don't care who they are, how poorly they do in school or what kind of psychological problems they may have. If we focus more on their capabilities and how to nurture those capabilities instead of always focusing on what they can't do, perhaps then we can truly help them achieve some sort of success. If a child is always led to believe that they are inferior, that they are different and need to be segregated because of that difference, then they will begin to believe it. Unfortunately, these self-contained special education classes can promote isolation and begin a downward spiral of low self-esteem. It is extremely difficult to undo the damage that years of isolation can do. Brooke is still much younger than her chronological age, and I partially blame this on those years of isolation. Once she was placed in a self-contained classroom, she never had the opportunity to connect with her peers. It has hurt her tremendously.

I could write forever about what I believe to be the pros and cons of special education. But the bottom line is that a child with SM should not be in placed in a self-contained special education class solely on the diagnosis of SM. Unfortunately my daughter had a significant learning disorder and my only options were inclusion or self-containment. On her entrance into high school, I had opted to place her in a self-contained classroom, where she would have a better chance of receiving her high school diploma, which she was able to achieve, thanks to her wonderful high school teacher. If I would have opted for inclusion, I knew that she would not be able to keep up with the class and would most likely receive a special education diploma. In hindsight, I should have gone for the latter. I can see now how important it was for Brooke to be in inclusion where she would have had at least the opportunity to gain social skills and learn from watching and listening to her peers. For her, socialization was and is a much more important skill to learn than social studies or science. She was never going to be able to fully understand these complex subjects and, in the long run, socialization skills would have helped her much more. Too much precious time was wasted on trying to pass statewide exams when all she really needed was basic life skills. I can honestly say that Brooke has not retained much of what she was taught in school.

The major problem that I encountered with the combination of the SM and the learning disorder was whether or not there would be an accurate assessment of her intellectual abilities. For example, during an assessment such as the neuropsychological exam, if she did not respond when a question was asked of her, was it because she didn't know the answer? Or was it because she was too anxious to let it be spoken from her mouth? And more importantly, if she didn't know the answer, or simply needed the question re-worded in a way that she could understand it, would she let that be known to the test giver? I am sure that there were times when she would have given an appropriate answer had she been able to relate to the test giver that she didn't quite understand the question. If you took the SM out of the equation, would her learning disability still be present? Of course it would; however, I believe that had she been able to express herself to her teachers, she would have had an easier time academically. Incidentally, Brooke, at 23 years of age, is now undergoing another neuropsychological exam. I am positive that this will now be an accurate assessment – as

Brooke is much more accepting of her disorder and will be able to speak up should she not understand what is asked of her.

The special education system in our public schools needs to be fixed, especially in the secondary education years. There is an injustice done to so many of our children on leaving school and entering the real world. There are too many talented, smart young children caught in the special education system who can contribute a great deal to this world if they are only given the chance. On exiting school, many of these children are totally unprepared for the real world and it is the parents who are left to pick up the pieces. And it doesn't stop there. My experience with the state agencies who were supposed to help our daughter transition out of high school was beyond frustrating. The agencies that professed to help my child were, in actuality, the ones discriminating against her. Parents need to be their children's advocates, throughout the school years and beyond.

To this day, Brooke continues to struggle – at 23 years old. However, she has made gains, gains that many education professionals predicted would never happen. It is hard work to help a child of this sort to be successful, and very easy simply to give up. A woman whom I had met through a SM support group had a daughter similar to Brooke. She, like Brooke, had other issues besides the SM which made the situation that much more difficult to treat. This woman had four other children – all of whom were successful in their education and careers. One child was a doctor, another a lawyer. She had told me how proud she was of all of her children, but that she was most proud of her daughter with SM, because she had to work the hardest to achieve her goals.

When a child starts out life with a deficit, they have to work twice as hard in order to achieve any sort of success in their life. It takes just as much hard work and determination for that special ed. student to receive their standard diploma as it does for that college graduate to achieve their Master's degree because of the simple fact that learning is so difficult for them. To put it in perspective, it would be akin to taking that straight 'A' student, and suddenly giving him homework assignments in a completely different language. This is what learning-disabled children face each and every day. Unfortunately, society forgets that life isn't a level playing field and very often views an achievement of a high school diploma as simply not impressive. But if you are a parent of one of these very special children, you know how impressive it truly is.

My daughter may never be a college graduate, she may not have a successful career or make a lot of money, but I have raised her to be a hardworking, disciplined, compassionate, lovely human being. So to the teacher who told me that I would never know what it feels like to be a successful parent or to experience the feeling of pride as a parent, you couldn't have been more wrong.

CHAPTER 13

Parents' Experiences of Selective Mutism

Bronwen, Alberta, Louise, Elaine, Mark and Julie (parents)

In this chapter, six parents – Bronwen, Alberta, Louise, Elaine, Mark and Julie – write about their own personal experiences of having a child with Selective Mutism, describing their own coming to terms with the condition, their struggles in gaining diagnoses and getting support for their children, and the indubitable pride they have in their children as unique individuals.

BRONWEN'S STORY

It has taken Haydn's dad and me a long time to understand the complexities of having a child with SM. In the toddler years he was viewed as stubborn and shy. It was often complicated by contradictory behaviour. For example, we went camping and Haydn made a friendship with another child but as they were not going to meet again there was less pressure.

I wish I had the knowledge I do now back in the beginning. Healthcare professionals were struggling to give us a diagnosis and so we were definitely struggling against the tide. The paediatrician kept suggesting adopting a 'wait and see' approach. At times it felt impossible. This was partly because the primary school were so good and we were almost managing most of the time. It was more evident that we were struggling when routine changed at school. For example: sports day and class assemblies. If things were routine for Haydn, then generally things were manageable.

We also grew to understand when appointments were not going to be of benefit for Haydn. For example, as he was a very restrictive eater we were given a dietician appointment for Haydn. I attended alone because I knew he would resent missing school, which has always been massively important to him, and while immaculately behaved publicly he would contribute nothing at the consultation. I, however, found the appointment incredibly worthwhile. It was reassuring and informative and I left knowing that I was a good mother who had a challenging situation to deal with.

I would also say, as a parent, fight as hard as you have to. Haydn has a great paediatrician. He disliked her immensely as a younger child. He generally does not feel this way towards many people but he viewed her as the person who made everything challenging and difficult. After he received his statement, he became more tolerant of her as he viewed the appointments as a tick box exercise to secure getting the help he needed at school each year. I have learned to be tough and I fight hard for anything I feel we need. Haydn's paediatrician is inevitably very busy but I pursue her intensely until she returns my calls. I have only done this on two occasions when I wanted a referral to a speech and language therapist and on another occasion a neurologist for his continuous nervous tics, but I was persistent and it paid off.

Breaking down barriers is particularly important for our children. Haydn viewed the headmistress at primary school as unreachable. However, the headmaster at Haydn's secondary school taught all the children in their first year of secondary education Maths regularly. This meant all barriers were broken down and he seemed very accessible and approachable to Haydn.

I remember being incensed on one occasion when it had been agreed that a dysfluency referral might be beneficial for Haydn. This is linked up with speech and language therapy. CAMHS and speech and language therapy decided that they felt this referral would not be beneficial. I actively challenged this decision. How dare they come to this opinion when they were looking at out-of-date records and had not reviewed my son for a significant number of years! Not surprisingly, when challenged, they reconsidered and the referral was processed. We asked politely how they had come to this decision and requested the rationale involved. Even writing this now fills me with fury, as these are our children's lives we are dealing with, and their wellbeing is our priority.

People's ignorance has amazed me. I have witnessed well-respected teachers who have academically achieved great success teach Haydn for a year and, at the end of that year, their knowledge, appreciation and approach to managing SM have remained incredibly limited. I was sad on these occasions but in other years teachers have absolutely amazed me with their support, encouragement and sensitive approach.

Haydn was not in a situation where more than one language was spoken within the home, was not living in a hostile or volatile home – and initially we were not a diagnosis of 'autism spectrum'. Therefore, people failed to understand how we could be in this situation. This was compounded by the fact our son liked school, had an excellent attendance record and continued to make steady progress academically. Currently he is doing his GCSEs.

At the point of diagnosis we were told at clinic appointments by Haydn's paediatrician and CAMHS (childhood and adolescent mental health service) that we were good parents. I think at that point we really needed to hear that. The feeling was that he was difficult to diagnose from an autism spectrum perspective because we had managed to work so hard on the challenging aspects of his life. However, I believe I understood and accepted the need for us to be observed as part of the assessment to obtain a diagnosis. It was quite threatening but I recognized that the healthcare professionals were just doing their jobs.

Haydn's class friends and their siblings and parents have always been very accepting of his inability to speak in certain situations. However, the judgements came from those who didn't know us so well. For example, the other class in the same year group at primary school. Understandably they didn't have a full appreciation of the situation Haydn deals with each and every day. Again, parents could be judgemental.

I have a number of friends who have not understood Haydn's SM. Because they have not spent the time trying to understand what SM is they have a limited appreciation of what we all deal with as a family. Or, most importantly, what Haydn deals with. They have remained in our lives but I tend to meet them for coffee when the children are at school rather than doing family activities together.

Equally, I have some amazing friends who never judge and remain enormously supportive and loyal. At times I have needed their support and as my parents are no longer alive I have valued their advice and been very grateful.

I have always worked part time since Haydn was born and while I recognize he needs quiet time at home, I also believe this has been an important part of teaching him to build on his independence. I have had to work on these skills whereas they come more naturally to others. For example, I have taught him to use the self-serve till at the supermarket so he can function independently as an adult. Now he is getting older I would say it has taken us a little longer to do many things independently but we have gone at a pace that was appropriate for our child. He had a house key later than many of his friends but equally he is far more careful with it than many of them. Some friends passed judgement that we didn't do it as quickly as them but I believe we managed things as we needed to!

I also recognize that I went through that inevitable stage of answering for Haydn. Now, however, I try very hard not to. I just recognize that others may have to be satisfied with a non-verbal response. The only exception to this is parents' evening where Haydn will occasionally need to write something down and I do speak on his behalf but we always discuss it beforehand. He also keeps things simple. For example, if we go to the pub for tea I know he will choose pizza and garlic bread so it makes it very easy for me to take over and order on his behalf. I am trying very hard to take a step back and see if Haydn can manage these situations independently and we have varying levels of success.

ALBERTA'S STORY

In my home there are four people, all related but uniquely different. Each one has a special component inside them that helps to make our family complete. There's me, my husband, my daughter, and our son. I feel that each one is here to help someone within it thrive. Somehow within the throes of life's ups and downs we make things work.

I hope in this short piece of writing to share with you one member of this family's journey in this topsy-turvy, unpredictable world. I hope to share with you one small element of a courageous girl's slow progress in this world even when the odds are stacked at their highest against her.

I have the privilege of having a daughter who has a condition called SM. I had never heard of this disability before and when it was first mentioned to me I admit I was very confused. In fact I thought that the child psychiatrist had made it up! Selective what? Another made up condition for something professionals didn't have the answers for, I thought. So, being a naturally curious and unbelieving mother, I did my own research and found out just a little bit more about SM than the professionals dared to tell me.

Slowly, as I began to gather the facts, I reluctantly conceded that they were right – she did have it. My first thought was 'At last, now I know what's wrong'. My next thought was 'Well, now that I know, what am I supposed to do?' No one seemed to know. But as in many situations, experience can be the best and hardest teacher. So I asked questions, tried various other technical sounding things and through trial and error discovered an important element of bringing up a child with SM. And that is acceptance. That was the first vital step in the journey to making our family work.

Accepting her for who she is the most significant part of enabling my daughter to thrive. So I learned to let my objectives go and stop bombarding her life with premature tactics to change who she was. I knew there would be time enough for interventions and the like. But I realized just for now she needed to know she was loved for who she was. And what better place to make this happen than in the familiarity and security of her own home?

I realized that at home she was at her best. And every mum wants to bring out the best in their children, right? So I made it my 'high priority project' that the home would be a place in which she could relax and recharge her emotional batteries. At home she could be herself, unencumbered by social pressures.

I noticed that when she was at home she relaxed!! The anxiety magically disintegrated as she walked in through the front door. I felt the home environment created an invisible therapeutic healing balm for her condition. Its familiarity was essential to her being able to survive when the pressure to speak and interact with others outside the home got too much. At home she would tell me about thoughts and feelings that she was unable to express during the day. I would listen to her hopes and dreams and sometimes the occasional barrage of unrealistic teenage rantings. I would be available to hear whatever she needed to say, whenever she wanted to say it. Her need to communicate was met in the conversations she had with me. This daily interaction was helping to weave together the threads of a disorganized fabric to make our family work.

I knew that social media was a necessary part of her world so that she could connect with others who held the same interests as herself. So, I made sure she had access to it whenever she wanted it.

I used to worry about her not being able to speak if some tricky situation occurred and I was not there. But with her condition I am comforted by her innate ability to read what others mean and not what they say. Over the years she has developed an ability to be able to see through others' motives. This skill brings along with it an invisible radar that helps her to syphon out the people who have her best interests at heart and those who don't.

When she was younger she would bring friends home on the odd occasion to celebrate some pre-teen event. Those were great days and she allowed her friends into her private space and world to get to know her properly. Devoid of anxiety, pretence and awkwardness she's a great girl! Sadly, many of those friendships have dwindled due to teenagers just doing what they always do, getting on with life.

This has caused great loneliness in a girl who finds it difficult to speak to others. So she fills her life with things that help to lessen the emptiness a little. In its place, she has become a hoarder. She fills her room with things. In her bedroom the wall is littered with posters of her latest craze. There is a large collection of Monster High Dolls that occupies the top shelf of the bookcase, an even larger collection of notebooks arranged haphazardly on the last shelf. There are myriads of clothes stuffed in drawers and hung up in her over-packed wardrobe. Lastly, and the most prized of her possessions, there is a life-sized pillow of an Anime character who substitutes as a boyfriend called Len.

There is one thing that she does at home and in public. Would you believe she dances!? My lovely daughter dances! She dances alone in the privacy of the living room as well as in the crowded room of a cosplay (costume play) convention in front of hundreds of people. If you're not familiar with what that is. Look it up! I promise you it will be an enlightening education. Just accompanying her to these events helps to make things work for our family, as this is something she does that we can all share and celebrate together.

So, all in all, with the coming and going of each of the instances in our life as a family I have learned that in order to bring about the best in this special child that I have, I have to make sacrifices. I have to ensure that the home is always her haven, where she can be herself at all times and be loved for just being who she is. At times I don't always get the balance right. But when I do she feels safe, she grows and flourishes. And when we do it well enough our family works.

LOUISE'S STORY

Jasmin developed Selective Mutism (together with separation anxiety and social phobia) over a period of time, but was more noticeable and unofficially diagnosed at aged eight when she moved to her local primary school. Her father and I had divorced two years earlier and it had been a particularly traumatic time, also the start of prolonged conflict between us over Jasmin's difficulties and needs and how to treat them. Like most parent stories I seem to hear or read, Jasmin was misunderstood, often regarded as rude, stubborn, controlling and was sometimes punished. This gradually changed throughout her primary school years, with support from CAMHS, and as I fed back information to teachers from knowledge gained mainly through, SMIRA and the Level I course 'Working with Selective Mutism'. I attended a few of the annual SMIRA conferences and remember at the last one feeling slightly isolated, for some reason, and wondered if I was connecting to the other parents.

Jasmin was, and still is, a very bright, creative, highly sensitive and popular girl who had some close friends. At school she was silent and her demeanour quite frozen. Yet at home she talked freely with family and close friends when they came to the house. Looking back, the behavioural techniques learnt were helpful, in that they enabled Jasmin and her teachers to find some comfort and ease in the classroom, but for Jasmin they were not sustainable. To change her behaviour, her own beliefs had to be changed from within so that her behaviour and attitude became natural and, most importantly, transferable to any environment or situation. It was necessary for her to want to change and to be empowered as an individual. I wanted her to lead a fulfilling life, to choose fulfilling relationships and of course to be as best prepared for her own parenting as she could.

Preparation for secondary school was structured with visits building up over the final term and even an extra visit for more anxious children. Jasmin's first day at secondary school was in her own words, 'overpowering' and made her feel 'numb'. It was also her last day. The following two weeks she was a sobbing heap of duvet as she knew if she dared stick one foot out that that was one step closer to school.

The experience of the first day at secondary school, and her feelings, were too overwhelming for her and she froze and retreated to safety: her home. I stopped work for a while to focus on strategies with the school to encourage her back in. My stress levels were sky high together with my anger with some, for not really understanding, and frustration with Jasmin for not going to school. The LEA (local education authority) became involved and I felt under immense pressure. Looking back I can see that in order to venture out of the house, Jasmin needed to feel some degree of safety within her own mind, which she just didn't have, so all the efforts to get her back into school at that time were in vain.

I will never forget the words spoken from my mother's Greek hairdresser; when his granddaughter was upset, he would simply sit her upon his knee and gently stroke her hair. It made me think about other cultures and wondered how they would deal with a situation like this; probably very differently. I suddenly felt deeply ashamed that I was not attending to my daughters real needs. She was expected to go to school, like all the other children, and needed to fit in, however traumatic an experience it was for her, but she was unable to do so. I longed to take my place under the duvet but I couldn't; finding new solutions and strategies drove me on.

As a working, single parent I could not possibly home educate and knew that the LEA had to provide schooling. Jasmin was provided with five hours of home tuition per week. She built up a good rapport with the tutor and spoke to him from the outset. However, by Christmas Jasmin had withdrawn from all social activities and only left the house when I dropped her at her nan's when I went to work. By the following spring she couldn't leave the house at all and would only see friends if they came to the door, although often she would run away and hide. Anxiety had taken hold and she had experienced her first panic attacks.

CAMHS told me they would be using an 'intensive approach' with Jasmin. It proved aggressive, intimidating and ultimately it failed.

On one visit she was cornered in the kitchen, was told that they needed to get her to start talking to them, all the while her hair was draped over her face so she couldn't be seen and she was stiff with fear. Not surprisingly, Jasmin retreated from them on subsequent visits until she literally locked herself away in a room. This became the focus of the following meetings and I became caught up in my own battle with them. So the new behaviours she was developing as a result of protecting herself from CAMHS then became their next issue to resolve. It was spiralling out of control and I was forced into a defensive and protective position and was regarded as an obstruction to their work. Furthermore, I felt that my attempts to explain our traumatic past, to make some connection to the behaviour, were silenced. I was literally told to put the past behind me.

I decided to seek out private help. I found a local child and adolescent psychotherapist. After my first couple of meetings with Kim, I felt I had walked out of a fog and was seeing the scenery for the first time. I was acknowledged. Some meetings later, including two meetings with Jasmin's father (who then rejected this route), Kim formulated a clinical picture and presented it to me. Another door had been opened and I could see Jasmin's difficulties in the context of a bigger picture: the family. Her Selective Mutism, OCD behaviours and anxiety were symptoms of a broader and more deep-rooted situation.

I realized then that Jasmin's difficulties started long before the Selective Mutism appeared and were evident in her development of OCD around the age of three years. Triangulation (where a child is caught between the conflict of the opposing parental and relational stances between the adults which is then internalized and causes unmanageable stress) had occurred in our family and Jasmin was showing signs of a regressive attachment towards me – 'the safe object'. I would add that I was unaware at the time of this 'conflict' as it was so deeply ingrained in our relationship. There is no doubt that Jasmin experienced trauma over a period of time, when her father and I divorced, and her development of Selective Mutism at aged eight was underpinned by powerful anxiety. Kim's role was to find the source of this anxiety and Jasmin's emotional and psychological inability to tolerate social situations. Kim wrote a 14-page report on Jasmin's difficulties where he talked of triangulation and attachment and where she is 'more likely… to express her symptoms when this attachment is challenged by anyone she experiences as unsafe'.

Jasmin was an untrusting child and the professionals involved had firmly secured her position behind a locked door. I had taken on a defensive and protective role, and I don't think I was in a position to help her with her powerful emotions and processing them, despite my desire and all my efforts. I found myself caught between the intrusion of the professionals and the cutting off of my own emotions in order to manage the situation.

After the CAMHS approach, she refused to see any more professionals, so I worked with Kim for the next year on my own, all the while Kim building up her trust and curiosity enough in order that she would want to see him. Kim started to work with me on a Case Treatment Planning approach. This meant that he was helping me to help Jasmin. The other professionals were still very much involved but I had to become the go-between and would often be triggered into my own fight or flight mode – mostly, I would say, fight.

It was during this year that I learnt that I had focused so much attention on helping Jasmin that I was not looking out for my own needs; this was a crucial starting point in Jasmin's recovery. My own life experiences had compounded and looking back, I hadn't recognized that I needed my own support as well as my own recovery space and time.

Jasmin's recovery was also conditional on her close environment. By environment I mean the physical and mental sense of safety at a minimum, but also three key ingredients, which I believe to be essential: trust, acknowledgement and empathy; just like a plant needing light, warmth, air and nutrients. Up until this point, they were lacking in different amounts. I consider that building trust is imperative in engaging a child, as well as the parent(s), and that without trust there is no foothold. This was obviously a process and didn't happen overnight.

Through my trust of Kim, I was able to model a trusting relationship and in time Jasmin built her own trust and curiosity enough to start visiting his clinic. She made her own decision to go, when she was ready. Empathy is wrapped up in trust but it just wasn't obvious to me in the professionals' 'tick box' system. However, I now understood and felt the true meaning of support.

At this time, acceptance of Jasmin's condition, and to make it known that she wasn't born with anxiety or SM, was vital. Up until now she had felt, in her words, that there was something 'wrong' with her, she felt like she was 'different' and 'weird'. Allowing her to experience anxiety and SM as something she had developed, and that it was external to her, gave her a great sense of freedom. This was demonstrated by her starting to recall memories and how she felt (although not necessarily put together). It was an emotional time as she began to talk about events from her earlier days and the vivid dreams she was having. Anger was expressed in addition to some more powerful emotions; she seemed to be coming more 'alive'; like a plant her leaves were starting to unfold.

There seemed movement from a static position, of which the effects were fairly quick and dramatic. I worked on modelling feelings and tolerating them and Jasmin really started to open up and talk to me about past experiences and just about anything. She was able to express herself because she knew she was safe to do so.

This intolerance of unpredictable reactions, also her own, now seems to be significant to me.

I started to talk about the 'now' and not get drawn into the 'what if' with her. Also, I verbalized a lot about 'when you feel a bit better, we can…' Gradually she started to have visions herself of what she would like to do when she felt a bit better and she was then telling me what she would like to do. For the first time she not only realized that she could change, but she wanted to change, and Jasmin was blossoming.

Jasmin was provided with online classroom-style learning. She was given a laptop and headphones and a timetable and now attends lessons live from home. They are small classes and pupils can interact via writing or using the mouthpiece on the headphones, or both. This education has been invaluable for Jasmin and she has progressed well academically and has a circle of online classroom friends. It provides a structure to her day and she is highly motivated by it. She took a GCSE last year and is due to take three more this year as a year 10. The secondary school provides an invigilator for exams and she takes them in her home. This year she will take them in an educational establishment in her own room.

For the last two years, Jasmin has attended Kim's clinic. Apart from local walks this was the only place she had attempted to go for a long time; she was virtually housebound. On the country drives that we started to do two or three times a week, she wouldn't even let me stop at a petrol station for fear of being too close to someone else.

On her first visits to Kim, he explained about panic attacks and what happens physiologically to the body. This had never been explained to us before and it helped in taking away the emotional impact and realizing that it was a harmless physical reaction.

Over the following months, Jasmin gradually built up confidence to leave the house more often and to go to public places by using a step-by-step approach. These would be steps that Jasmin had chosen so that she was in control; this started with a trip to a garage where she got out of the car and came into the shop with me. We were then able to go on holiday and she would venture out of the cottage in the daytime and visit shops and the beach. Previously, we had to go out after dark and sit on the beach alone. I noticed after a while that she was talking to shop keepers and strangers fairly freely. This seemed to be happening as her anxiety reduced. She told me recently that she didn't like to be called Selective Mute anymore as there were literally only a small number of people she could not speak to: her GP, social worker and Kim; professionals connected to her recent past, who were still working with her now. Anybody new she meets now, she can speak to and she has ventured out to more and more new places.

An interesting event occurred recently, whereby we were waiting in the doctors surgery, when a couple of Jasmin's old school friends walked in. She fled from the surgery and out onto the street. Afterwards, she said that she felt nothing; no anxiety, no panic, she just fled. Kim explained this as a 'dissociative response in that the feelings were "split off" and not felt, but that she had an automatic flight reaction, triggered by an association with the situation'. Despite this, Jasmin was able to return to the doctors' the following week having decided with Kim that she should have some 'distraction' when something like this happens. This distraction could be an activity or, ideally, a mental distraction in her head.

A very important stage of her recovery, still to complete, is to communicate all that she wants to forget and attach her feelings to it through a specific channel; she doesn't deserve to hold this burden in her head as it belongs elsewhere. There is still some way to go, but Jasmin is gradually integrating back into the community and she is engaging in a school integration plan, ready to start as soon as she is able to.

ELAINE'S STORY

My daughter, Tracy, is nine and started to show signs of SM around the age of three when she started playgroup. She developed separation anxiety and started to become very shy with certain people and in certain places. She wouldn't join in with group activities like singing and dancing in playgroup yet she loved to do so at home all the time. I thought this was strange, but apart from that she seemed perfectly normal.

As the years passed the shyness got worse with extended family and friends – but especially strangers and doctors and dentists. I had to stop taking her to the dentist because she refused to open her mouth. This frustrated me and even though we threatened to punish her, she still wouldn't comply! I had no idea then how scary this was for her. I only thought she was being disobedient and defiant.

It also became very difficult for her when we were visiting her grandparents who we didn't see very often. She was unable to hug them or say hello or goodbye or to say thank you when they gave her something – a drink, a biscuit, or money. To me this behaviour was unacceptable and she was being rude. We tried our best to reason with her but nothing changed – it only got worse. Finally she started refusing to stay overnight with both sets of grandparents and her cousins. She just didn't want to go – even when we assured her that her older sister would be going too and she would look after her. We'd drop her off but, within a couple of hours, or by bedtime, we'd receive a phone call asking us to come back and pick her up – she wanted to go home!

Around this time I became concerned that this wasn't the normal shyness that both my husband and I experienced as children. She wasn't growing out of it – in fact she was getting worse. That was when I found out about SM on the NHS website. It recommended a course of speech therapy to help her overcome this completely and go back to the confident person she was before. That was 18 months ago, but no matter what her speech therapist does, she still isn't making progress. They really don't know what to do with her and are suggesting stopping the sessions because she is due to start seeing a psychologist soon who should know more about anxiety and should be better equipped to help.

It's so sad because I really thought this would work but it hasn't. The changes have been very small and very slow – so to most people, they still see Tracy as an extremely reserved, shy person who is unable or unwilling to talk but inside she's bright, exuberant and full of nonsense. Also, it has taken her months and months to build up a rapport with her speech therapist and even now she's still not able to speak to her on a one-to-one basis – only in relaxed group sessions at school with her friends joining in and the focus isn't just on Tracy!

Oddly enough, Tracy is happy and feels confident at school with her friends and generally has no problem speaking. She does struggle with asking for help, going to the toilet and talking about bullying to the teacher, as well as reading out loud in class. She can often only manage this at a whisper. I know now that she has a real problem with anxiety – mostly in social situations, but also excessive worry about her health.

This resulted in a meltdown recently as it has been suggested by a paediatrician that she may have a mild form of autism and they want to test her for it. Two speech therapists are to be involved in conducting the test and it has to be recorded with family members present to make it less distressing for her. It was to be held at school and for some reason Tracy was convinced it was happening on a particular day. She utterly refused to go to school – locking herself in the bathroom and eventually screaming with all her might to show us her fear of going ahead with this test. She's afraid to admit there's something wrong and afraid of what might happen if it turns out she is autistic. She just wants to be normal like everyone else and most of all to be left alone without all the fuss and stress that is going on in her life at the moment.

I'm at my wits end because I feel that no one knows what she is going through – or myself and her dad. The stress is overwhelming and I just wish it would all go away and we could go back to leading normal lives again, but it won't! People think we are pandering to her and being far too soft; and that she's refusing to speak because she's stubborn and rude and we're allowing her to get away with it by not punishing her. If only they knew how far from the truth they are. If they could live in her shoes for a day they would soon see that she's not making it up – it's not just 'in her head' and she desperately needs support and encouragement not criticism and judgement.

I just need to know that things will get better and she will be able to lead a normal life. What if she's still like this when she starts high school? That's only 18 months away from now. If she worries about how people view her in primary school – it's going to be so much worse for her in high school. Will she ever get better and be able to go out in public, talk to strangers, pay for things at the shops herself, go to the doctors and the dentist, go to parties and sleepovers and actually enjoy herself? I know there's no way of knowing for sure but I have to hope and believe that she will be happy and healthy, and the anxiety will eventually ease.

MARK'S STORY

As a child, growing up was a perfectly happy time for Nicola. She was full of life and her formative years and development were textbook for a three- to five-year-old.

Then one day on an outing with her grandma, Nicola suddenly clammed up in the company of a person that she didn't know. We believe this was the start of her SM. She was five years old at the time. Although she still spoke freely in social situations, we did notice she was quite 'choosy' about whom she spoke to. For the next five years or so we weren't unduly concerned. We thought she was just a quiet child.

However, in year 4 at primary school, we noticed significant changes in Nicola's behaviour. For example, she would go to school in her school uniform wearing trousers, which was perfectly acceptable and within the school rules. Then, on returning home, she would get changed and put her school dress on. She would engage in routines that involved running around the garden in the early hours of the morning – on some occasions half-dressed. As parents, we feel sure these were coping strategies and thought-blockers that she employed to try to rid herself of the anxiety and fear of having to speak at school the next day.

We were noticing more and more of her rituals and routines that she was engaging in – for instance, making endless lists of things to do and memorizing television scripts. More upsetting and disturbing were her sudden physical outbursts. She used to hang on to the night for dear life to block out thoughts of the next day and the trauma and stress a new day would inevitably bring with it.

As Nicola progressed through primary school we did notice her inability to process information. She would be more comfortable with rote-learning rather than gestalt learning. For example, it took her many years to work out how to tell the time. She was also unable to distinguish between left and right and found mental arithmetic impossible.

SM was a term we had never heard of until we saw a BBC documentary in 2010 called 'My Child Won't Speak'. As we watched with great interest, our then 14-year-old daughter Nicola pointed and said, 'That's me!'[1]

At last we were able to attach a name to our daughter's condition. Shortly afterwards our next appointment followed at the Child Adolescent Mental Health Service (CAMHS). We duly explained to the clinical team we were sure Nicola had SM.

'I'd rather be in a wheelchair than have this,' Nicola once said. These are words that will be etched in my subconscious forever. If only the SENCOs had recognized the early signs and the presentation of symptoms – shyness, reticence and her extreme reluctance to communicate – and if only the teachers had not marginalized her because of her silence that has almost certainly compounded her anxiety, she may have been spared the breakdown and suicidal thoughts that happened later on.

Nicola is now in her 19th year and still soldiering on, fighting very hard to search for the key that will unlock her potential. As parents, we are extremely proud of her.

JULIE'S STORY

I remember clearly taking our daughter to a mother and toddler group with a friend and her daughter and Justine simply couldn't deal with it to the extent that she just made this awful, loud monotone sound (which I subsequently learned was her way of blocking out things she found overwhelming) and couldn't bear any of the other children near her, even our friend's daughter. I would say this was the first time I was aware that she had a different take on things to other children her age.

---

1 Danielle, who was one of the three children who actually appeared in the *My Child Won't Speak* documentary (Goddard and Peel, 2010), has contributed to this book, in various chapters, including providing some of her own life story in Chapter 17.

When she started playgroup, I was called aside one day and asked if I had noticed anything about our daughter because she would not respond to any of the staff, nor the other children, and they had never heard her speak. They suggested I come and work at the playgroup so that I could be with her, which, with hindsight, I wish I had done. At that time I felt it would not help her cope in the longer term if I was always there. After a period of time I moved her to a smaller playgroup with fewer children and staff and she coped with this better, although I don't think she ever spoke to anyone there. If ever there was the slightest change in routine or they had photos done, for instance, she would become obviously overwhelmed and very, very distressed and shut us out completely too, as parents, until she could process her distress.

When she started school it was pretty tough and the teacher actually said to me that they had 'never seen a child like her before' and that they 'had tried being nice to her and tried shouting at her' but she still would not respond to them. On the way into school her body language would change dramatically and she went more and more inside herself even though her older sister was at the same school. Justine was obviously extremely distressed and I was told to take her in the toilet before I left every morning, so that they obviously didn't have to worry about that. They told her sister that she had to hide from her in the playground because they obviously didn't want her to comfort her. She would not eat so at this point so I started collecting her at lunchtime for home lunch. They told me I had to tell her what she would be doing each day because, they said, 'she does not do anything we tell her'. I learned many years later from Justine that she adopted the habit of copying work from the children next to her because she couldn't understand what they wanted her to do and didn't want to be shouted at all the time if she didn't do any work. When she moved from reception into year 1, the teacher used to completely ignore her when she went into the classroom. When I challenged the teacher she told me, 'She will not speak to me so why should I speak to her?' When we were waiting to go into the classroom in the mornings more than once I would hear other mother's tell their children, 'Don't go near her, there is something wrong with her.' It broke my heart and I made the decision to remove Justine from the system to home educate her.

Even though I did this following the correct procedure the school still 'set' the education welfare officer onto me and the head of the school very unprofessionally asked our year 5 daughter in front of her whole class what was happening with her sister and what was wrong with her. At no point did they advise me that she might need extra support, or how to go about getting it for her myself. In general, I feel the education system has failed Justine tremendously over the years.

While she flourished at home, we decided to fight to get her statemented so that she would have support at such time she felt ready to re-enter mainstream schooling. Eventually she was statemented to receive full-time one-to-one support. My main argument in her case was that the only way she could access the national curriculum was with support. She went back to another very small school at the end of year 5 where she had a very supportive teaching assistant and, although she found many things difficult (she desperately needs routine and things to be in the right place, etc.) she really enjoyed her time there.

It has been suggested to us on many occasions that our daughter is on the autism spectrum though this has never been diagnosed. She was diagnosed with SM and social phobia by a CAMHS psychiatrist. It is my understanding that many of the traits of SM are very similar to those of autism. However, the Social Communication Disorders Unit at a major London hospital told us last year that they couldn't assess her for possible ASD because she 'refuses' to communicate with them. It is very frustrating that, even at that level, people still have the attitude that a child so terrified that they can't speak or even look at someone is somehow 'refusing' to communicate.

Parenting a child with SM can be pretty lonely. Most people will talk to your child for a certain amount of time and when they still don't respond they just give up and often avoid you like the plague too. I remember an old school friend of mine actually said to me once, 'I won't be coming round anymore because she obviously does not want me there and behaves like an animal hiding under the table when I come in.'

CHAPTER 14

Therapists' Experiences of Selective Mutism

Marian Moldan, LCSW-R (Director, Childhood
Anxiety Solutions); Judith Rosenfield, M.A., CCC-SLP
(Director, King's Speech and Learning Center)

In this chapter, two therapists – Marian Moldan and Judith Rosenfield – write about their experiences of successfully working with clients with Selective Mutism. Marian experienced Selective Mutism herself as a child and wrote about her own experiences of her early school life in Chapter 4. Marian demonstrates the innate skills that adults who had SM as children can possess when working therapeutically with anxious children. Next, Judith provides a number of successful case studies and, valuably, includes the approach she and her colleagues used in each case.

MARIAN MOLDAN

I don't think the structure of my treatment with this population is so different from others specializing in the treatment of Selective Mutism. I start where the child is successful. I collaborate with the family to build a hierarchy with their current successes as the starting point. I embed rewards in the structured activities that help them to practice their hierarchy of verbalizations many times over. I collaborate with the family and extended relatives as well as school personnel in order to help this child generalize their speaking skills into the home, school, and community. Once the child is speaking consistently without the parent in the session, I tend to observe the child's pragmatic abilities. Does the youngster or young adult use language to problem-solve, to negotiate problems, to compromise, to ask for help if he is sick, hurt, or in danger? Does this youngster have a mean length of utterance longer than a word or two? Can this youngster request or take turns when speaking? Can this same youngster use academic language in the classroom in both verbal and written form? Or have the years of being mute left gaps in their pragmatic and academic language skills? Youngsters and adults are put into SM groups in order to practice filling these gaps. These homogenous groups become a safe place to practise and receive support in the company of those who understand.

There are those who describe therapeutic treatment as part science and part art. My science comes from conferences, books, and professional experience of working with selectively mute children and adults for at least 30 years. My art comes from having recovered from Selective Mutism as a child. Peppered throughout the scientific techniques and interactions are those innate understandings of having once been just like the client before me.

I understand that most selectively mute children need a 'warm-up period' whereby they can acclimate to a new setting without immediate intrusion. As a result, I spend the better part of the intake session speaking to the parent(s) while the child plays silently alongside the parent. By respecting the contact functioning of such a child, the anxiety threshold seems to decrease after a short time. Typically, at some point during that first session, the child may whisper something to the parent or non-verbally appear more comfortable. At that moment, I ask the child and the mother, 'Would your child like to continue drawing or would he like to play a game? You can tell your mom and she will tell me.' I take care to study how the child responds. If he continues to watch me warily, I will look down.

Typically the child whispers something to the parent who repeats it to the therapist. Games are structured to require some form of communication starting where the child is successful in the session. After they whisper to the parents, that is the starting point for continued verbalizations, whether whispered inaudibly to the parent or whispered a bit louder. With every turn comes the reminder, 'You can tell your mom and she will tell me.'

There is nothing in the literature about selectively mute children and the need to win. However, pulling from my own history and the countless other selective mute children with whom I have worked,

I understand that most work hard at competing and trying to win a game against others. Parents will often report that at home, these same frozen children will scream, yell, cheat, and tantrum in order to win a game against others. With this knowledge, I embed the reward within the game by casually stating that when each player rolls the dice, if they can say the sound, letter, number or tell their family member their number they get an extra turn. If not, the player gets one turn. I don't recall any youngster not working to get this reward when it was combined with a speaking step that they could accomplish with very little help.

Over time, even in the first session, while playing and interacting, as the child speaks more there comes a new progression. Either the child drops his hand from his mouth, speaks a bit louder, or shifts his body a tiny bit to face the new person in his life. When I hear his word, number or sound, typically I act as if the child had said it to me by casually responding, 'Oh, yes. You did get a six. Thanks for letting us know. Oh boy! I'm getting nervous because that means you get an extra turn and I may end up as the loser here!'

I also understand that taking the step to verbally respond to a choice question takes a huge leap. It involves allowing someone to hear my voice. Simultaneously, it also involves opening myself up to the chance that I may say something wrong and be judged harshly. With this understanding, I typically ask others in the family almost any question first; and then, initially allow the youngster to copy their responses in order to lower his anxiety threshold while taking the initial steps facing the fear of verbal communication.

Due to my history, I appreciate the written word. I understand how the written language may go through a similar process as the use of verbal language. Both may have gaps resulting from years of unpractised academic language. Teachers often report that once the child is speaking, and the teacher can attend to his writing skills, this skill appears delayed. Often the selectively mute child can be seen copying from others. Other SM children can be seen sitting still with a blank paper on their desk and pencil in their hand while everyone else has been writing for a while. Once the selectively mute child begins to write, the words are few, lacking details and descriptions. It is a challenge to write anything, requiring much practice and support. It is even more challenging to write an opinion piece. Likewise, the task of elaborating on an event in written form is experienced as difficult.

Just as this population needed support and practice in verbal language, so too do they need the same with the written language. Youngsters are encouraged to bring in assignments and homework to therapy. The therapeutic environment is transformed into an emotional classroom as we work together to repair the fractures in their writing skills. Teachers collaborate with this aspect of the therapeutic process by giving the child far more time to develop a written and spoken presentation to be worked on.

All of the interventions, techniques, and assignments are developed to meet one's individual needs at any given time. Hierarchies and rewards are determined by the unique abilities and desires of each person in the office. Goals, expectations, and rewards change as the person changes. Woven within science, professional observation and technique are fibres borne out of my own selectively mute childhood and adolescence.

JUDITH ROSENFIELD

Nora's story

Nora was seven and soon to be entering second grade when her mother enrolled her in a two-week music and drama camp at our centre. I allowed her to enrol with a sibling since I knew that would contribute to her comfort and ultimately to her success. Nora's mom reported that Nora had been selectively mute for several years. She was described as a sensitive child and required much care each day to attend to all of her needs as she transitioned from one environment to the next (i.e. what most mothers would refer to as their 'high maintenance' child).

I typically don't dictate to my staff how to manage their creative groups, but this was different. SM is a very delicate condition and warrants unconditional acceptance of the child. Their care needs to be delivered with as much sensitivity as the child possesses. I gave Shay, our music director, one set of instructions: 'Don't make Nora sing, and don't make Nora talk.' From there, I let Shay's magic unfold.

To hear him call out 'Nora-rhythm!' throughout each song warmed my heart. Setting the goal to contribute to a group as a valuable team member without any mention of a voice was the ticket to Nora's success. She mastered her job as chief rhythm maker by playing the drums. It was only two days later that she began talking spontaneously to the other children in the group, and would speak privately to Shay, Miss Catherine (another music instructor), or me. By the end of the two-week session she was singing the chorus to Good Lovin' by Young Rascals just as loud as anyone in the group, 'Yeah, yeah, yeah, yeah, yeah,' and even did so during the Share Day presentation to the parents! Early in September, just two weeks into the school year, I received the following email from Nora's mother.

> Nora is doing great! I don't know what changed in her, but she seems much more confident lately. As far as I know, she has not spoken to her teacher directly yet, but her teacher says she is very happy and chit chats with all of her peers. After two years of athletic training with the same coach she has finally directed a question to her coach.

I know what changed Nora without a doubt – it was the rhythm! 'Nora – we need rhythm' must have still been echoing in Nora's ear as it continues to echo in my ears to this day.

Nick's story

Nick was a handsome and athletic looking 14-year-old, who, at a glance, could have been any American teen heartthrob. Who knew he would become one of my most challenging cases to treat as a speech-language pathologist? Not only did his autism spectrum disorder cause a disconnect with his emotions and insight into his social challenges, but his impaired language processing made it very difficult for him to talk about abstract topics such as past and future events. There was a huge discrepancy between his communication abilities at home where he was most comfortable, and any context outside of the home, where he was typically mute. Thus, I needed to prioritize managing his SM in my approach to social language therapy (speech pathologists call this pragmatic language therapy to address *how* we use communication). My challenge was simple. I would need to release Nick from his state of 'shut down' by offering a no-pressure approach to conversational practice coupled with a bombardment of confidence boosting.

In my initial sessions with Nick, I had him share photos and artwork (he was a talented artist) from home as a means to bridge the gap between past and present. What I learned in addition to Nick benefiting from visual images was fascinating. Nick's face lit up while describing his family trip to one of his favourite places in the country, rich with memories of visiting his grandfather and being outdoors in a warm climate. He described everything from a sensory perspective and elaborated as I had never witnessed in our prior exchanges. His voice was strong, his speech was clear, and his language was grammatical and meaningful. He described the warmth of the sun and the smell of the ocean. Nick was not just a visual learner – he was a sensory learner!

Knowing what made Nick tick was crucial for future intervention. I began using hour-long weekly sessions to develop Nick's small talk skills while playing basic card and board games. I ordered one of his favourite foods – e.g. pizza – each week to create positive sensory memories. I progressed on a continuum of games requiring minimal speaking (chess) to games involving speech on each turn (Apples to Apples). No mention of speech expectations was conveyed. Things were moving along nicely. Playing board games proved to be effective in strengthening our bond, and eliciting more speech. However, I soon felt that my efforts had reached a plateau in that I still didn't observe any initiative language, only responsive. I was ready to set the bar a little higher, and try something new.

I invited Nick to a teen and young adult speech event to practise either small talk or presentation skills. I carefully set things up for success. I instructed him to present a tutorial on how to draw using a whiteboard to keep things simple while at the same time presenting on a favourite topic in which he is most confident. I could sense that Nick was more anxious than usual when he arrived by the intensity of his facial expression. Nick's affect was always flat, and I had yet to see him smile, but this night felt different to me as I felt my own anxiety elevate. I could feel his pain. I called on Nick to come up to the front of the group of about six others after everyone else had volunteered to present. I will never forget how terrified he became. His hands were visibly shaking as he perseverated on his attempt to draw a simple picture by making random marks on the board and immediately erasing them. His lips became 'blocked' as a severe stutterer may experience on a word beginning with a 'p' sound. The room was silent. Fortunately for Nick, he was in a safe place with no snickering or commenting. Another student thought quickly and offered to show an amusing demonstration of how to draw a puppy.

She offered much needed comic relief to the group, but I wanted to cry for Nick. I called his mother the next day to see how he was. He had not mentioned it to her, reflecting how much hurt, shame and fear he must keep bottled up inside on a daily basis.

I took Nick's failure as my own, but knew I had to practise what I preached – that only the client should set the pace for change. I was moving much too quickly. It was clear that Nick would need much more practice holding the floor in a basic group conversation before being thrown to the wolves again to present to a small group. His mother agreed to enrol him in our weekly social group for teenage boys where he continues to make tiny but steady gains in social communication by taking advantage of natural opportunities to connect with peers with absolutely no pressure to perform.

David's story

David was 17 years old when I started working with him in school. His speech-language goals were to improve his vocabulary and reading comprehension, but when I asked him in our first session of the school year, 'What interferes the most with your success at school?' he confided that he was very quiet, and sometimes didn't talk at all. He reportedly had been like this ever since he could remember, and denied any trauma in his life. David agreed to my help under one condition – I only see him individually and not in a group.

David was very insightful and could explain in detail contexts that made him feel secure versus those that were threatening to him. He explained that he can speak in a one-to-one context with a close friend (and he had several friends), but will immediately shut down with just one more student joining in.

I was eager to learn more about David and to see if any other school personnel knew what we were dealing with. My first instinct was to protect him from any unfair discipline for what may be misperceived as uncooperativeness. I knew he hated gym, so I spoke first to his gym teacher. She explained that he stays by himself, but changes for class and makes an effort to participate despite his muteness. At times she modifies his class requirements to allow for his anxiety.

I then spoke to the school principal who indicated that he was aware of David being terrified of the cafeteria. So, he cuts him some slack when he finds him hanging out with one particular friend in various hiding spots throughout the school. Being new to the school, I was so relieved to learn how accommodating the staff had been thus far. It would make my job easier as I worked with David across school contexts to know that I could count on compassionate teachers to help create opportunities for David's success. Our first couple of independent assignments looked like this.

- *Week 1:* Try to say one word when a third student joins a conversation you are having with a friend.
  One week later: Goal achieved!

- *Week 2:* Try to say one full sentence when a third student joins a conversation you are having with a friend.
  One week later: Goal achieved!

The next jump in progress came accidentally when another student knocked on the door thinking it was his time for an appointment. I was pleasantly surprised when David greeted him verbally and with a full smile. I looked at him as if to ask if he was okay and he nodded, 'yes.' The boys explained that they knew each other from class. David was himself and fully participated in a more traditional language lesson with his classmate. He was even silly at times, engaging in off-topic chatter, which was a welcomed change.

I was anxious to build from the recent momentum, but didn't want to push things too soon, or jeopardize his trust in me. I decided to take a chance and called David to speech therapy at the same time I called two other students from class. I quietly told him when no one was paying attention that he could leave if he wanted. He replied, 'No, I'm good.'

I was careful not to put David on the spot in return for his courageous decision to stay in the group. Once he knew that he was safe and that I was not going to make him do anything he didn't want to do, I saw the pressure lift by his more relaxed body posture. He participated; however, I could tell by his brief utterances and his lack of expression that he was not completely himself. Nevertheless, just agreeing to be part of a group was huge progress. David heard my message from an earlier session, 'If you want to stay the same, keep doing what you are doing. If you want to get better, then just do anything, no matter how small, differently.' In turn, I heard his message loud and clear. Yes. My friend was here to get better.

Kimberly's[1] story

I remembered feeling a little disorganized the day Kimberly came to see me for her initial consultation. I was running late, and then, once started, I talked excessively. Reflecting back, I felt her nerves. So, in an effort to make her feel at ease, which was my number one goal, I didn't allow for any awkward moments of silence. By babbling about myself, I took the spotlight off of her. It helped for her to see my human side, and also know that there was no pressure to perform.

Kimberly opened up almost immediately and confided that I was one of the few adults she had spoken to in years, other than her family. She was in her 40s and had three children. I also learned that she had Asperger's Syndrome, including a significant sensory processing disorder, and that she was perpetually referred to as 'shy' and hated it. Other than some social skills groups as an adult, Kimberly had never received therapy for communication problems related to either Asperger's or SM. She was hungry for some help, particularly now that she had become a published author and was being encouraged to host a tour of book-signing events. Did the marketing rep ever read her book, *Under the Banana Moon*, her memoir?! I immediately put her at ease by saying the words, 'You don't have to do anything you don't want to do.' Though it sounds so basic, it is easy to forget that you are in control over your life when experiencing obsessive negative thoughts. Hearing it from a professional seemed to grant her the permission to be free. My goal would be to empower Kimberly to regain her control over her life, and to honour wherever she is in that process. We started with the practice of small talk skills to lessen some of the anxiety regarding what to say to less familiar people.

Small talk skills (Small talk 101)

- ▲ *First step:* How to start a conversation:

  Talk about the 'here and now'. Talk about a common bond. Talk about a hot news item (never talk about the weather unless a hurricane is coming!). Offer a compliment. Find out needed information.

---

1 Kimberly also writes about herself, throughout this book.

⮝ *Second step:* How to maintain a conversation:

> Comment to share information versus asking questions, which may lead to a dead end. Use the three-sentence rule: elaborate using three full sentences to answer who, what, why, where, how, or when.

After an initial jump in progress, Kimberly confided that she was beginning to avoid certain people and contexts due to her fear of closer connections. Again, Kimberly's control needed to be restored. She needed a rehearsed line to use in the event that she needed to decline an invitation. In other words, reminding herself that all she had to say was, 'No thanks, I can't this week,' would help her feel more secure. We also decided to change the focus of her small talk practice out in public from 'making social connections' to 'carrying out a mock anthropology assignment'. Her new goal was to learn more about people, their roots, and their customs. The problem was solved, and Kimberly was on her way to becoming a small talk graduate.

Our next phase of treatment addressed the need to expand Kimberly's social network to help with career options through texting, Facebook, and other social media. In a few short months Kimberly had a website to showcase her artwork and published books, became a master of texting, and was frequently sharing photos, resources, and messages with friends and family on Facebook, Twitter and LinkedIn. Aside from gaining personal satisfaction from opening up a new social window, Kim found her career as a published author and artist began to flourish. She was now 'in the game'.

Our official therapist-client relationship came to an abrupt end due to a lack of funding one year later. Fortunately, we have maintained contact, which has allowed us to work on several publishing projects together, as well as developing a long-lasting friendship. I have learned to change my expectations of a friend to accommodate for her SM. I know if I call her she will answer, and if I email her, she will promptly reply. However, if I dare attempt to plan to see her in person, I will get denied. I would normally take it personally that I must correspond only on a friend's terms, but I don't with Kim. I don't get hurt. I just get disappointed because I miss her! I like to connect in person with people I care about, but she does not. In her mind, she can't, and that's just the way it is right now.

CHAPTER 15

A Teacher's Experience of Helping a Child Find Her Voice

Hélène Cohen, Learning Support Co-ordinator
(St. Lawrence College Junior School, Kent)

Working with Chloë has been one of the most rewarding, frustrating and emotional experiences of my teaching career. It was certainly the longest! I had encountered children with Selective Mutism before, when teaching in secondary schools; however, they were the ones who had managed to use the transition from primary to secondary to find their voice. Therefore, the Selective Mutism was no longer evident by the time I was teaching them.

Allow me to introduce myself. I am Hélène Cohen, 'Miss', or Mrs Cohen to thousands of children, many of whom are now adults. I have been teaching for 30 years, initially in the secondary sector, but more recently at a small, independent primary school. Working with all aspects of learning support has been my main interest, although I am also a teacher of English, leading the subject in my current school. That's probably all you need to know about me.

So, back to Chloë. I shall be calling her this, having asked her to choose her name for the purpose of this account. That epitomizes our relationship – everything up front, no tricks, no lies. She is the focus, after all.

I first met Chloë soon after I started at her school. She was in the reception class, and her teacher expressed a concern about a little girl who wouldn't speak in school. She would happily, indeed noisily, talk at home, but only around a very select few people. Not knowing where to start with this, I went on a course. I decided that three of us should go: her current class teacher, the one who would most likely teach her the following year and me. Thus I met Maggie. Maggie Johnson was running the course and it was she who opened my eyes to the fundamental nature of Selective Mutism: anxiety. This was a revelation to me, as Chloë could be seen playing happily with friends, especially when she thought we weren't looking! While appearing extremely shy, she always seemed happy in school.

Initially, I worked with Chloë from a distance, offering support to her teachers, as they attempted the various steps as laid out in the *Selective Mutism Resource Manual* (Johnson and Wintgens, 2001). All was going well, slowly but well. Chloë started to record her reading at home to be played back to her teacher; she would quietly talk with a select few of her closest friends in school – definite progress. Then changes happened in her home life, and the little talk there was became less. I was also aware that Chloë would be moving up to KS2 (Key Stage 2), across the road and with a very different regime, so the transition needed managing. There would be more teachers, most of whom would be new to her, and more movement around the school on a day-to-day basis. Added to this, Chloë was evidently an intelligent girl. I decided to work with her on a weekly basis, to build a relationship, so that she would have continuity when transferring to KS2. I always took her out with another child, to help her to feel more secure. This is when I saw, first hand, the full extent of the anxiety behind Selective Mutism.

We used to play games that would develop her logical thinking skills. This would require Chloë to make choices, which is where the anxiety showed. While whichever friend was joining her that week (there were three who would take turns) would happily select a response, placing a tile in the square of her choice, Chloë would sit, anxiously tearing at a tissue, reluctant to commit to her choice unless 100 per cent certain. She would work away at the tissue, gradually shredding it, and select her response by holding this tissue and tile in both hands and slowly move her whole body gently forward until she touched the square where she needed to place her tile. Her face looked anxious, her shoulders tense – I find it hard to describe in words just how closed in and full of anxiety the movement would be. During this time I needed to do an assessment of her receptive vocabulary, as it was hard to place her academically due to her anxiety about getting an answer wrong. Using a picture-based assessment, where I would say a word and Chloë would need to select one of four pictures that best fitted the word, her score was average, a standardized score of 102 where 100 is exactly average. For this assessment, Chloë only answered when absolutely certain of the answer and did this showing immense anxiety. My experience and intuition meant that I felt that this was not a true reflection of her ability.

This is a concern for those who display Selective Mutism. The underlying anxiety means that a test situation will often not reflect true potential, so such a child could easily be placed in a set at school at a level below her ability, which will further undermine self-esteem. This can easily become a downward spiral, as self-esteem is essential to successful learning as well as to breaking the silence of Selective Mutism.

As I worked with Chloë, I gradually gained her trust. The aforementioned honesty when working with Chloë was essential for this. I always outlined what we were doing, talked openly with her about her voice, and appealed to her innate sense of fun. This was helped by the introduction of home visits during the holidays. In her own environment, while she still didn't speak in front of me, her sense of mischief started to shine through. We tried the various Sliding-in™ techniques as outlined in Maggie's programme, but Chloë was not yet ready for this. Being sensitive, she picked up on how much her mother wanted her to succeed in speaking outside the home and that in itself added to her own pressure and anxiety – all resulting from the mutual love between her and her mother. So instead, I drank coffee with Chloë's mother and we would chat, so that Chloë could become more comfortable around me.

There were small steps of progress surrounding the transition, the first being Chloë's 'accidental word' in school. Here are the notes of the incident:

> Today, at lunch, R saw Chloë being a bit silly and she was crawling on the floor, so he asked her if she was okay and she said, 'Yes, fine'. Then quickly put her hand to her mouth, as if realizing that she had said it out loud. R then asked her to fetch him a glass of water, which she did – albeit slowly. He then continued to eat his lunch quietly, without trying to make any conversation. C will inform Chloë's mum of this incident. Hopefully Chloë will be able to reflect favourably on this.

This utterance was denied by Chloë, and still is to this day, although assurances were given that this didn't mean that she would now be pressured to speak in school.

Having established earlier than usual who would be Chloë's teachers in year 3, I ensured that all of the KS2 teachers and TAs (teaching assistants) underwent some basic Selective Mutism training with Maggie, so that none would put undue pressure on her and all would have some understanding of how communication would work. In year 3 we also started on a range of activities, such as blowing bubbles and other silly games, all of which took away the pressure of making choices. It was also agreed that I should be in the pool with Chloë for swimming lessons, supporting her and another child to help them to become comfortable in the water. All of this seemed to help Chloë develop confidence around me and this was first seen when I re-did the receptive vocabulary assessment. This time, albeit reluctantly, Chloë agreed to have a go even when unsure.

This had a tremendous impact on her standardized score, which went up by 15 standardized points, a score much more in line with my understanding of her natural abilities. This in turn was a super boost to her self-esteem and marked the start of her real cheekiness when working with me – it turns out that Chloë cheats, not to win, but to ensure that I lose!

The transition to year 3 was positive. I was able to monitor her progress more closely, being based in the KS2 part of the school. Chloë's confidence gradually grew and she would sometimes 'forget' where she was and was even seen running, when she thought no one was watching. This confidence was noticeable in several ways. In year 3, Chloë's movements became bigger: from the closed in, anxious movements, tearing (or as we referred to it, killing) a tissue, she would now make 'body sounds', tapping, stamping, pinging a ruler on the table, and would even reach across to write on the class whiteboard. Her silent, puppet-operating performance of 'Head, Shoulders, Knees and Toes' to her entire class was extremely entertaining and she even played the piano in assembly as everyone was filing in. Added to this, she started to record herself making the body sounds, and allowed me to play these to a select few members of staff. She also, through the dedicated work of an exceptionally patient teacher, started to join in with PE and Games for the first time. Every step of progress, for example with throwing and catching a netball, would then be shown to me so that she could build on this, and not deny her achievements. Her mother would then ensure that she rehearsed these skills at home, away from prying eyes.

Notice how casually I threw in that Chloë played the piano in assembly. This was huge! It also involved tears – not hers. Her mother had, as agreed with Chloë, waited outside. I was in the hall. I managed to hold it together the whole time I was in Chloë's presence, then quietly slipped out after her performance. The full force of the emotion and the enormity of what Chloë had achieved then hit me, as I cried with her mother, quietly, outside the assembly hall. This epitomizes the intensity of working with someone who has Selective Mutism. The emotional investment is high, but the rewards are higher.

This leads me to make mention of how we communicated, negotiated and came to understandings. It was largely through writing and drawing. This would be done on mini whiteboards to allow for wiping things away. Chloë liked to be in control of the whiteboard. If I set out choices, she would draw little boxes in which to record a tick or cross to show her preferences. Whenever I drew a box, it was never neat enough for her exacting standards, and would be erased and replaced with one drawn by Chloë! Through this communication, I learned that she was texting some year 6 girls, and had wished she had spoken the first time they had played together. This not only shows just how important each first encounter is, but how Selective Mutism is not a choice, not stubbornness, but deep-rooted anxiety.

Then the first real sound that I heard from Chloë, her giggle! Like champagne being poured from a bottle. I have already mentioned her sense of fun, so the talking tasks were built around this. The friends chosen to join in were all gigglers, and as Chloë relaxed, so her laughter escaped. This helped her to move on to some silly sounds – 'huh', tongue clicking and sucking against the roof of her mouth.

These may all be tiny steps, but each marked huge progress for Chloë. Working with those who have Selective Mutism requires constant patience alongside tiny steps that each move things forward. It's so important to keep some momentum and not stay still, however tiny the steps may be.

To further build on this, I became her form teacher in year 4. The only subject I taught her was spelling, as we don't have all subjects taught by the form teacher in our school, but it meant that she and I could touch base throughout the day. 'Thumbs up' became Chloë's first form of communication with the now increasing number of teachers that she encountered daily.

We built on this with technology. The first step was Chloë recording things at home for me to hear, including conversations with her mum and sister, reading and then questions for me, so that we were conversing remotely. Initially I heard these recordings alone, then with Chloë in the next room and eventually with her in the same room, so that she, her voice and I were in the room together.

The emotion of hearing Chloë's voice for the first time was overwhelming, so I was relieved to have been alone for that. Having focused on the whole 'underplay' element – 'no pressure, your voice will come in time', etc. – had she witnessed my delightfully tearful response, it would have been hard to convince her that we were relaxed about her Selective Mutism.

We then agreed who would be allowed to hear the various recordings, each initially being heard without Chloë present. The teachers would let Chloë know when they had heard her voice, and even those who thought they could distance themselves were moved beyond their expectations by the impact her voice had on them. Her voice, an ordinary little girl's voice. What had we all expected? I don't know. Yet we all had the same first response – she sounds so normal!

Recording Chloë's voice progressed over the time she was in the junior school. We used it in a structured way so that Chloë could demonstrate her learning to her teachers. This included explaining 'forces' to her male Science teacher; reciting numbers in French – a super French accent – and even telling us when things were troubling her. Throughout all of this, Chloë was supported by her friends. Everyone in her class was reminded that Chloë hadn't yet found her voice, but would do so in time, so that the openness was there throughout.

While Chloë was in year 4, I saw a BBC television programme on Selective Mutism (Goddard and Peel, 2010). In this there was a child called Red who would communicate with her grandfather by texting. I thought this would be a good idea to introduce at school, as it would allow 'in the moment' communication between Chloë and her teachers. We'd tried a mini whiteboard, but these 'show me' boards are still a fairly public form of communication, which was quite daunting for Chloë. I purchased two extremely basic phones, one black and one pink, that each had the other's number saved so that they could be used solely for texting each other. This proved a success. Chloë was able to answer questions in class and even let me know if something was bothering her. Hers was the pink phone, naturally! The amazing thing is how accepting the other children always are. The worries of their reaction to a child having a phone in school, albeit a basic one, were short lived. Having seen it, and had the reason for it explained, they simply accepted it. This is true of so many interventions for learning support.

I remained Chloë's form tutor for year 5. We had a fun activity of writing riddles and her classmates would be called on to offer theirs to the group. How could Chloë join in? Chloë and I agreed that she would record her riddle on a talking postcard, which I could then play to the class. This would be a big step for Chloë, as most of her form had been at school with her for several years by then without ever having heard her voice, so this needed to be considered carefully. Eventually we agreed that we would use the talking postcard with several children first, so that it wouldn't automatically signal that the voice was going to be Chloë's. Then when the day came to play Chloë's riddle she would first leave the class, ostensibly to run an errand for me, so that she could be out of the room when it was played. Then, after the class had heard it, I would explain that it had been Chloë. I made one mistake. I forgot to tell her closest friend what I was doing. All went to plan and Chloë went to fetch something from my office. I played her riddle and noticed that Chloë's closest friend was looking daggers at me. Credit due, she didn't say a word to indicate whose riddle we were hearing. She just sat there, staring at me, pure anger in her eyes. After solving the riddle, one by one children started to ask whose riddle it was. I looked straight at Chloë's friend and explained not only whose riddle it was, but that she knew that I was playing it to them, which was why she was out of the room. Her friend relaxed immediately and I apologized for not having forewarned her.

Key to this stage was to explain to the class that they were not to make a fuss about this when Chloë returned. This is the crux of what she had been dreading, the attention made of her once everyone realized they had heard her voice.

Later in the same year I introduced an inter-house poetry recital. Every child in the school had to learn a poem by heart and recite it to the rest of the year group, then four children in each year would be selected to represent their house on stage, in front of the entire junior school. Chloë was to be no exception, so she duly learned her poem – naturally a silly one – and recorded it. We played that recording to the whole of her year group, with her in the room, another huge step forward. Every teacher and TA was allowed to hear this, so that now her voice had been heard by many. Chloë was widening her circle of friends and even speaking with some of them in school, out of the hearing of adults.

Transition time again. As Chloë started year 6, we needed to consider her best interests for secondary school. It was felt that she would benefit from moving school, having a fresh start, as the key obstacle to her talking was now the fact that she hadn't already done so and it would be a break from the norm for her. At a new school there would be no expectation of her silence, making it easier for her to speak. Our main target was for Chloë to be able to speak when starting secondary school. To that end, the summer break between years 5 and 6 included several home visits.

We started by developing the use of the phone. Initially I wasn't allowed to speak, just listen. I would text Chloë a question, 'What did you have for breakfast?' Chloë would have time to prepare her answer, then text me so that I knew the phone call was coming. I would answer the call and say nothing while Chloë spoke. This was using speaker phone at her end. The call would be ended. Gradually I was able to say 'Hello' and 'Goodbye', and then ask the question while on the phone, making it more like a conversation, albeit very structured. One advantage of the phone call is that it could happen throughout the school holiday, so that there was no break in communication. When I went away, we could still have our regular 'chat'.

As stated before, we have to keep the momentum going, moving forward in these small steps, so I brought the use of the phone into the home visits. For some time now we had been playing the card game 'Fish' as the talking task. Progress had been slow but constant, so I arranged for a home visit on a day when I could spend as long as was needed. Here's how it went:

> We started by generally chatting, that is to say that I chatted with Chloë's mother while she and her sister played. We then moved to the game 'Fish', using the Sliding-in™ technique. I stood just outside of where they were playing, round the corner but within the room itself. I could just about make out Chloë speaking very quietly, but what was really noticeable was that her younger sister initially reverted to whispering herself. Being only six years old, when she forgot that I was there – as she couldn't see me – she started to talk properly. This was an important observation, as it showed how her sister had been mimicking Chloë's behaviour, making herself at risk of Selective Mutism. Stopping the game, I spoke to Chloë alone and explained to her what was happening with her sister. As stated before, I have always been extremely open and honest with Chloë and she acknowledged that her sister was doing what I'd said. Although concerned that I might be putting pressure on her, I felt it important that Chloë understood this impact of her own difficulties.

I then got Chloë to go upstairs and use my phone as a recording device to simply say her numbers, Ace to King, as used in 'Fish'. After she'd done this a few times, and her voice had become normal on the recording, I suggested that she phone me from her room on my mobile. Initially she did this evidently using speakerphone, so I suggested that she put the phone to her ear and repeated the numbers after me each time. I said, 'Ace', then she said, 'Ace'; I said, '2', then she said, '2' etc. She did this in a clear, normal voice, responding to me each time. I then got her to repeat the process standing in the upstairs hall, then sitting halfway down the stairs, then in the doorway to the lounge – with me reassuring her that I had my back to the doorway – then partway in the room, then sitting on the couch behind where I was, and doing it without the phone, repeating the words after me. Then I got her to stand directly behind me and repeat the words after me. By this time the words were in a very squeaky strained voice, but they were voiced not whispered. Chloë and I then played a game of 'Fish', where she was looking at me the whole time while saying the card she wanted. Again her voice was very quiet and squeaky but it was a definite voice and I could understand which card she was asking for each time. We then played the game once more with her mum and her sister joining us. Then before I left I got her to say, 'Thank you' for the cookies I'd taken in, and say goodbye to me.

I still don't know how I did that in such a nonchalant manner. My heart was racing and I wanted to shout my delight at this progress, but I knew that any indication that this was a big deal would blow it! I calmly walked to the car, drove round the corner and out of sight of her house, then allowed the pent up emotion to flow through my tears. Such feelings could only be shared with one who'd understand, so I phoned a close colleague who'd been sharing this journey. Together we could allow the necessary outpour.

Year 6 was a year of key development, with colleagues emailing me examples of her progress. Chloë completed tests and exams, answering all questions, allowing her to achieve grades closer to her abilities; she joined in a dance routine in the school talent show; she was on stage for the sharing assembly, and played a recording of herself saying 'Moo' – she was a cow – in front of not only the entire junior school, but many of the parents too; she had a go on the 'Bucking Bronco' at the summer fete, for all to see and joined in the Science revision quiz, pressing her loud buzzer and holding up an answer on a 'show me' board.

The transition wasn't straightforward and necessitated an appeal to get her into a school that was small enough to allow her to flourish. Our contact has also not ceased. How can it when it has been so intense? She is speaking at her secondary school. However, the anxiety doesn't miraculously disappear. As I said earlier in this chapter, Selective Mutism is not a choice. Her speech is quiet, and mostly in response to direct questions. She misses her friends from our school, although has become closer to one of the two girls who moved to the same school as her. The anxiety now shows through feeling unwell. Initially she was physically sick each day. This is no longer the case, but she still struggles to eat properly throughout the school day, depending on a good breakfast and food as soon as she returns to the security of her home.

I don't know if Chloë will ever talk calmly with me, but while I can't deny that I would love to be able to chat easily with her, it doesn't matter. It's about Chloë. It always has been. It's always about the person with the difficulty, it has to be. That's the nature of the job. Our part is to come up with the steps that will facilitate progress, being patient throughout and keeping our emotions away from the child. The rewards are worth every second of time, drop of patience and tear shed.

CHAPTER 16

How Different Life Would Have Been Without Selective Mutism

Carl Sutton; Dawn (parent); Liz, Wendy and Kimberly

SM has caused me to suffer profoundly at various points in my adult life – most notably with clinical depression. Without SM I believe I would have been spared years of entirely avoidable suffering. I am not unique as depression plagues many adults with SM, regardless of how their SM came about. As such I am a strong proponent of treating SM in children as early in their lives as possible to avoid mental health issues in later life. Selective Mutism certainly is treatable, given the right approach, as the previous two chapters clearly demonstrate. My life experience is one example of a 'worst-case' scenario in which I received no help or support whatsoever for SM in childhood.

It is difficult to describe my life without SM or to guess what it may have been like because it has been part of my life for so long. However, without SM I believe that I would have fulfilled my childhood goal of becoming a professor (in Computer Science). While I got much of the way toward my goal, I had to leave academia because I was struggling so much with SM that I became mentally unwell. Regardless of my becoming unwell, however, a professor would have to be able to give lectures – something that was impossible for me personally.

As a PhD student the one and only time I tried to give a lecture – at a conference in Vienna – was a disaster. I faltered over my words for 15 minutes of the allotted half hour then shame-facedly left after being asked *no questions*. I felt distraught and, in privacy, burst into tears in a toilet cubicle, after which I left the university building and wandered aimlessly through the city. Eventually, feeling like my life was over, I wandered into a beautiful little baroque church – Peterskirche[1] – which is just off one of the main pedestrian thoroughfares in central Vienna, called the Graben. On entering that church, I had what could be likened to a religious/spiritual experience, despite having no spiritual or religious inclinations to speak of. Whether it was the beauty of the interior of that church, the level of despair I was feeling, or the fact that an organist was playing rapturous music from some place entirely out of sight, I was filled with a profound feeling that 'come what may, everything will be okay'. This message is one that I have often reflected on and try to carry with me always. Indeed, for the most part, despite the challenges in my life, my life has, indeed, been okay. I have returned to this church on three further occasions so far.

More to the point I believe the mental distress I experienced, particularly in my 20s, may have been averted with more awareness of SM and appropriate support in my childhood. In fact, at no point in my life have I been directly 'treated' for SM. As a child this was because my muteness was never seen as something to be helped. For instance, as a teenager and young adult, my mother and stepfather didn't seem to notice (or care) that I mimed and hadn't spoken a single syllable in the house for year after year. Later in life, as an adult, despite my trying to seek relevant support from a number of sources, there seems to be no specific support to be had for this condition and I have thus (as all adults with SM have) had to strive to defeat this condition without imaginative professional support.

As an older sufferer of SM, much of my experience of SM was during a time when this condition (formerly Elective Mutism) was relatively unheard of. As such, services didn't exist because I was suffering with something that very few had any

---

1   See www.peterskirche.at.

expertise in working with. Young children of the future could fare better and be spared much of my experience.

For those too old to have received intervention as children, those who slip through the net, and those who do not respond to 'treatment' however, it has to be noted that funding for mental health services is inadequate. The provision of mental health services is a competition and, as such, limited funds will always be spent on conditions which are ostensibly more harmful such as self-harm, antisocial behaviour and eating disorders – disorders which may make an individual a danger to themselves or others. Given SM is generally portrayed to be innocuous (rather than the *horrible* mental health condition that it can become) it is very low down the pecking order for provision of services.

SM severely affects the life outcomes and mental health of many young adults, in a very detrimental way. Running a support group and being a point of contact for many adults with SM, their parents and mental health professionals, I am also personally aware of adults in their 30s and 40s, confined to their homes (through SM, agoraphobia and depression), solely dependent on their aging parents and unable to fend for themselves.

The other 'what if' for me is 'what if' I hadn't been so ashamed all my life of suffering from SM? What if I had felt that it were more acceptable to be different to everyone else? I could, in fact, have lived relatively happily with an inability to speak, if I had never perceived other people to see it as an issue. After all, many people happily live with deafness, encountering many of the same barriers in life that sufferers of SM do. In fact, for a number of years it occurred to me that I should be a Trappist Monk, because at least in that setting my behaviour would have been ordinary and acceptable.

In my young adulthood, for instance, one of my profoundest worries was that I would never marry or have a family of my own because I was suffering from something I was so ashamed of – something which, I believed, nobody could accept me for. However, I am now married and I have an adult daughter I am very proud of, and my SM when it crops up is acknowledged and accepted within my closest family. It is finally clear to me that SM is something that I should never have been ashamed of in the first place.

Thus, while it has taken me years to feel comfortable enough to promulgate my experience in the form of a book, as I am here, I will, finally, assert that I am not ashamed of it. I have suffered from something that profoundly affected me for years, for which there was no available support or 'treatment', and, within that, I have done the best that I possibly could and achieved the most that I possibly could. What, therefore, should I be ashamed of?

For adults with SM there can become an element of self-acceptance, in much the same way I have accepted my own SM. I do not believe that I will ever be entirely free of this condition, but I also feel that I should be accepted for who I am – speech or no speech. Alongside self-acceptance, however, adults with SM and those who had SM in childhood often have an urge to change things for the better for the children of the future. This is the same for me also and is the reason why I started iSpeak with Cheryl and the reason (besides having a profound need to get my own story out) for putting this book together.

Following are some personal thoughts on how different life could have been without SM. Please note that a number of people who candidly contributed to other chapters found this chapter too emotionally difficult to take part in.

The experiences begin with Dawn and her profound worries for the future and sense of loss on behalf of her gifted son for all the things he may not be able to achieve due to a condition that few professionals seem to take seriously enough.

DAWN'S STORY

Writing about how Tom's life would have been different without SM is definitely the hardest thing to write. It stirs up lots of emotions.

It makes me so sad to see Tom, now 13, struggling with something the rest of us just take for granted: speaking. Even the most introverted people can reach out to say to another person: I'm hurt, I'm scared, or I'm lonely. Tom can't. He will never be able to say 'I found that interesting' or 'boring'. He will have answers to questions screaming in his head, but will never be able to say them out loud.

It makes me angry! Why does he have to have this? What caused it? Will it ever get better? Will the world never know just how extraordinarily clever Tom is? Will he never be able to use that fantastic brain to make a difference to the world, to leave his mark, and leave his legacy? Nobody, apart from his family, will know how funny he is, and what a dry sense of humour he has. Nobody, apart from us, will know anything about him because he can't speak.

If Tom didn't have all the problems he does he'd have loads of friends. Academically he'd be a superstar. He'd go on to be a maths professor. He would be happy and love life…

But this is the real world and, at this moment in time, Tom's life couldn't get any further away from my wish for him. In the real world I just want him to be able to leave our house and be able to speak enough to get by. I don't care if he's not a chatterbox. I just wish he'd be able to say 'thank you' in a shop – or even just be able to go into a shop. I wish Tom were able to connect with the world outside our door, because, unless some miracle occurs sometime soon, Tom is never going to be able to do any of these things. Plus I worry about who is going to help him when we are not here? It shouldn't be like this! Why is there no help available for children like Tom? Why isn't he deemed important enough? Why does no one take SM seriously? Why do the 'professionals' he has encountered have no understanding of SM? It's so wrong. It destroys our children's lives.

LIZ'S STORY

I have often wondered how my life would have been if I hadn't suffered from SM. If I could have been helped earlier would I have achieved more? I know, for certain, that I would have been happier and my choices may have been made more with confidence rather than fear.

I used to daydream a lot when I was a child. I lived in my own little world – I felt a lot safer there. I loved long car journeys when I could sit and make up stories in my head. My vivid imagination made me a very creative person and even in school my teachers recognized that I was developing a talent for music, art and writing. I have taken up writing from time to time in my adult life and have found it a great way of expressing ideas and thoughts that I have not been brave enough to speak about.

Despite all the dreams, when I left school I went to work in an office. Answering phones, attending meetings and working with colleagues weren't suited to my extremely introverted nature and I often struggled and felt that I was slow and inadequate. I had quite a few office jobs. I always wanted to achieve more but my SM, lack of confidence, and anxiety let me down. I hated making mistakes and couldn't recover or learn from them easily. I just worried that I was failing and had a tremendous sense of guilt about this. I remember overhearing a recruitment consultant describe me on the phone as someone who 'would not set the world on fire' – in my own mind that's exactly what I wanted to do! But to the outside world I appeared to be morose and indifferent.

For me, learning about SM was the first step in battling against it (I had felt so much guilt in not doing as well as I could have done and I felt a great burden of responsibility) but still I failed to do the simplest of tasks that other people seemed to manage with ease. I couldn't talk to anyone about this as, even to me, it sounded ridiculous that I was afraid to speak to some people. Even to say 'hello' took a lot of effort. But then I discovered that I was not alone. If I had known this sooner my life would have been so much easier to cope with. I feel so sad for the little girl that I once was, who was so scared to go to school; for the young woman who dreaded work and despite feeling stressed and sick, still carried on; and for the woman who wanted to socialize but could never think of the right words to say.

I now realize that there are many people who have suffered and are still isolated and suffering the way I did and it would have taken just a little more understanding of this condition and help at an early age to improve their lives.

Quiet children are often overlooked. Shyness is seen as something they must get over, but when it persists it means that the child feels unsafe and fear and anxiety can take root and become part of their everyday lives, just as it did mine. I wish I could take back the years I spent being anxious and have enjoyed more of my life. I would have liked to have achieved more in my working life. I spent a lot of time observing – being the onlooker, too afraid to join in.

We all have our insecurities but they should never put limitations on our lives. There are still a lot of intelligent and creative children with SM who are struggling and unhappy, and who knows how many of them could 'set the world on fire', if they were given the right help.

WENDY'S STORY

It is difficult to imagine what I might be like without SM because it feels so much a part of me. I wouldn't be quite the same person without it; I would have a different personality. That's how it feels anyway.

Selective Mutism influences a lot of the choices I make, and largely because of it social avoidance has become a way of life for me. I always have to think about how I'm going to cope with the social aspect of whatever situation I find myself in, and that limits my activities.

I don't kid myself that my life would be idyllic if I didn't have SM, but things might have become easier for me over time. I would still be on the autism spectrum, and I would still face challenges that so-called 'normal' people do not necessarily face. I daresay that if I hadn't had SM I would have made a lot more social mistakes. My not speaking very much and my not talking to very many people has possibly protected me well from putting my foot in it too many times and from offending too many people and having to deal with the consequences of that. But it has also protected me from learning from my mistakes and from getting the necessary social experience and practice to be able to improve my people skills. I would have needed a thick skin, which I haven't got. But I might ultimately have ended up with better social skills, with more social confidence and without all the shame and embarrassment that I feel at still being like this in middle age. I might have found a way of being able to hold my own socially and not need to feel so much anxiety about being around people. If I didn't have SM I would not still be as easily walked over as I am, as I could have learned my own way of asserting myself.

I have never stopped feeling like a child. If I hadn't had SM I might have been able to feel more like an adult. I might have been more free to do adult things like finding a job or an occupation that suits my way of being and to find where I 'fit' in the world. This would have also given me greater financial independence than I have ever been able to achieve. Perhaps I could have felt more empowered to make lifestyle choices for myself, like where I wanted to live, whether I wanted to live alone or with other people and how I wanted to live my life.

If I hadn't had SM I may not have been as socially isolated as I have been. I would never have been a social butterfly; I am by nature a loner, an introvert and a somewhat private person. But being as isolated as I have been was not entirely a choice on my part. It is almost impossibly difficult to make friends when you can't talk to people. Having SM has undoubtedly affected my relationships with family members. Without SM it would have been easier for me to maintain relationships with my mother and with my sisters. As I haven't lived with them for some time and I don't see them often, it has become difficult for me to talk to them when I do see them. It has also become difficult for me to speak to my sons as they have become adults, even though we do all still live in the same house. This coupled with the fact that I still feel so childlike, means that I don't feel I have much say or much control over how my home environment is and I often feel powerless and afraid. If I didn't have SM I would have got into more conflicts with immediate family members, but ultimately I might have been more successful at setting appropriate boundaries for my children and at maintaining relationships with them as they grew up.

I do not aspire to be 'normal'; my aim is to become the person I have the potential to be. I am still learning who that person is, but one thing I do know is that person is not a neurotypical and I wouldn't want to be now. I can appreciate my uniqueness. It would no doubt be easier for me to 'become myself' if I didn't have the challenge of living with Selective Mutism and if I wasn't so afraid of the world and of the people in it.

When I look back at my life, I am struck by how lifelong my difficulties have been and by how far back my problems go. That being the case, I think it is time for me to cut myself some slack. I can only be who I am and so long as what I am doing (or not doing) is relatively harmless, I need to find a way of being able to say to the world, 'This is who I am, take me or leave me'.

KIMBERLY'S STORY

'Somebody pair up with Quietty, so she doesn't end up standing there alone like a kid on a playground with nobody to play with!' (Laughter all around.)

This statement came from a hypocritical teacher I was blessed with in 2007. She preached about the horrors of lung disease. Not a way to watch someone die, she said. She'd watched family members struggle to breathe, she said. This teacher had a nasty cough. She took frequent breaks to chain-smoke cigarettes outside the classroom door. I was taking her Certified Nursing Assistant class. I was 43. She was in her 50s. This teacher named me Quietty. I was proud that I raised my hand even when I didn't know the answer. I participated more in that class in four weeks than I had in an entire year of grade school! But still she chose to target me with disparaging remarks and a humiliating nickname.

Without SM, I would still have been on the autism spectrum, but chances are this teacher would not have singled me out. Ironically, because she chose me as the target for her bullying, I was unable to say, 'That's so unprofessional. What kind of teacher are you?'

Am I perceived as weak? An easy mark? I don't feel that way. Without SM, let's see… First of all, I'd probably have gotten into a lot more trouble than I did growing up!

Because of Asperger's, I don't always 'get' if someone is flirting with me, or asking me out. There's a delay – and then, if I realize what's going on, it can't be acted on because that's when SM kicks in, so that I can never reciprocate my feelings to the interested party. I think back to people who've expressed interest in me, and the ways I could've responded if I'd had a voice that didn't betray me.

For starters, the ones that come to mind are Danny, Lenny, Mario, that guy at the movies, and that delivery guy! WHAT IF I'd had a voice (once I realized what was going on)? Well, SM has certainly kept me chaste, hasn't it?

In high school I was sometimes invited to parties: a couple of girls' night sleepovers, an 'end of school' celebration at a cool guy's house… Although many people have done these things, I haven't. I could only shake my head NO. It's fair to say that without SM, I would have more memories spent with other people, doing things that other people take for granted as coming of age activities.

There are things so painful to recall (that SM has stolen from me) that some memories are too painful to share. Hey, if you've read any of my other chapter contributions to this book, you're probably thinking, 'She's been painfully honest, raw and open! Why hold back now?!' I'll tell you why. Writing the other chapter topics were easy compared to writing this one. How can I imagine if a part of me never existed? Well I've got a great imagination and a sharp mind, so I'm trying. Here goes…

Without SM, I would've spoken up when I was being wronged. I would've had more opportunities, and less abuse. No screaming in my head that dissipates like smoke, unacknowledged. I could've been HEARD.

I'm going to share one gut-wrenching experience. When my husband was dying of a cruel terminal disease (between 2000 and 2005) I discovered the music of Adam Duritz, who recently 'came out' as having mental illness, which may explain, in part, my strong identification with his lyrical song writing, so filled with symbolism, mourning, and whimsical moving imagery. The teacher – my adult bully – I would have two years after my husband's death was right about one thing: watching someone die is hard. It's cliché, but Adam's music got me through. To this day he writes songs with layered meanings that underline my present life experience. My daughter is transgender and wants a sex change. Wouldn't you know it? Adam's most recent album has a song about transgender.

I've seen Adam perform dozens of times. It's always a special experience. A few years ago I had primo seats at a concert. Between sets, Adam would walk down the aisle next to my row, and get a drink of water. After he had walked past my friend, Al, and me for, like, the sixth time, Al who is the opposite of introverted called out, 'Hey Adam!' He turned. Adam was standing one foot away from me.

I wasn't star struck. I was dumbstruck. Al high-fived Adam. My voice was stuck. Minutes later, Adam passed us again. Once more Al called out, 'Adam!' Adam stopped. Again he was one foot away from me. I could see every dreadlock up close. It was my opportunity to tell him how much comfort his music gave me during such a terrible time in my life. It was my opportunity to tell him that his music continues to help me in my personal life. 'Excellent show, man,' said Al, as they shook hands. Adam thanked him, paused, and headed back to the stage.

So there's a glimpse at how my life would've been different without SM. I would've said those things during that pause. I would've said that even when one lives in a house of the dying, music lifts you to a place of the living – with all the raw living emotions that go with that. Being silent doesn't mean I'm empty.

When I walk through malls, I hear music playing over the speaker system. Inside my head, I'm singing those songs. In my imagination people walk by, turn and stare because I'm singing without a care. I see looks of amusement as people SEE me. I daydream like that, when a song's on in the car. Inside my head I'm that person at the red light, singing with the radio. Yeah, without SM, I'd be that person. But I'm *this* person and that's very OKAY.

CHAPTER 17

Life Stories

Carl Sutton; Danielle, Beth and Rachel

In the final chapter of the book, we look at three life stories of adults (Danielle, Beth and Rachel) who experienced SM as children/into adulthood. In the same way that I would suggest that my own life story eventually had a positive outcome, each of these stories does also. In fact, all three of these stories culminated in the person concerned becoming, of all things, a public speaker or taking on a media-facing role.

In fact, regarding further seemingly unlikely outcomes for children/adults with SM, Helen Keen (as I indicated in a prior chapter) became a comedienne and radio presenter; Mab Jones 'Daring Wordsmith' became a performance poet; and Katrice Horsley was the UK's National Storytelling Laureate between 2012 and 2014. Additionally, Kirsty Heslewood became Miss England 2013.

What such stories demonstrate, surely, is that change is possible for some people with SM, although one should not lose sight of the fact that for many young adults with SM even basic public communication seems out of reach. It is also important to note that, while supporting parents via iSpeak, I have encountered young children whose communication needs are abandoned by both psychological and speech-language services as early as seven years old because they are seemingly 'unresponsive to treatment'. This book has highlighted the fact that SM can continue until middle age or even late adulthood, so being so dismissive of young children when the outcome may be lifelong mental health issues is abominable. Stories with positive outcomes are great, but one should not forget that not all outcomes for people with SM are so good.

SM is not, by any means, a pleasant experience. While many children with SM may recover in childhood, for those whose SM persists it can become an egregious experience. My own experience has left me with an element of Post Traumatic Stress Disorder (PTSD) in that I very often re-live and re-experience the level of isolation and stress that I experienced in my early 20s, because I had no support back then. There was no professional support available and I could not ask for help from my parents. While I may have come to terms with my experience, have written about it candidly throughout this book and state categorically that I accept myself for who I am, the experience is something that no amount of counselling or CBT will ever alleviate. I very strongly feel that much of my experience could have been averted with sufficient support (had such support even existed in my case) in childhood. This is the most important message of this book as far as I am concerned and I shall repeat it one last time: help and support children with SM in early childhood to avoid issues later on.

Regarding the following three stories, Danielle, who has also contributed in numerous places in the book provides a summary of her experience first. Danielle, while recovered from SM to the extent that she regularly contributes in the media to raise understanding and awareness of SM, still experiences severe anxiety in her daily life. Next Beth writes about her own experience, in which she found religion to support her recovery, and about her newfound enjoyment of public speaking. Finally, Rachel writes about her own very difficult experience. This particular story also provides a recent historical context to the experience of SM, as you will read.

The standout message of Rachel's experience and, it is hoped, of this book is that with determination – preferably with support as it can be extraordinarily more difficult without

– people with SM can live fulfilled lives, and that, as Donna Williams wrote in the foreword, Selective Mutism, like any other condition, does not have to define any person who experiences it.

DANIELLE'S STORY

For as far back as I can remember, Selective Mutism has been a massive part of my life, from the early years of having to deal with it in its entirety, to taking drastic action in my teens to beat it, to now, battling severe anxiety on a daily basis as a result of it.

During my early school years, I was naively unaware that I was different from my classmates. I never struggled in school, always had lots of friends, and had great support from the teachers, despite their lack of knowledge of SM. Junior school for the most part was a similar story, I had great friends and supportive teachers. My issues really came to a head when I was faced with a supply teacher who appeared to not know about my SM, or at least not know the extent of it. During our first lesson, which was English, we were given a written task to do. To encourage us, the teacher had promised us stickers and so, after we had finished the exercise, we were to go up to her desk and show her the work we had completed. One by one, my friends went up and got their stickers. When it came to my turn, I went up to the teacher to show her my work and, once she'd marked it, she asked me which sticker I'd like. I pointed to one of them but, instead of just giving me the sticker I'd chosen, she insisted that I tell her which animal was on it first. Obviously, that was not going to happen under any circumstances and so I returned to my seat, the only one out of all my friends who did not get a sticker, despite having done the same amount of work as them. As trivial as it may seem now, to a nine-year-old child, this was a massive deal. It was in this one moment, that I realized how different I was from my friends and classmates. The supply teacher's campaign to try and make me talk did not end there though, the situation became more severe during a lesson later on in the day. We were given an oral exercise to do, not the best task for a child with SM. However, these exercises were not usually an issue for me as I'd been given a whiteboard by my regular teacher at the beginning of the school year.

We were put into pairs and given the task to do. As always, I teamed up with my best friend. We started to complete the exercise with me writing my contribution down on my whiteboard. Within minutes of starting however, the supply teacher came over to us, confiscated my whiteboard, in doing so taking away my only way of communicating, and moved my partner to another group, leaving me on my own for the rest of the lesson with nothing to do. Even at this young age, I could feel the anger inside me growing. How could one woman be so ignorant?! I spent the rest of the day desperately struggling to hold back tears, not knowing how to deal with the anger I felt. As soon as I got home, my parents put in a complaint to the school and, the following day, my headmaster called me out of class and apologized to me for what had happened, informing me that the supply teacher would never work at the school again. For me, the damage had already been done though. In that one day, any childhood innocence I had had about my SM had been taken away from me, and I began to realize how different I was from my classmates.

This type of incident became all the more common once I'd moved up to comprehensive school, with some of my peers also feeling the need bully me (see Chapter 8). I had a particularly difficult relationship with my maths teacher when I started year 8. He seemed to feel the need to make me feel isolated, at one point even forcing me into an emergency appointment with a psychiatrist because, no matter what anyone did or said, I physically couldn't leave the house as a result of something that had happened during our previous lesson. At one stage, I was being bullied in between lessons by a girl in my year, bullied during lessons by my maths teacher and, if we had a supply teacher that day, potentially facing bullying from them too. Needless to say that school was the last place that I wanted to be!

Towards the end of my first year in comprehensive school, aged 12, I started having severe panic attacks every day due to the situations that I was constantly being faced with in school, with bullying being particularly prevalent during this time. I missed most of the last term of year 7 because no one knew what to do to help me get into school. By this time, I'd seen seven different psychiatrists, none of them having much, if any, knowledge of SM whatsoever. When I moved into year 8, I had a new head of year who took me under her wing and helped me into school every morning and generally looked out for me. Without her, I doubt that I'd have managed to get through the school gates at all.

By the time I'd got to year 9, I'd been diagnosed with moderate depression, was seeing my tenth psychiatrist, and was on beta blockers and Valium to control my anxiety. I continued to have panic attacks every day and, as the bullying from teachers and pupils alike became more intense, so did my anxiety. It was after another hellish day that I made the decision, despite being advised not to by my psychiatrist, that I wanted to move schools. My parents and I sat down there and then and searched for schools on the Internet. I quickly ruled out all the state schools in the area as I knew people from my junior school attended them. We managed to find a much smaller independent school that on the outside appeared perfect. I knew that the only way this plan would work though was if I was able to talk the minute I set foot in the school on my visit. Somehow I managed to do this and, not long after, I started at the school. Although my anxiety still affected me severely, the not talking aspect of my SM was well and truly behind me and I managed to lead a fairly normal school life, despite my on-going battle with severe anxiety and depression.

Within six months of starting at the school, in November 2008 just days before my 15th birthday, I was contacted by a producer from the BBC, asking me if I'd like to take part in a documentary about SM. Even though I hadn't long got over it myself, I jumped at the chance of sharing my experiences in order to help others. The filming of 'My Child Won't Speak' was a long and, at times, very difficult process. Although in the final cut of the documentary, my story got about 20 minutes of air time, we actually filmed around 150 hours' worth of footage, between March and August 2009. The hardest session of filming for me was undoubtedly the session that we filmed in the shop, with me attempting to buy a chocolate bar. What wasn't shown in the final cut was that for a couple of hours before the filming took place, I was working with a psychologist who had been taking my heart rate at various points during the day. I was also wearing a heart rate monitor during the filming. This only added to the stress I was going through and that, coupled with the fact that I was being followed around by a massive camera and sound equipment, was too much for me. I became incredibly angry, partly at myself for not being able to complete the task, but also at the producer for putting me in a situation where I felt vulnerable. In the documentary, you can see me refuse to answer any of the questions I was asked and eventually walk away from the camera. At this point, the psychologist, who had travelled from Bristol for the day just to film with us, called me into her car and started talking to me about my heart rate, showing me diagrams mapping the increase and decrease as the situation in the shop intensified. She managed to calm me down enough to carry on with the filming shortly afterwards. The main thing that kept me going through these difficult periods of filming was the thought that what I was doing could potentially help other people. For me, that was the only motivation I needed to carry on with the filming.

I've continued to try and raise the awareness of SM over the past few years by sharing my story. I've written a few blogs for various different mental health related websites, one of them being published in a local newspaper and, in early January 2015, recorded 'Finding Your Voice,' a documentary about SM for BBC Radio 4. Helen Keen, who was the presenter of the documentary, is a massive inspiration for me and so I was really honoured to be able to record an interview with her. I intend to continue talking about SM in the hope that one day, SM will be common knowledge amongst everyone.

BETH'S STORY[1]

I suffered from SM right back in my earliest memories – being afraid to speak, watching the world as if through a pane of glass, not knowing how to connect with other children. I don't think any one factor caused it – possibly a combination of an introverted, very independent personality, and being a middle child. I had a great-uncle who remained voluntarily mute throughout his adult life, so perhaps some genetics were involved too. I grew up in a wonderful, loving family, and suffered no identifiable trauma.

During my first few years at school I very rarely spoke, and subsequently had no friends. I found it virtually impossible to express my feelings, although I could usually answer a direct question if asked. I remember sitting at the dinner table desperately wanting to know what day we were going on holiday, hoping one of my brothers would ask my parents, as I couldn't get the words out. I tried to avoid drawing any attention to myself, and spent a lot of time wanting to be invisible.

---

1 Beth Moran is the author of *Making Marion: Where's Robin Hood When You Need Him?* Lion Fiction (2014).

I suffered from recurrent ear infections as a child. My mum knew to ask if my ear hurt when I hovered about in the kitchen instead of hiding in my room. I never spoke to my lovely grandparents, or wider family, unless in response to a direct question. Growing up I found social situations incredibly difficult.

When I started junior school, a new girl moved onto my street, and becoming best friends with her transformed my childhood. With my friend, I was confident, sometimes loud and often mischievous – though, even as a teenager, she commented that I sometimes came round to her house, hung out for a while, and left again without saying anything!

Throughout my school life, basic things like answering my name in the register left me nauseous and anxious. I would leave a shop rather than have to address the shopkeeper and found most social situations terrifying. I did, through my friend, develop a small group of other friends with whom I could mostly be myself. I had a lot of fun with them. However, I never wore clothing with a label or wording on it; I never listened to music without headphones; and I tried to keep any aspect of my life that could be open to judgement as hidden as possible. I also found noise and crowds distressing.

I dropped a grade in two of my GCSEs because, during the exams, my pen ran out, and I couldn't put my hand up and ask for another one.

In the year I graduated from university I moved to a new city, started work as a research scientist, married and had a baby. This was my toughest time. My old friends were travelling, or out partying, enjoying the usual life of twenty-somethings. I loved my job, and my new family, but felt extremely lonely. At that point I still didn't know what it was that prevented me from connecting with people, or why I had times when I simply couldn't speak.

After moving nearer to my hometown, when pregnant with my second child, things improved, although the fears were still there. Health professionals and new friends thought I suffered from depression, as I seemed so quiet and rarely smiled, no matter how I felt inside. I often came across as standoffish, weird, grumpy or uninterested until people got to know me. It's only in recent years I realized my struggle with friendships was because I closed myself off through fear. Basic tasks like getting the attention of a waiter or phoning a plumber were major challenges for me, causing a lot of stress. I know my children missed out when they were younger as

I couldn't approach other parents at the school gates, so they had a very limited number of friends invited round to play. If a stranger spoke to me in the street, I would freeze, unable to answer. Going to the hairdresser was a nightmare. If I saw someone I knew out and about – even someone I would class as a good friend – I would hide, unable to cope with the possibility of passing the time of day.

The road out of SM was a long slog, and one I haven't finished yet. The central factor in overcoming my fear of being noticed and judged was my Christian faith. I can remember a light bulb moment as I walked to my local shops, one of my children in a pushchair, hoping not to see anyone I knew. Suddenly I had a revelation – I believe God loves me, he knows me better than anyone and made me 'me' on purpose – so, if other people, who don't know me as well, don't like me or think I'm any good, they must be wrong!

I would repeat this to myself over and over as I faced social situations: 'I don't have to be ashamed of who I am or what I say'. I also worked on not calling myself a 'freak' or saying 'I hate being me!' when I failed to talk, or when I did and then worried about what I'd said. I replaced it with positive words instead: 'I may have said something stupid, but that's okay. I don't have to be perfect.' I also had some fantastic counselling in my mid-20s after my problems began to affect my voice physically – it became so weak I struggled to use the phone, causing problems in my job as an antenatal teacher. The counselling helped me consider how much our words – and the way we say them – are part of our identity; and to address some self-esteem issues.

I began to set myself daily challenges. The fact that fear controlled huge parts of my life grew increasingly frustrating and upsetting. Every day I did something that scared me: I made a phone call, drove on a busy roundabout, said hello to a mum in the school playground. And gradually, put together, these things began to work. I even dealt with a chronic spider phobia to the amazement of my family! Eventually I made a decision never to say no to anything simply because I felt afraid.

I started public speaking in my early 30s, and to my surprise found not only did I enjoy it, I was actually quite good! It was chatting to people afterwards that I initially found difficult. I now speak in a wide variety of situations: at conferences, on local radio, and even on a stage at our town carnival.

Around four years ago, I had a real break-through moment, when, for the first time, I initiated a conversation with a stranger. Up until that point, I had only addressed someone I didn't know if I really needed to (like a receptionist at the doctors). I had never started small talk or made a passing remark. On this occasion, I made a comment to a cleaner in a campsite toilet – a nothing, everyday occurrence to her, but a huge deal to me! I walked out of that toilet ten feet tall! It still surprises me when I find myself chatting with people I don't know.

I am still facing challenges – one of the biggest of which is my facial expressions. When I taught myself to smile a few years ago, I was amazed at the positive reactions I got. I have received a lot of hurtful comments over the years about this issue, and nowadays I probably find smiling appropriately more tiring than talking. I have some catching up to do because I missed out on learning the normal rules and social nuances that others develop as children. I still find crowds can make me very anxious.

But my life is unrecognizable from how it used to be. The biggest message of my story is that change is possible, and it thrills me to be able to stand up in front of other people and share that truth with them.

RACHEL'S STORY

I was born into a lower middle-class family in the mid-20th century. My earliest memory, at around the age of four, is of my father complaining I was a nuisance and a mistake. I was afraid of my father as he always seemed angry with me and I would hide behind a chair when he returned from work. Aged about five, my mother sent me to buy a loaf. I had never left the house alone before and returned without the loaf after running away from a large dog on the street. My mother flew into a rage, shouting at me and striking me and ordered me to go back out to the shop. From that moment, I sensed the world as an unsafe place. I had a strong sense of being unwanted and in the way at home.

When I started primary school I was amazed to see that my new teacher had taken so much trouble to set out an exciting array of activities in the classroom. My teachers were kind and good-natured and I did well at my work. School was a happy place for me and I made lots of friends. I remember myself at this stage of my life as a lively, outgoing and inquisitive child. Nevertheless, I continued to be afraid of my father's constant criticism, shouting and smacks. I found his name-calling upsetting – e.g. 'thickhead' and 'clot' – and received blows to my head if I voiced an opinion. My mother too seemed critical and cold. I believed I must be stupid and bad. Choosing to be quiet and invisible at home felt safer, and my parents praised my quietness to other family members. Later in life, I realized that my mother rarely left the house, was dominated by my father and avoided engaging with persons outside of the immediate family.

At grammar school, I gradually began to experience difficulty in speaking. The school's strict regime, bullying teachers, and not feeling accepted by girls from more middle-class backgrounds made me feel that anything I said would be ridiculed as stupid. Fearful of certain teachers, I was punished for avoiding their lessons and hiding in the cloakroom. My school performance plummeted and teachers viewed me as failing. In private, I was reading avidly, including literature classics, science and philosophy. As my teenage years progressed, I became mainly comfortable talking with people on a one-to-one basis. I enjoyed friendships with other girls on the fringes of social life at school and also found connection and comfort through sexual exploration with local teenage boys. Throughout this time, my parents disapproved of my studying, reading, having friends, my interests and my desire for a career. My father once dragged me out of the local reference library after school where I loved to go to pore over the large encyclopaedias. I saved my tears for the privacy of my bedroom at night.

Ordered to leave school early and get a job to pay my parents back for bringing me up, I left home and worked in menial jobs in a big city, sharing bedsits with a friend. Continuing my studies part time, I eventually achieved my dream of higher education when I was accepted at an all-women's college. Living on campus in a hall of residence far away from anywhere familiar to me, I 'froze' and found myself unable to speak to other students or lecturers. Although longing to make friends and belong, this scenario created a vicious circle whereby I was criticized for being very quiet and always being alone. This unwelcome, negative attention exacerbated the situation and I became less and less able to speak and, as a result, was completely shunned by the other students. I was sent for by the principal and told to pull myself together. There were no support systems in place for students. With nowhere else to turn, I approached my GP who referred me to a psychiatrist. The psychiatrist promised to help if I went into his hospital.

I thus became a patient in a rambling Victorian psychiatric hospital. Promises to help me were reiterated by the doctors, but no explanation was ever given as to how this would take place. The doctors told me I was depressed. For the next year I lived on a ward of about 50 women. My treatment included some 30 drugs per day including Largactil, electro-convulsive treatment (ECT) under general anaesthetic three times per week, and two bouts of narcosis (deep sleep treatment) which involved being kept asleep for periods of time using drugs such as sodium amytal. I was given chloral hydrate every night at bedtime. Insulin coma treatment was the norm on the ward and I was pressured to agree to this, but refused. There were no talking treatments. Nevertheless, I remember the hospital as a caring community. I found all the doctors and nurses to be kind, caring people. Still in my teens at this stage, they were almost like surrogate parents. The hospital was also a community with social film nights, sports and many other activities. I felt welcomed and safe and my extreme quietness was accepted. I also developed a relationship with a male patient.

After almost a year, I left the hospital and resumed bedsit life, finding work in quieter environments. I made many new friends and stopped taking the prescribed drugs. As I moved towards my mid-20s, my fear of speaking and being in groups of people gradually diminished. I found the courage to return to my studies and while occasionally struggling to speak in lectures and seminar groups, I found acceptance, understanding and friendship. In a few short years, times had changed. Attitudes were more relaxed and student support systems were beginning to emerge.

I went on to enjoy a career that included teaching and lecturing as well as other high profile posts in which I deliberately challenged my speaking difficulties. I loved my work and developed strategies to help myself such as careful choice of where I would be seated, using a microphone, careful preparation of material, speaking first in group discussions to break the ice, always arriving early and being ultra-reliable and well organized. I learned to take the view that if something didn't work, I would do better the next time.

Marriage, children and a happy home life were also strengthening factors. Now retired, I enjoy being able to pursue my interests and have an active social life. The inability to speak has faded. I feel my experiences have made me a more empathetic person. I have always tried to encourage those who appear to be ill at ease in certain situations.

Helping a New Partner Join a Family Where There is a Child with Selective Mutism[1]

Maggie Johnson (Principal Speech and Language Therapist, Kent Community Health NHS Foundation Trust) and Vivienne

Generally, children with Selective Mutism (SM) are most comfortable around those they have always lived with. This commonly includes parents, siblings and other familiar individuals who have always resided alongside the child – for example a live-in grandparent. Integrating a new, less familiar, adult into the home environment can therefore be problematic.

When in a comfortable, familiar environment (usually at home), children with pure SM will speak and interact in ways that are both age appropriate and characteristic of their own personality. However, there is a discernible cut off point between the child's immediate family and people outside their comfort zone. When people outside the child's nuclear family enter the home, the child will tend to experience a marked rise in anxiety. This is when the characteristic symptoms of SM start to appear. Typically the child appears more subdued than usual; facial expression may be frozen (unable to smile or react); there is a failure to speak (frequently, even when the child is spoken to); the child may markedly avoid eye contact; may become distressed; may fail to eat while being watched; may try to hide or avoid entering the room; may attempt to whisper to a familiar adult only. Young children may freeze completely when spoken to by an unfamiliar adult. All these responses can seem

---

1 This appendix is included with the permission of SMIRA (the Selective Mutism Information and Research Agency) as it is also a SMIRA leaflet.

like rejection or dislike of the outsider if the child's anxiety is not properly understood.

Integrating a new partner into a family which includes a child with SM can be particularly stressful, both for the child and main carer. In part, this can be because there is an expectation for that partner to assume a parental role and form a bond with the child as soon as possible. When this does not happen, frustration can build in both the natural parent and new partner which only feeds the child's anxiety. If there is a concern or expectation that the child will be resentful of the new relationship the SM behaviour is likely to reinforce this belief and be mistaken for defiance. The natural parent's attempt to explain the situation can appear at best over-protective and at worst, disloyal to the new partner.

Thus, successfully integrating a partner into a family with a selectively mute child can be a challenge! But if it is carried through in a sympathetic step-by-step fashion, a trusting relationship can be achieved.

Dos and don'ts

Do...

Explain in detail about your child's condition and back this up with written information. Encourage your partner to go online or do some reading about SM (see useful references at the end of this appendix).

Remember that your partner may initially get the impression that the child dislikes him or her and may be feeling confused or disappointed; a selectively mute child that doesn't speak, pointedly looks the other way and never smiles, may give that impression! It is important that you stress that the child is simply reacting to his or her feelings of anxiety.

Understand that it may take time for your partner to digest all this information which may go right against their natural instincts. But however hurt, helpless, angry or frustrated they may feel, it is vital to remain calm. Any disapproval, disappointment or unreasonable demands will make it even harder for the child to relax and behave normally in their company.

Remove all pressure on the child to speak until he or she is comfortable enough for this to happen naturally. You and your partner should continue to speak to the child and include him or her in all family activities as usual but avoid direct questions and make it clear that your new partner is more interested in enjoying their company than hearing them speak. It is good to include siblings (when present) as this provides familiarity and may draw the child's focus away from your partner; this will ultimately help the child get used to their presence.

Always respond positively and warmly to any attempts by the child to communicate either verbally or otherwise! Pointing, nodding, drawing, listening to a story and sharing activities and interests such as football, cycling, swimming and so on are all valuable forms of communication, each a step nearer to talking.

Whenever possible, you and your child should take short breaks away from the company of others; this will allow him or her to talk freely to you and convey urgent needs, without having to resort to whispering in your ear. This is particularly important when relatively long periods of time are spent in company.

At first, allow long periods of quality time together with your child, in the absence of your partner; this will reduce anxiety; allowing your child to return to his/her normal self and speak freely. Ideally your partner can gradually be included in these periods, first by occupying themselves nearby, then as an observer, and finally by taking part in your game or activity as the child gets used to speaking at normal volume in front of them.

Reassure your partner that the child's inability to speak and interact freely is only a temporary setback and with time, perseverance and patience the situation will resolve!

Likewise, explain to the child that talking and relaxing will get easier in time.

Do remain in charge of your child. Retain full responsibility for the day-to-day discipline and management of your child. Handing over control to your partner is likely to greatly increase your child's anxiety. For many children, SM tends to be highly contextual in nature: an adult taking on the role of an authority figure tends to be more intimidating than one acting as a trusted friend; that is why it is important for your partner to concentrate on building a trusting friendship, rather than quickly assuming a parental role, bearing in mind the child also has an absent father or mother with whom he or she may or may not have a talking relationship.

Do inform your child's nursery or school about the change in family circumstances, as this may influence your child's behaviour outside the home. SM children find all change difficult, even the little things in life, but with time to prepare, understand and adjust, they can happily adapt to a new situation.

Don't...

Don't feel that you have to choose between the child and your partner! Try and get your partner on side, his or her co-operation will ultimately bring the family closer together in the long term!

Don't ask leading questions such as 'Why don't you like John?'

Young SM children are unlikely to be aware of the concept of anxiety, so won't to be able to explain their behaviour in terms of feeling anxious. In fact they are unlikely to be aware that their behaviour is odd at all! Behaviours such as avoiding eye contact, failure to speak and frozen facial expressions are instinctive reactions to anxiety-provoking stimuli. There is no conscious thought involved on the part of the child; in other words these behaviours are not premeditated! If it is suggested that the child dislikes someone, it is likely to lead to confusion on the part of the child and he or she may simply agree with you because you're an adult!

Don't be pressured and try not to be upset by relatives or friends that advocate a zero tolerance, quick fix approach. SM is not widely recognized or understood by the public at large, so for those unfamiliar with the condition, it is tempting to think that it can be easily dealt with by confronting or correcting the child. This will make matters worse as you will no doubt have discovered already! Any parent with experience of a selectively mute child will tell you that patience and perseverance are required, over a prolonged period of time.

Useful references

▶ The free advice leaflets at: www.smira.org.uk (go to Downloads Section for SMIRA leaflets and Useful Information).

▶ *My Child Won't Speak* – documentary made by Landmark Films, shown on BBC 1, Feb 2010 and available on YouTube.

▶ *Can I Tell You About Selective Mutism?* by Maggie Johnson and Alison Wintgens (2012) London: Jessica Kingsley Publishers.

▶ *Silent Children* DVD available from SMIRA www.smira. org.uk.

▶ *The Selective Mutism Resource Manual*, second edition by Maggie Johnson and Alison Wintgens (2016) Milton Keynes: Speechmark Publishing. Especially the chapters on Frequently Asked Questions; Creating the Right Environment: The Starting Point for Home and School; and Facing Fears.

APPENDIX B

The Reasons Why I Dislike School

Lorraine (written when she was 12)

The teachers are unhelpful and the other pupils are horrible and irritating.

Most of the rules are pointless and are just there to make us mindless robots so that we don't get 'out of control'.

There are many alternatives to school that I would be much happier with but no one's taking any notice.

It takes up too much of my time. It starts too early. It finishes too late.

I hardly learn anything and learn more from the Internet and books.

You get punished for not understanding something or not being good at a particular subject.

I don't enjoy any of the lessons – either due to my teacher, the people in my class, or the fact that the way subjects are taught just does not interest me.

The teachers don't understand that some people learn differently to others.

The point of school isn't just to educate us – it's also to keep us under control and train us to be obedient.

Everyone thinks they're better than everyone else so they feel that they don't have to treat people with respect.

I dislike getting pushed into walls and not being able to breathe when everyone is trying is trying to get to lesson.

You get nasty rumours spread and horrible nicknames made up for you. These stay for the whole time you are at school and they're never forgotten.

At one point I had so much homework plus three projects to do all at once. It can be overwhelming.

When it's been snowing and it's icy everywhere, we hardly ever have snow days. I always slip on the ice and the upperclassmen think it's funny to throw ice – not snow but ice – at you.

If you're different in the tiniest way then you'll get bullied. The teachers also don't like you looking the way you want to e.g. dyeing your hair is against the rules.

It's freezing inside the school and yet you're not allowed to wear coats or cardigans.

The school never listens to anything you have to say and if you make suggestions on how to improve things you get punished.

You're not allowed privacy.

It's unhygienic. You find chewing gum that's been there for years under the tables. At one point there was a sandwich in the sink.

If you are unhappy in your education and you're just waiting for it to be over then you're not going to remember what you've been 'taught' and you'll just fail.

It influences suicide, self-harm, mental illness and underage smoking.

When you're forced to do something then you probably won't try hard with it.

BULLYING, DISCRIMINATION and SOCIAL PHOBIA.

Einstein hated school.

You don't NEED to go to school to get a good education.

I would like to go to a democratic school as these accept improvement ideas from the students as well as the teachers. They aim to let children grow to be unique individuals and have less requirements and restraints as public schools. Sadly the nearest democratic school is in London and only accepts primary-aged children.

I also like the idea of a Waldorf school. They are similar to democratic schools in the way that they like their pupils to be themselves and let them choose how they want their education. But, sadly, there isn't one of these in Birmingham either.

I think that I would enjoy being home-schooled also. I wouldn't have to spend as much time on it as I would with going to a public school and it would probably be a lot easier as a lot of things I mentioned in my earlier list wouldn't apply.

There is also something similar to home-schooling called 'unschooling'. The student would take classes at home and would be able to choose what they learn and not have to follow the curriculum. There are also online schools where you can take classes on the Internet in the comfort of your own home and you can work at your own pace.

References

Anxiety and Depression Association of America (2015) *Social Anxiety Disorder and Alcohol Abuse.* Available at www.adaa.org/understanding-anxiety/social-anxiety-disorder/social-anxiety-and-alcohol-abuse, accessed 19 July 2015.

APA (2013) *Diagnostic and Statistical Manual of Mental Disorders (V).* Washington, DC: American Psychiatric Association.

Attwood, T. (2008) *The Complete Guide to Asperger's Syndrome.* London: Jessica Kingsley Publishers.

Black, B. and Uhde, T. (1995) 'Psychiatric characteristics of children with Selective Mutism – A pilot study.' *Journal of the American Academy of Child and Adolescent Psychiatry 34*, 7, 845–856.

Cline, T. and Baldwin, S. (2004) *Selective Mutism in Childhood* (2nd edition). Oxford: Wiley-Blackwell.

Cunningham, C. E., McHolm, A., Boyle, M. H. and Patel, S. (2004) 'Behavioural and emotional adjustment, family functioning, academic performance, and social relationships in children with Selective Mutism.' *Journal of Child Psychology and Psychiatry 45*, 8, 1363–1372.

Elizur, Y. and Perednik, R. (2003) 'Prevalence and description of Selective Mutism in immigrant and native families: A controlled study.' *Journal of the Academy of Child and Adolescent Psychiatry 42*, 1451–1459.

Goddard, E. (Producer) and Peel, B. (Director). (2010) *My Child Won't Speak* [Television documentary, 17 February 2010].Oxford: Landmark Films.

Goleman, D. (1996) *Emotional Intelligence: Why it Can Matter More than IQ.* London and New York, NY: Bloomsbury Publishing PLC.

Johnson, M. and Wintgens, A. (2001) *Selective Mutism Resource Manual.* Milton Keynes: Speechmark Publishing Limited.

Johnson, M. and Wintgens, A. (2012) *Can I tell you about Selective Mutism?* London: Jessica Kingsley Publishers.

Johnson, M. and Wintgens, A. (2016) *Selective Mutism Resource Manual* (2nd edition). Milton Keynes: Speechmark Publishing Limited.

Kolvin, I., Trowell, J., Le Couteur, A., Baharaki, S. and Morgan, J. (1997) 'The origins of Selective Mutism: Some strategies in attachment and bonding research.' *Association of Child Psychology and Psychiatry (ACPP) Occasional Papers (Bonding and Attachment) 14*, 17–25.

Lesser-Katz, M. (1986) 'Stranger reaction and elective mutism in young children.' *American Journal of Orthopsychiatry 56*, 3, 458–469.

Lesser-Katz, M. (1988) 'The treatment of elective mutism as a stranger reaction.' *Psychotherapy 2,* 305–313.

Moran, B. (2014) *Making Marion: Where's Robin Hood When You Need Him?* Oxford: Lion Fiction.

Motavelli, N. (1995) 'Fluoxetine for Selective Mutism.' *American Academy of Child and Adolescent Psychiatry 34,* 701–703.

NHS (2015) *Selective Mutism.* Available at www.nhs.uk/conditions/selective-mutism/Pages/Introduction.aspx, accessed 19 July 2015.

Remschmidt, H., Poller, M., Herpertz-Dahlmann, B., Henighausen, K. and Gutenbrunner, C. (2001) 'A follow-up study of 45 patients with elective mutism.' *European Archives of Psychiatry and Clinical Neuroscience 251,* 284–296.

Simone, R. (2010) *Aspergirls: Empowering Females with Asperger Syndrome.* London: Jessica Kingsley Publishers.

Sluckin, A. and Smith, B. R. (2014) *Tackling Selective Mutism.* London: Jessica Kingsley Publishers.

Steinhausen, H. C. and Juzi, C. (1996) 'Elective mutism: An analysis of 100 cases.' *Journal of the American Academy of Child and Adolescent Psychiatry 35,* 5, 606–614.

Steinhausen, H. C., Wachter, M., Laimböck, K. and Winkler Metzke, C. (2006) 'A long-term outcome study of Selective Mutism in childhood.' *Journal of Child Psychology and Psychiatry 47,* 7, 751–756.

Sutton, C. (2013) *Selective Mutism in Adults.* (MSC Dissertation, University of Chester). Available at www.ispeak.org.uk/Download.ashx?PDF=/Downloads/PS7112_Dissertation.pdf, accessed 15 October 2015.

Tzabar, R. (Producer) (2015) *Finding Your Voice* [Radio documentary, 10 February 2015]. London: BBC Radio 4.

Walker, P. (2014) *Complex PTSD: From Surviving to Thriving.* CreateSpace Independent Publishing Platform.

Williams, D. (2015) *Selective Mutism.* Available at donnawilliams.net: www.donnawilliams.net/selectivemutism.0.html, accessed 19 July 2015.

Wong, P. (2010). 'Selective Mutism: A review of etiology, comorbidities and treatment.' *Psychiatry 7*(3), 23–31.

Index